STELLA BUDRIKIS

Madness and Marvels

The Lives and Times of C. Y. O'Connor and Dr Henry Barnett

First published by Stella Budrikis 2024

First edition

This book was professionally typeset on Reedsy.
Find out more at reedsy.com

For Gary, who helps me stay sane
when life seems a little crazy.

Contents

Preface

When life itself seems lunatic, who knows where madness lies?
Dale Wasserman, 'Man of La Mancha'

The genius of engineer Charles Yelverton O'Connor is commemorated in Western Australia in the naming of schools, a suburb, a federal electorate, and several suburban streets. The National Trust has an annual lecture series named after him. Most poignantly, his name has also been given to the beach where, early one morning in 1902, he took his own life with a gunshot to the head.

His death has become one of the iconic moments of West Australian history. So much folklore has grown up around it that it's difficult to sort fact from fiction. It has been the inspiration for several plays, a documentary film, and a novel, as well as being commemorated by a popular sculpture in the waters off Fremantle.[1]

But O'Connor is remembered for far more than just the tragedy of his death. Besides overseeing the construction of the Mundaring to Coolgardie water pipeline, still recognised as one of the world's great engineering marvels, he also designed and built Fremantle harbour in the mouth of the Swan River, proving wrong the naysayers who said it couldn't be done. Much of Western Australia's rail system was also established by C. Y. O'Connor.

The very success of O'Connor's career raises questions about the way his life ended. How did someone of such talent and competence come to believe that his life was no longer worth living? Did he really think, as the folklore often suggests, that the pipeline scheme had failed? Did the pressure exerted on him by the press and other detractors, during those final years when the pipeline was being built, break his spirit? Or had the signs of distress been there earlier? How did the political and social environment of the time (especially the gold rushes of the 1890s) affect him? Wanting answers to such questions led to my decision to research and write about C. Y. O'Connor's life. Yet the task seemed daunting.

The same questions have been pondered, and answers proffered, by several professional historians and biographers in the past. Alexandra Hasluck wrote a brief but authoritative account of O'Connor's life, published by Oxford University Press, in 1965.[2] Merab Tauman's scholarly biography, *The Chief*, which appeared in 1978, filled out many of the details.[3] Her meticulous research is inspiring, given that she wrote the book before the advent of the internet, with its facility to search out documents online. At the time she was writing, there were still people alive who remembered O'Connor.

Tony Evans' *C. Y. O'Connor, His Life and Legacy,* published by UWA Press in 2001, brought the research up to date. I can only agree with Kim Beazley, in his review of the book, that 'there is unlikely to be a better biography of C. Y. O'Connor.'[4]

What, then, could I as a writer add to the picture?

Early in my research, I learned that the O'Connor family rented a home, 'Park Bungalow', from a Dr Henry Barnett, the superintendent of the Fremantle asylum. I was intrigued and began looking for more information about the O'Connor's landlord.

Philippa Martyr's paper, *Unlikely Reformer: Dr Henry Calvert Barnett (1832-1897)* revealed Henry Barnett as an adventurous, creative, forthright and sometimes obstinate character, with strong views on how the asylum, and society, should be run.[5] He was an amputee, and many stories, plausible and implausible, circulated about how he had lost his left leg. For many years he played an integral part in the life of the Fremantle community and the wider West Australian colony. Until his death in 1897, Dr Barnett's name was almost as familiar to West Australians as that of C. Y. O'Connor.

Like O'Connor, Barnett was a north of Ireland Protestant, well educated, with an impressive range of interests and skills. Like O'Connor, he had character flaws, and a propensity to evoke both admiration and conflict. And, as with O'Connor, there were elements of tragedy about his life. The two men, though very different in personality, were both visionaries in their own fields.

While there's no evidence to prove O'Connor and Barnett were close friends, it seems likely they had a cordial relationship. Their lives certainly intersected frequently in the tight-knit society of the West Australian colony, through dinners and balls and garden parties, Sunday worship and membership of sporting clubs.

Yet circumstances, and the priorities of the government and the society in which they lived, pitted the interests of one against the other. While O'Connor was handling hundreds of thousands of pounds in funding for the harbour and other projects, Barnett spent years pleading for a meagre increase in funds to upgrade the asylum. The gold-driven boom in Western Australia's population, that filled the coffers which paid for engineering marvels, led to the asylum becoming disastrously overcrowded.

The idea of writing a book that would interweave the two men's stories, and in the process reveal how they interacted with each other and the community in which they lived and worked, appealed to me.

Initially my focus was on a period of almost seven years, between mid-1891, when O'Connor arrived in Western Australia to take up the post of Chief Engineer, and Dr Barnett's death late in 1897. These were the years in which their lives overlapped. The period coincided with O'Connor's role in building Fremantle Harbour, as well as much of the railway system.

Without O'Connor's harbour and rail, Western Australia would have struggled to develop as rapidly as it did or capitalise so effectively on the prosperity of the gold rushes. Without the success of the harbour project, it's unlikely that either the West Australian government or the London bankers would have had confidence in this 'shire engineer from New Zealand', as the *West Australian Sunday Times* once derisively called him, to handle a project of the vast size and huge expense of the pipeline.

The 1890s were a time of rapid change and growth for the previously insignificant and isolated colony of Western Australia. Responsible self-government had been granted in October 1890, with the newly elected government under John Forrest feeling its way through multiple challenges.

As I researched and wrote the first draft of this book, I became aware of other themes running through the story. A strong current of racism permeated West Australian society in this era. Its effect was felt both by Indigenous people and by Asian immigrants. Neither O'Connor nor Barnett was racist, at least by the standards of the day. But they were not impervious to the effects of the racism around them.

The 1890s also saw the rise of a campaign for the right of women to vote in Western Australia. It was a much quieter, more dignified affair than the campaign led by the suffragettes in Britain, but it was effective much sooner. At least some women had been given the vote by the time of the referendum on Federation in 1900. I decided to include something of these threads in the book as important background to the society in which O'Connor and Barnett lived.

Originally, I planned to end the book in 1897 with Dr Barnett's death. The same year saw the unofficial opening of Fremantle harbour, and O'Connor's investiture as a CMG (Commander of the Order of St Michael and St George) in London. It was a natural climax to the story. But after finishing the first draft, I revised this plan. It seemed unfair to O'Connor to leave him suspended in a moment of apparent triumph and hope for the future, when I knew that moment to be ephemeral. It also seemed unfair to the reader who, aware of the story of O'Connor's death, would be left wondering how he could have reached that low point from such a pinnacle.

So, I added a final chapter, which covers the course of events between 1897 and 1902, though in a more condensed form than the rest of the book. For those who want more detail about the building of the pipeline, and other aspects of O'Connor's life and career, I recommend Evan's and Tauman's biographies.

I also took the advice of one of my early readers to 'begin at the beginning' and tell the story of the two men's lives from their childhood, rather than trying to include their back stories in the main text as I did originally. I think this has greatly improved the readability of the book and provides better insight into the characters and motivations of the two men.

Notes to the reader:

This is a work of non-fiction, and nothing has been made up. However, I have sometimes taken the liberty of editing the formatting of material quoted, to make it easier to read, where I could do this without any change to the meaning of the text.

The official Hansard records of speeches made in parliament in this era were reported as indirect speech. I've converted some of these to direct speech. Thus, *The Premier said...He thought there had been a great deal of money spent on that building by the Government*, becomes *'I think a great deal of money has been spent on that building by the Government,' the Premier said.*

I've occasionally made similar changes to newspaper reports of speeches and interviews.

Hansard reports also often included long paragraphs full of colons and semicolons. I've removed some of these from the middle of sentences and replaced them with commas or full stops. And I've expanded the abbreviation 'Hon. Member' to Honourable Member'.

However, I've left the original spelling and punctuation in quotes from most personal letters and reports, as this often conveys something of the level of education, formality and state of mind of the person writing them.

In the nineteenth century, words like 'color', 'endeavor' and 'favor' were spelled without the 'u' that is customary now. I've kept these spellings in quoted material.

It was difficult to know how to refer to C. Y. O'Connor. Calling him 'Charles O'Connor' felt odd, since he is so widely known by his initials. During his lifetime, official documents and newspaper reports almost always called him "Mr O'Connor' or 'the Engineer-in-Chief', or 'the Chief Engineer'. In the end, I decided to refer to him simply as O'Connor (or the Engineer-in-Chief, or the Chief Engineer, capitalized) except when talking about his personal and family life, where I've sometimes used 'Charles'. Likewise, I've used 'Dr Barnett' most of the time, reserving 'Henry' for his personal life.

ONE: The boy from Belfast

In the early weeks of 1832, residents of Belfast in Ireland scanned the daily papers and listened to circulating rumours with a growing sense of dread. A strange and deadly new disease, cholera, was sweeping across Europe from Asia, killing thousands. Already it had reached Scotland. How long could it be kept from creeping into a port town like Belfast?

Sarah Barnett, wife of Belfast dentist Richard Barnett, shared the community's anxiety. With two young boys to care for and a third child due any day, she had good reason for wondering what the future would hold for them all.

On 10 February, Sarah gave birth to a healthy boy, to whom she and Richard gave the name 'Henry Calvert'. Their first two sons, Richard and John, were named after their paternal and maternal grandfathers. Henry was a common enough name in Belfast. But the Barnetts' reasons for choosing the name Calvert for their third son went unrecorded. Perhaps, as loyal Presbyterians, they had in mind the minister Henry Calvert, who arrived in Antrim in the 1600s, to help establish the Presbyterian church in Ireland.[6]

Despite the best efforts of the Belfast authorities to quarantine the city, the first case of cholera appeared less than three weeks after Henry's birth. It spread rapidly in the overcrowded slums and tenements that housed industrial Belfast's working class. By the summer of 1832, it had spread to the whole of Ireland.

When the epidemic came to an end in November, nearly three thousand Belfast residents had been infected and more than four hundred had died, including one of Sarah's brothers, William.[7,8] Henry's immediate family were spared, but the first year of his life passed in an atmosphere of unease and sadness.

Henry's father, Richard Barnett, the son of an influential merchant family, had set himself up as a dentist in Belfast in 1825, 'having acquired a thorough knowledge of the…profession in its various improved branches'.[9] Three years later he married Sarah Milford, the daughter of another family of Belfast merchants. In time, he came to own several properties around the town.

During Henry's childhood, the middle-class Barnett family lived in a pleasant home in Chichester Street, near the Belfast town centre and not far from the port on the river Lagan.[10] Their neighbours included a doctor, a dancing master and a vet, along with various 'gentlemen' of no named profession.[11] By 1844, three younger sisters (Helen, Isabella and Margaret) and two brothers (William and Albert) had been added to the family.

Belfast was unusual in Ireland in that it was highly industrialised, specialising in the production of linen thread and cloth. It was also unusual in being led by middle-class merchants and manufacturers such as the Barnett and Milford families, rather than by aristocratic landowners. The town was predominantly Protestant, though it had a sizable Catholic population.

What would later come to be known as 'the Protestant work ethic' was strong in Belfast, with both labourers and managers working long hours. Nevertheless, the arts, music, literature and sciences thrived, and the town liked to think of itself as 'the Athens of Ireland'.

Henry's father, Richard, had an interest in natural history, so it's likely he sometimes took his children to visit the Royal Botanical Gardens, when they opened to the public on Sunday afternoons. In this green oasis, young Henry would have been surrounded not just by carefully tended trees, shrubberies and flowerbeds, but by specimen plants from around the world, donated by travellers and explorers. Many were labelled with their botanical names and the exotic places from where they had been collected. Perhaps it was here that Henry developed his lifelong love of flowers. Here, too, he might have formed the desire to see the world beyond Belfast and Ireland.

That desire would have been nurtured by watching the ships coming and going from the port, carrying cargoes from all over the globe. During his childhood the channel formed by the Largan River was being straightened and deepened to allow ships to come right to the town centre. Belfast might have been grey and industrial, but for a young boy with an inquisitive nature there was always something interesting to observe.

Henry received his early education from tutors at home. When he reached high school age, he was sent to the school of theologian Dr William Molony, in Carrick Fergus, which his two older brothers, Richard and John, had attended. The school boasted that it provided 'all that may be required to facilitate the future advancement of the pupils in mercantile, military and professional life.' A resident French gentleman taught French every day, and 'in addition to the ancient and modern languages, music, drawing and dancing are continually taught.'[12] While Henry may not have relished learning Hebrew, Greek and Latin, he enjoyed music and dancing, and developed his skills in rowing, fencing and cricket.

In 1845, just as Henry entered his teen years, the Great Famine began. Potato blight, originating in north America, spread via Europe to Ireland. It devastated the potato crop on which a third of the Irish population depended, for food or employment or both. Infectious diseases such as typhoid and cholera followed, ravaging a population weakened by hunger. Over a million people died, while at least the same number fled Ireland. It was a disaster that would leave a scar on the psyche of the whole country.

A middle-class family like the Barnetts would not have gone hungry. Ireland was still growing and exporting other crops such as wheat and fruit, as well as dairy products, and the Barnetts had money to buy food. But Henry could not avoid seeing the ragged, emaciated people who began to crowd the streets of Belfast, looking for work, looking for relief, looking for a ship to take them away to England or America.

In May 1847, a woman was found dead on the pavement on Chichester Street. She and her husband and child had come from Lisburn, south of Belfast. Too weak to continue, she lay down on the street and died from fever while her husband was seeking help.[13]

People in Henry's parents' situation did what they could to help relieve suffering, by busying themselves with fund-raising for the local hospitals and workhouses, running soup kitchens and serving on relief committees. But it was a time of increasing sectarian tension. Henry may well have heard sermons, delivered by Presbyterian ministers, blaming the famine on the supposed laziness and lack of initiative among the Catholics.

Angry Catholics, especially those wanting independence for Ireland, accused the British government of deliberately starving the Irish. They suspected (sometimes rightly) that the Protestants providing aid were using it as a way of proselytizing. Though, as an adult, Henry remained a Protestant, he would choose to keep his own beliefs quite private.

Henry finished school in 1849, as the potato blight began to recede. His two older brothers had both gone to medical school in Edinburgh when they left school, but Henry was restless and wanted to travel before settling into more studies. He joined the *Salem*, a cargo ship headed for Quebec. Although his parents may have preferred him to finish his education and take up a profession, he wasn't exactly running away to sea against their wishes. The *Salem* was part-owned by his father and managed by Captain Josias Milford, almost certainly a relative of his mother.[14]

The outward journey proved uneventful. But when the *Salem* reached Quebec, the crew found the port in the grip of a cholera epidemic. After being detained in port for months, they took on a cargo of timber and began the return journey to Liverpool. Their vessel ran aground off the Gulf of St Lawrence and had to be towed back to Quebec. While the ship was being repaired, the adventurous Henry bought a birch-bark canoe and went exploring up the Saint Lawrence River.

The *Salem* eventually sailed from Quebec again, with Henry Barnett on board. But the crew's troubles were not over. A tremendous storm off the Banks of Newfoundland left the *Salem* without lifeboats or water-casks and with damage to the rigging. In icy conditions, with the crew on half-rations because salt water had got into the provisions, the ship limped back to Liverpool.

Disenchanted, for now, by life at sea, Henry returned home. During his time away, the newly completed Queen's University Belfast had opened, and he was able to undertake his medical studies without leaving Belfast.[15]

The yearning to be at sea soon returned. In 1855, after being accepted as a member of the Royal College of Surgeons, he joined the Peninsular and Oriental (P & O) Steampacket Company as a ship's surgeon.[16] His travels aboard the steamship *Bengal* took him to ports across Asia: Bombay, Calcutta, Colombo, Singapore, Hong Kong and Shanghai. He also visited Egypt and the Middle East.

In 1856, he responded to a call to serve as doctor to the American and English merchant community in Foochow (Fuzhou). It was not an easy time to be in China. The country was in the grip of a civil war, known as the Taiping Rebellion. On one occasion, a close friend of Henry Barnett, Howard Cunningham, was speared in the abdomen when he went to defend his Cantonese servant against Fokien attackers. Cunningham died in Dr Barnett's arms later that evening.[17] As the only doctor in the area, it fell to Henry to perform an autopsy and send a report to the American embassy.[18]

During his time in China, he would experience Chinese inter-ethnic rivalries, the trickery of con-artists and attacks by pirates. He subsequently developed a view of Asians that was neither unduly romantic nor ignorantly prejudiced.

While in Foochow, he was still able to satisfy his appetite for exploring unknown territory. In 1858, he accompanied an American missionary, Edward Wentworth, on an expedition up the river Min to Yeng Ping, at that time unreached by westerners.[19] Wentworth was intent on distributing Christian literature to the villages along the way. It was, at times, a hair-raising journey, over rapids and through rocky gullies. Henry quipped that he should expect a medal from the Missionary Society for his services when they returned.

His main interest, though, was in the scenery and vegetation through which they were passing. At times he was overwhelmed by the beauty of it. 'I don't wonder that the Chinese call their country the Central Flowery Land', he exclaimed to Wentworth. He collected seeds which he later sent to his father, who in turn donated them to the Royal Botanic Society in Belfast.[20]

After three years in Foochow, and suffering poor health, Henry set off, via Manilla, to California. Accompanied by his dog, Belle, and a companion from Hong Kong named Shortrede, he made his way on horseback to the goldfields and then to Yosemite, a trip he would later describe as one of the best he ever made.[21]

At Yosemite, he and his friend encountered a party that included a Colonel Lawrence and his sister, a man named Duff, and a daughter and niece of Colonel Fremont. (Fremont, a somewhat controversial explorer and military man, would later found the Californian Republican Party and nominate for president of the United States.) They camped and travelled together in the wilderness for several days, eating around the campfire at night and sharing stories and songs.

Henry was impressed by the grandeur of the landscape, which was still in its pristine state. He was also impressed, and delighted, by the hardiness, and cheerfulness, of the young women in the party, who seemed unfazed by having to sleep on the ground, even in the rain.

Henry and Shortrede left the rest of the party when it returned to Colonel Fremont's home. Colonel Lawrence later accompanied the pair on a trek to see the 'big trees', the giant sequoia trees at Calaveras. Henry was awe-struck. 'I despair of giving you any idea of these glorious trees', he wrote to friends in Belfast. 'I had heard of them, read of them, seen pictures of them, but never imagined anything like them...The pyramids did not astonish me so much.' Again, he collected seed cones and sent them to his father for the Botanic Gardens in Belfast.

Having crisscrossed the southern United States, he returned home to Belfast and then went on to Edinburgh, where in 1860, at the age of twenty-eight, he became a licentiate of the Royal College of Physicians.[22]

Still looking for adventure, he sailed from London to Melbourne in 1861, and travelled on horseback around outback Victoria, New South Wales and Queensland, still accompanied by his little dog Belle. The descriptive articles he wrote about his travels in country still largely unexplored by Europeans, were published by English magazines and journals. They would earn him a Fellowship of the Royal Geographic Society.[23]

By 1864, he was back at sea. While working as ship's doctor aboard the *Malabar* along the West African coast, he met the woman who would become his first wife, Annie Lee Frost Matthews, nee Copplestone.

Henry was traveling to West Africa to take up a post with the P & O Company, while Annie and two of her children were on their way to Sierra Leone to join her husband, a naval officer named Thomas Leethem, aboard the hulk *Isis*. During the voyage, Henry and Annie developed a friendship that he would later describe as 'intimate', and Annie confided in him that her husband badly mistreated her.

Henry left Sierra Leone aboard the *Malabar* twenty-four hours after arriving. But on his return to the port, he visited Annie. He found her in a terrible state, lying in bed with a fever. She said the climate was bad for her health and again complained of her husband's cruelty towards her. She desperately wanted to return to England to her parents but had no money.

Henry, feeling sympathetic, offered to lend her what she needed, and she accepted his offer. Some months later, when he arrived back in Liverpool, Annie was waiting for him.[24]

In April 1865, Thomas Leethem filed for divorce from Annie, citing Henry Barnett as co-respondent. Leethem alleged that Henry and Annie were living as man and wife in an adulterous relationship. Both Annie and Henry denied the allegation of adultery, though they shared the same address. The divorce was granted in 1866. Custody of Annie's children with Leethem remained with their father, as was customary at the time.[25]

While waiting for the divorce to become official, Henry and Annie rented a house in Milford, in Pembrokeshire, Wales, where Henry set up in private medical practice. Now aged in his mid-thirties, he seems to have been unready to settle into routine domestic life. In January 1867, while Annie was heavily pregnant, he got into an argument with his landlord, a shipbuilder named Roberts.

When the case came to court in December, Henry alleged that he had asked Roberts to leave the house after Roberts had insulted him. Roberts had struck him about the head with the handle of his umbrella, causing deep wounds and lasting dizziness and memory loss. Henry appeared in court looking frail and had to remain seated in the witness box while giving evidence. He called several medical witnesses to corroborate his claims. Roberts argued that he had acted in self-defence after Henry had behaved aggressively towards him.

During the hearing, Henry and Annie's domestic arrangements at the time of the assault were exposed and discussed. Annie was called as a witness, though she hadn't seen the assault happen. She agreed that Henry had suffered lasting effects from his injuries. Under cross examination she also revealed that Henry had sometimes been 'very irritable', even before this event.

The jury found in Henry's favour but awarded damages of a mere one farthing (a quarter of a penny, the minimum possible.) They may have felt that Henry was putting on an act, appearing frailer than he really was. But it's also likely that they were showing their disapproval of a man who had been living openly with another man's wife.[26]

Henry Barnett and Annie were married in a registry office in London in 1867, not long after the assault by Roberts. But the social stigma of being married to a divorcee affected Henry's practice, while his innate need for adventure left him restless. He applied to the Colonial Office for a position overseas and accepted the post of Resident Medical Officer in rural York, southeast of Perth, in the remote Swan River colony. The following year, he and Annie and their two children, Alexander and Florence, boarded the barque *Lady Louisa* to travel to Western Australia. The voyage would bring about dramatic and far-reaching changes to the lives of both Henry and Annie.

TWO: Stormy times

The Barnetts quickly established themselves in the life of the small community in York. The district was large and the medical practice a busy one, enough for two men, it was said, though Henry was replacing the only doctor.[27] But soon his own health problems began to interfere with his ability to work.

During the voyage to Western Australia, Henry had injured his left knee when he fell over a ringbolt on the ship. Complications set in, and it became clear that the leg would have to be amputated. An above-knee amputation was performed at the Perth Public Hospital in January 1869.

When the stump failed to heal, Henry insisted his reluctant doctors perform a second, and then a third, higher amputation. The doctors said a further operation would kill him. Knowing the risk of sepsis spreading beyond the leg, and feeling close to death, Henry argued it would be lifesaving.[28]

It did indeed save him, but the amputation affected every aspect of his life, physically, mentally and socially. Rehabilitation services were non-existent. It was up to Henry to manage his own recovery. He hired a manservant to push him around in a wheeled chair and gradually he became proficient at using crutches. Annie was expected to help with dressing his wounds.

During his convalescence, Henry distracted himself by writing letters, poetry and short stories, many of which he submitted to the local newspapers under the rueful pseudonym 'Uniped'. He took an interest in, and made suggestions on, topics as varied as the best way to conduct elections, how to prevent the spread of fire in Fremantle, and the geology of the coastline in relation to harbour improvements.

He and his family eventually returned to York. But now that he could no longer easily ride a horse or walk long distances over uneven ground, Henry had lost the mobility necessary to serve a widely spread rural population. He asked to be moved and, in May 1872, he was appointed Colonial Surgeon for Fremantle and Superintendent of the colony's only asylum in that town.[29]

As colonial surgeon, Henry Barnett was responsible to the colony's Principal Medical Officer for managing most aspects of health in Fremantle. He had a role in providing sanitation and infection control, immunizations, quarantine and inspection of ships' crews. Until he was relieved of the responsibility in the early 1880s, he was also the visiting medical officer for the prison in Fremantle and the Aboriginal prison on Rottnest.

Superintending the asylum in Fremantle was seen as a part-time position. His role was chiefly to admit patients sent there by the courts, and by medical colleagues, and decide when they could be discharged. In 1870, psychiatry as a discipline was in its infancy. Henry had no specialized training and little experience in dealing with mental illness. But it was assumed that any competent doctor could manage an asylum.

He took on the role with a level of dedication that undoubtedly exceeded what was expected of him. In fact, his determination to bring about improvements to the asylum led to him becoming a thorn in the flesh of the government in the years ahead.

Although he had less travelling to do, the onerous nature of these posts meant that Henry Barnett had little time to spend at home with his family, which now included four children. The Barnett's third child, Henry (Harry) had been born in Fremantle in 1869, while they were waiting for Henry senior to recover from his surgery. Their youngest child, Isabelle Margaret Olive (known as Olive) was also born there in 1871.

Much of what little spare time Henry did have was taken up by other pursuits. He joined the Fremantle Literary Institute, and within a few years had become its president.[30] He became known for his skill in reading aloud poetry and other works, a form of entertainment popular at the time. Even before he left York, he had been appointed a Justice of the Peace and he sat regularly on the bench of the magistrates' court in Fremantle.[31] In October 1872, he was appointed to the newly constituted Medical Board.[32]

Annie occasionally took part in musical events, such as a fundraising concert for the literary society, but her role in the community was much less remarked upon than Henry's.[33] While she enjoyed singing, and had a good voice, her ability to sing comfortably was affected by shortness of breath caused by her increasing problem with dropsy, a form of congestive heart disease.[34]

Annie had been happy to be a doctor's wife, but she resented being nurse to an invalid while Henry recovered from his surgery. She found Henry more irritable and demanding than he had been, as he adjusted to the physical and psychological effects of losing a limb. Her own health problems received little sympathy from him. She apparently found some secret satisfaction in giving several bottles from his wine cellar to the servants without his consent, though her generosity backfired when Henry accused one of them of stealing.[35]

By 1876, Annie had begun a very public affair with a younger man named Thomas Stockley King, a Fremantle merchant. They were often seen walking arm in arm together. King was reported to have visited Mrs Barnett several times late at night. Henry ignored the liaison for as long as he could, but Annie's rejection of him for a younger, fitter man rankled.

After discovering amorous letters in Annie's possession, along with a photograph of King marked 'To be ever worn near my heart', Henry confronted Annie and told her he wanted nothing more to do with her. He drew up an agreement with her for their separation. If she would give up her affair and live well away from Fremantle, he would support her financially. Such agreements between disillusioned spouses were not unusual at a time when divorce was difficult and expensive.

Henry also obtained an agreement from King, through an intermediary, that he would have no further meetings with Annie. King helpfully handed over to Dr Barnett the amorous letters he had received from Annie. They were later used as evidence in the Barnett's divorce case.

Despite the agreements, the affair continued. In January 1877, Henry

Barnett created a stir in Fremantle by firing three shots from a revolver at his rival, while King was walking with Annie Barnett. Henry had earlier threatened to shoot King if he didn't give up meeting with her.

Although neither King nor Annie was wounded, Henry was charged with discharging a revolver with intent to kill. His lawyer argued in court that there was no evidence that the revolver was even loaded. The doctor had intended only to frighten Stockley King.[36] This was almost certainly true. Henry was an experienced hunter, well used to handling guns. If he had really intended to kill King, he would not have missed. The case against Dr Barnett was dismissed. Stockley King left the colony for good a few months later.

In September 1877, Henry petitioned for divorce on the grounds of Annie's alleged adultery. Theirs was the first divorce case to be heard in the fifty-year-old Swan River colony and the legal profession, as well as the press, followed the proceedings closely.[37] The fact that Henry was represented in court by the colony's attorney-general, Henry Hicks Hocking, under instruction from his lawyer, Septimus Burt, and the case was heard by the latter's father, chief justice Sir Archibald Burt, demonstrates the importance of the case in the close-knit community.

Annie failed to give persuasive evidence that her relationship with Stockley King was platonic.[38] She tried, more convincingly, to argue that Henry Barnett had cruelly mistreated her in an ongoing way, by describing several episodes of Henry's alleged violence towards her. One witness, a female servant who had lived with the Barnetts during their first year in Western Australia, described the doctor as a 'contrary, disagreeable man' who had few kind words for his wife. But she said she had never seen him act violently towards Annie.[39]

Henry did not deny that on one occasion he had struck Annie across the face, when he discovered her writing a love letter to King after she had promised to abandon the affair. Annie described to the court how Henry 'jumped into the middle of the room' and 'sprang onto the bed' in the hotel room where she was writing the letter, before attempting to throttle her. She claimed that she had screamed for help, and two sailors had come to her assistance, pulling Henry away from her. Henry said the two men had merely told him to calm down. The sailors had since gone to sea, so could not corroborate either story.

Nevertheless, the judge felt that there was evidence of Henry's violence and ill temper towards Annie.[40] Chief Justice Burt was also critical of Henry's own adultery with Annie prior to their marriage. The case ended with a *decree nisi*. Henry Barnett was ordered to pay his ex-wife ten pounds per month for as long as she remained single, provided that she stayed more than ten miles from Fremantle. Once again, Annie gave up her children as a result of being divorced.

She died only two years later, in August 1879, from dropsy.[41] She was forty-nine. A newspaper columnist in 1917 claimed that Henry and Annie had remarried just a few weeks after the divorce. There is no record of this, though they may have reconciled.[42]

The year after Annie's death, Henry married Emily Winn Stephens, from the small farming community of Northampton, three hundred miles north of Perth. Emily had accompanied her sister, Mary Jane, and her brother-in-law, Samuel Mitchell, when they migrated with their children from Cornwall in England in 1875. Seventeen years younger than Henry, with a petite figure and kindly face, Emily took on the care of his four children. Their marriage was childless but apparently happy.

The doctor and his family had previously lived in a two-storey house in Cantonment Street in Fremantle, but with four growing children to accommodate, it seemed time to move.[43] In December 1883, Henry Barnett acquired three adjacent lots of land between Quarry Street and Fremantle Park (an extensive area of open ground) and began building a new home for himself and his family.[44] The block on which the house, Park Bungalow, was built was on a limestone rise, close to the park and the quarry that gave the street its name. The road that fronted the blocks, at right angles to Quarry Street, soon became known as Barnett Street.[45]

The building was completed in November 1884, at a cost of just under two thousand pounds. Within a year or so, the iron roof began leaking badly and expensive repairs were needed. The collar ties between the rafters had been omitted and this had led to the roof being defective. Dr Barnett sued the architect, James Manning, claiming that he had been negligent in supervising the builders, J. Harwood and Sons. The case was settled in Dr Barnett's favour and the roof repaired.

The house was built on tall limestone foundations. A steep flight of stone steps led up to wide verandahs which gave views of the Swan River and the ocean in one direction, the park and the Asylum in the other.

A photo of Park Bungalow taken in the 1960s shows it rundown, the roof rusted, the walls beside the decaying limestone steps overtaken by creepers and the verandah forbiddingly dark. But when landscape artist James Goatcher (1878-1957) painted it sometime after 1903, he portrayed the house set in a garden full of brightly coloured flowers, with sweeping steps leading to welcoming shade. Given Dr Barnett's love of flowers, this was probably how it looked when he lived there.[46]

THREE: Charles Yelverton O'Connor

In 1864, about the time that Henry Barnett and Annie Leethem met aboard the *Malabar*, another young Irishman was pondering what to do with his life. Born in County Meath, in 1843, Charles Yelverton O'Connor was ten years younger than Barnett. Like Barnett, he came from a respectable Protestant family, though the O'Connors were members of the Church of Ireland rather than Presbyterian.

The O'Connor family had connections to the Irish aristocracy by descent through the Yelvertons, on both his mother and his father's side. His mother's sister, Cecilia O'Keefe, was also married to a Yelverton, Barry John Yelverton, 3rd Viscount Avonmore. The O'Connor side of the family claimed to have roots in the ancient Irish kings of Connaught.[47]

Charles' first six years of life were spent in comfort in Gravelmount, a six-bedroomed manor house on a wooded hillside with adjoining land. His father, John O'Connor, leased the property from a wealthy landowner, Thomas Longfield. Some of it he farmed and the rest he sub-let to tenants. Elizabeth O'Connor, Charles' mother, was known for the lavish dinner parties she put on to entertain their extended family and members of the local gentry.

When the Great Famine struck Ireland in 1845, the O'Connor family were financially ruined. Charles' father John, the son of a clergymen, had strong Christian principles. In an effort to relieve the suffering of the impoverished people around him, he employed extra men on his farm, though he had no work for them to do. He brought in grain to feed those who were starving and was lenient in collecting rents from his tenants. As the famine went on, he lost most of his income.

The family gave up their lease on Gravelmount and all the stock and equipment was sold.[48] 'When Mr O'Connor left Gravelmount, the poor lost in him a sincere friend, who made many personal sacrifices on their behalf far exceeding his means in times of sore-pressing calamity,' the Meath Herald reported.[49]

John O'Connor found work as secretary to the Waterford and Limerick Railway Company, and the parents and two older sons (George and Lorenzo) moved to Waterford in the south of Ireland. But Charles and his younger sister, Frances, were sent to stay with an aunt and uncle, Martha and Samuel Garnett, at their country property, Summerseat, near Dublin. They would remain there until Charles reached high school age.

It is difficult to know what impact this would have had on young Charles. It wasn't unusual at the time for children to be sent to stay with relatives if their parents thought that it would be to their material or social advantage. It's likely that Charles and Frances were used to being cared for mainly by servants rather than by their mother and father. The lack of servants to care for the youngest children may even have contributed to the parents' decision not to take them to Waterford. But they were being removed from a household with five children and all the people they were familiar with, to one that had previously been childless.

Nothing suggests that Charles and his sister were treated with anything but kindness by his aunt Martha and uncle Samuel. They had the freedom of a country life that they would not have had in crowded Waterford. The Garnetts were well known for their stables, and Charles learned to ride and developed his life-long love of horses while he was living with them. But the separation from his family must still have been a dramatic upheaval for a child of his age.

Charles returned to the family for his high-school years. His two older brothers, George and Lorenzo, had both gone to Trinity College, Dublin, and then joined the military. Charles knew, even before he left school, that he wanted to be an engineer. At seventeen, he became apprenticed to John Chaloner Smith, the chief engineer of the railway company where his father worked.

Smith was known for his considerateness and his encouraging attitude toward his apprentices. Under his guidance, the young O'Connor soon demonstrated great ability, not just as an engineer, but also as a financial manager and supervisor. He could handle emergencies well, keeping a cool head, and he impressed his employers.[50]

After the death of both his parents in 1863, O'Connor decided, like many young professional men of that era, to move overseas. Work on constructing the railways in Ireland was coming to an end, and he was looking for new challenges. Initially he considered going to South America, but soon settled on New Zealand. He left Ireland in December 1864, at the age of twenty-one, with a recommendation from John Chaloner Smith.

Over the next twenty-seven years he worked his way up the engineering ladder in New Zealand, from assistant surveyor at a remote camp south of Auckland, to Marine Engineer for the whole colony.

During his stay in the Westland region in 1869, O'Connor was mentored and befriended by the district surveyor, Malcolm Fraser. The following year Fraser would become Western Australia's surveyor general. By 1891, Fraser had become 'Sir Malcolm' and had been appointed colonial secretary. Fraser would be responsible for notifying O'Connor, by telegram, of the vacancy for the position of engineer-in-chief in Western Australia.[51]

O'Connor met his wife, Susan Laetitia Ness, in 1873, while working in Christchurch. Susan's family had migrated from Northumberland to New Zealand when she was nine years old, and Christchurch had been her home ever since. Charles O'Connor had worked with her father, government architect William Ness.

O'Connor and Susan were married on 5 March 1874, the day after Susan gave birth to their first child, Aileen. Susan's parents were the only witnesses at the wedding ceremony. Why Charles and Susan left the marriage until such a late date is unknown. Was there a reluctance on the part of one or both to marry? Had Susan's parents been against the match? Or did Aileen enter the world sooner than expected? Whatever the reason, it was never discussed outside the family.[52]

A photo of the couple taken in 1874, possibly just after their wedding, shows Susan standing behind the seated O'Connor, one hand on the back of his chair. She looks down demurely. It was a pose common in photos of couples at the time. He sits, arms folded across his chest, legs crossed, and he frowns slightly at the camera, as if bemused or uncertain about being asked to pose for the shot.[53]

The first few years of their marriage involved much time alone for Susan, raising their growing family in small rural towns. Charles travelled widely as he helped to build roads, bridges, and ports around New Zealand. All the while, his standing as an engineer increased.

In 1879, while working on the harbour at Hokitika in South Island, he met the great English marine engineer, Sir John Coode, who had arrived in New Zealand to inspect all its harbour works. Coode was impressed with the young engineer and would support O'Connor's application for membership of the prestigious Institute of Civil Engineers the following year. Yet ironically, Sir John Coode's name would become a source of great irritation when O'Connor arrived in Western Australia a few years later.

In March 1880, two events occurred which shed light on O'Connor's philosophy and character. The family were busy preparing to move from Hokitika to Dunedin, where O'Connor had been appointed Inspecting Engineer for the whole of the South Island of New Zealand. On 20 March, a Saturday evening, a testimonial dinner was held in Hokitika in his honour. In a farewell speech, O'Connor gave credit to the miners he had worked alongside for the past fourteen years for helping him mature, from a boy with a collection of inherited assumptions and beliefs, to someone who could think and deliberate for himself.

> *'Can anyone fail, having thought a little, to find that the conservative prejudices of the one particular school in which he was brought up are not* all *right, and that beliefs and thoughts and practices which one had been carefully trained up to look upon with horror, were believed in and thought and practised by men infinitely wiser and better in*

> *every way than ones-self? Or, in a word, can anyone fail under such circumstances, to become less of the conceited, exclusive, and pedantic boy, and more of the hearty cosmopolitan, more of the liberal minded sympathiser with all created beings? I think not...'*

Much of the rest of his speech was taken up with a discussion of the dangers of uniformity in the education provided to 'the masses'. He also extolled the west coast scenery, its beauty and grandeur. Like Henry Barnett, he was awestruck by the beauties of nature. Unlike Henry Barnett, who was inspired to write poetry in response to being moved by what he saw, O'Connor thought it a source of inspiration for future poets and songwriters in New Zealand.[54]

O'Connor had never been to university, but his life in the mining camps had provided him with a broad and diverse education. While he clearly valued this, not everyone he worked with in future would appreciate his free-thinking, independent attitude.

On the Sunday morning after the farewell dinner, 21 March, the family's plans for moving were upended when eight-month-old Charles Goring O'Connor suffered extensive burns as a result of an accident with boiling water. The exact nature of the accident is unknown; one newspaper said he fell into the water, others that it tipped over him.[55] Scalding accidents to young children were not uncommon in this era, when most homes had no hot water on tap, and boiling water was carried around the house to where it was needed. Toddlers could fall into water being prepared for bathing or laundry. But for a child of young Charles' age, simply pulling a hot teapot off a table could be enough to cause severe scalding.

Baby Charles died early the following day. The O'Connor family were devastated. Their move to Dunedin was postponed for a week.[56] Yet it reveals something of C. Y. O'Connor's character that during that week he took time to correct a newspaper report of the farewell speech he had given on the Saturday. What had been printed was his notes, what he would have wished to say in farewell to his friends, he wrote, while his actual speech had been much briefer.[57] The letter was the product of a man who valued accuracy, but also of a man who dealt with strong emotions by keeping busy.

O'Connor continued to be promoted to positions of ever greater responsibility and authority. In 1883, he was appointed Under-Secretary for Public Works in Wellington. He gave up his plans for taking long-service leave overseas to take up the position.[58] In May 1890, he was made marine engineer for the whole country.[59] This took him from a desk job back to more practical engineering work, something he had been wanting to do.

Yet O'Connor was struggling with disappointment and dissatisfaction. In his appointment as marine engineer, he had been passed over by the New Zealand government for the post of engineer-in-chief in favour of a man who he felt was less qualified. His current position was insecure, and his salary less than he thought appropriate. He had a wife and seven children to support and was at an age where he needed to consider how he would fund his retirement. After having lived in New Zealand all of his adult life, he began to look overseas for a solution.

FOUR: Dr Barnett and his guests – 1891

Pedestrians walking along Quarry Street, in Fremantle, one warm summer evening in January 1891, might have heard singing and the strains of a violin coming from a substantial house set well back from the road. These sounds were not the cheerful fiddling and raucous songs that might be heard on any night of the week, outside the many hotel bar rooms of Fremantle. The music came from one of Dr Henry Barnett's musical 'at homes'.[60]

Earlier that day, the wide verandahs of Park Bungalow had been enclosed with calico, which excluded the rough and tumble life of the port town outside and improved the acoustics. Inside, the gaudy Japanese lanterns strung under the roof echoed the bright colours of the ladies' summer dresses, while flowers, potted plants, and bamboo added a tropical, festive touch.

Dr Barnett, now in his late fifties, with a receding hairline and greying moustache, observed the crowd of almost a hundred guests. They were listening attentively to the talented but mercurial Francis Hart singing a solo, accompanied on the violin by Mr M. B. O'Reilly, a newcomer to the colony.[61] Francis was husband to Dr Barnett's niece by marriage, Lilian, who was also present that evening.

Among the guests was another recent arrival in the colony, the new governor, Sir William Robinson. Here too were Justice Stone, and Major Phillips, the commandant of the armed forces, along with Dr Barnett's old friends, Archdeacon Watkins and William (Bill) Marmion, the member for Fremantle.

Unmistakable among the crowd was the mountainous form of the colony's recently elected Premier and treasurer, John Forrest. Standing over six feet tall and weighing sixteen stone, Forrest was no longer the fit and muscular adventurer he had been when Dr Barnett first arrived in Fremantle. But he still retained his popularity as a local hero. It was rumoured that Forrest, the miller's son from Bunbury, would soon become 'Sir John', in recognition of his new political status and his past services to the colony as surveyor and explorer.

Henry Barnett and John Forrest had known each other for a long time. Forrest had been an official visitor at the asylum in the early 1880s.[62] He had made regular inspections and was familiar with its layout and working. Whether he understood what it was like to be incarcerated in a place holding almost three times more residents than it was intended for was another question. Henry Barnett had certainly done his best to make sure he did.

These men and their wives, along with a cross-section of Perth and Fremantle's residents, mingled with an easy familiarity, born of the frequency with which they met each other socially. In this isolated colony, with its population of just over forty-five thousand people, the elite of every sphere of society formed a small and cohesive clan.

Making sure that all ran smoothly that evening was Emily Barnett. Emily was a dependable, respectable woman who quietly got on with things.

A solo on the violin by Mr. O'Reilly came to an end. As the applause and murmured appreciation ebbed, a quartet of singers, two men and two women, stood to perform 'I Love Thee So', a song set to music by the governor, Sir William Robinson. It was one of three of his compositions sung that night and seemed a fitting finale to the programme.

But the audience was not ready to go home yet. The floor was cleared, and an impromptu dance began, perhaps enhanced by some of the contents of Dr Barnett's excellent wine cellar. The musicians were happy to provide light-hearted music for dancing.

A sense of optimism pervaded the gathering that evening at Park Bungalow. Just months earlier, on October 25th, 1890, the British parliament had granted Western Australia the right to responsible self-government. The colony now had a two-house parliamentary system and its own constitution.

The new lower house, the Legislative Assembly, led by John Forrest, had ambitious plans for developing the colony and taking it into federation with the other Australian colonies.

These plans included building railway lines from Perth to Bunbury and the Yilgarn goldfields; extensions to several other existing rail lines; harbour improvements at Geraldton, Carnarvon and other ports; upgrading and extending the telegraph system; a lighthouse at Cape Leeuwin; and above all, creating a harbour at Fremantle suitable for ocean-going steamships. Improvements to the asylum were not high on the agenda.

* * *

One Saturday morning, not long after the musical evening, a visitor arrived at the heavy wooden gate of the Fremantle Lunatic Asylum on Finnerty Street. As he waited for someone to let him in, he pondered the gothic looking building behind the high stone wall. The word 'mournful' came to mind.

He was curious to see how the Fremantle asylum compared with other asylums he had visited in the 'more advanced' colonies of Australia, including Callan Park in New South Wales and the lunatic asylum at Kew, in Melbourne.[63] But mere curiosity wasn't the only reason for his visit. He intended to write an article for publication in the *Daily News* newspaper. Dr Barnett had been happy to agree to his visit and promised to show him around. The doctor had no qualms about using the newspapers to publicise the dire state of the colony's only asylum.

The gate opened and the visitor was shown to Dr Barnett's office by a staff member, dressed in what looked to him like a prison warder's uniform. The man most likely *was* a prisoner, seconded from the nearby Fremantle prison to work as an attendant in the men's wing of the asylum.

The few items of furniture in the doctor's cramped, oddly shaped office in a corner of the building, harked back to a bygone era. To the visitor, who used the pen name 'Traveller' in his subsequent account, the room resembled the rough accommodation of a second-class pub.

Dr Barnett arrived and introduced himself. The Belfast-born doctor still spoke with a trace of an accent. He outlined to his visitor the general running of the asylum and the many problems created by overcrowding and underfunding. He then led the way out of his office to the accommodation in the male section of the asylum.

This was in the original part of the two-storey building, constructed of local limestone by convict labour in the 1860s. Separate male and female areas were divided internally by a central staircase and externally by a six-foot wall. The asylum had been designed to house up to fifty patients. It now contained a hundred and twenty.

Everything about the place reeked of the convict era. It had been built primarily to detain mentally unwell convicts who couldn't be cared for in the prison. Many of those transported to Western Australia by the British Government between 1858 and 1868 had pre-existing mental health problems when they arrived, and many continued to need care after transportation came to an end.

Two of the elderly male patients introduced by Dr Barnett told the visitor they had been residents of the asylum since 1858, thirty-three years earlier. They had been accommodated in a temporary asylum prior to the completion of the present building.

From the beginning, the asylum had also housed civilian patients, male and female, alongside the all-male convicts. In 1886, control of the asylum passed from the imperial government in London to the colonial government in Perth. But the penal atmosphere remained. Patients were still officially classified as Imperial (if they were ex-convicts) or Colonial.

Dr Barnett's visitor noted the cell-like rooms, the bare wooden floor-boards, the broad-arrow markings on the bedding, the lack of anything stimulating or cheerful or inviting. He thought if the inmates ever had a moment of sanity, they would have been forgiven for thinking that they had been incarcerated, under sentence of death, for the most diabolical crime.

In one room they found a Burmese man named Sue Long. He was lying on the wooden floor, though there was a stretcher bed in the room. Dr Barnett explained that the unfortunate man had an abscess in his spine, and the unrelenting pain from this had driven him insane. The floor offered more support than the sagging stretcher. Apart from the bed and a blanket, there was nothing else in the room, just bare, whitewashed walls.

From that distressing sight, Dr Barnett led his guest past more dreary cells until they reached the exercise yard. Here, patients in all states and stages of illness sat huddled together aimlessly in the summer heat. A clean but inadequate cook house stood to one side of this yard.

The asylum took in not only patients with acute and chronic mental illnesses, but also those with congenital intellectual disability, and elderly people with dementia. Patients could also be admitted if they suffered from a physical illness with neurological symptoms, such as epilepsy, alcoholism, or tertiary syphilis. It was a place of last resort—most families preferred to keep their mentally unwell relatives at home if they could.

Dr Barnett showed the visitor one ward occupied by those who were so physically disabled, by age or illness, that they were confined to bed. As in the cells, the whitewashed walls were bare of anything to look at.

Beyond the exercise yard, past the featureless recreation ground on the male side of the six-foot wall, the visitor and his guide progressed into the outdoor area of the female side. Here they found thirty or forty women, ranging in age from fourteen to seventy. Young women in the throes of post-natal illness sat slumped besides elderly women with dementia. Other patients wandered restlessly about the yard.

A woman could be sent to the asylum by the courts for showing evidence of 'moral insanity', including frequent drunkenness, prostitution, vagrancy, or behaviour that her husband considered 'wild'. Dr Barnett was attuned to the problem of domestic violence and tried to ensure that women were returning to a safe place when they were discharged. He was not always successful.[64]

Apart from opiates and the sedative chloral hydrate, Dr Barnett had few medications available to him for treating his patients. Treatment, in theory, revolved around providing patients with compassion, kindness and a dignified existence in a clean, comfortable, structured environment.

In 1872, not long after he became superintendent of the Fremantle asylum, Dr Barnett had drawn up a list of 'Rules for the guidance of attendants'. Under the motto 'Gentleness. Firmness. Truthfulness' he listed six guidelines for the attendants to follow:

> *1. An Asylum is not merely a house for the accommodation of persons of unsound mind, it is an institution for the cure of those laboring under mental disease.*
>
> *2. Patients must be employed as much as possible. The more heartily Attendants enter into amusement and encourage occupation of the Patients, the more highly they will be esteemed.*
>
> *3. In dealing with the insane it is wrong to suppose that any special line of conduct is advisable; the more nearly they are treated as sane and reasonable beings the more easily will they be managed.*
>
> *4. No kind of deception should be practised towards patients, either with a view of rendering them more amiable to management or of inducing them to undertake work; all promises made must be strictly kept.*
>
> *5. Should violence towards a patient be proved against an Attendant, immediate dismissal will follow.*
>
> *6. The study of the Attendants must be to induce the Patients to apply themselves to some occupation; and the Surgeon will feel obliged to the Attendants for any suggestion tending towards improvement of the health or comfort of the Patients.*[65]

These rules remained the ideal to which Dr Barnett and his staff aspired and they were still displayed on the asylum walls in 1891. Putting them into practice, however, had become increasingly difficult as the asylum became more and more crowded.

Even employing adequate staff was difficult, due to the lack of funding and space to house them. The staff ate with the patients because their own dining room was being used for beds.

Year after year, in his annual reports, Dr Barnett pleaded with the government to do something about the situation. In 1888, after the Colonial Secretary remarked to his government colleagues that 'for the last ten years the necessity of the work has been dinned into our ears by the Surgeon Superintendent', the colonial government set aside a sum of nearly two thousand pounds for improvements.[66]

Plans were drawn up by the government architect, George Temple Poole, for a new wing on the south side of the building, with staff accommodation and extra wards. It was another six months before the tender was finally awarded to Bunning Brothers in June 1890, and the work completed. But the extra female ward and a room for the matron that it provided barely made an impression on the overcrowded conditions.[67,68]

As Dr Barnett and his visitor proceeded around the building and grounds, the doctor commented bitterly that the government, 'apparently can find money for everything except that required to ameliorate the condition of those who can have little pleasure in life, and whose very existence must often be one of grief to themselves and those associated with them.'

'Surely,' he went on, 'their diseased minds should be sufficient for them to endure without the additional wretchedness of having to put up with semi-prison life, in every shape and form.'

Yet it was impossible to provide anything better than prison fare while the government provided only forty-five pounds per year for the upkeep of each patient.

'So long as this prison element exists in our Asylum, the hope of inmates being cured must always be a small one, except in very rare cases indeed. In fact, it is evident our Asylum is intended to confine, certainly not to cure,' said Dr Barnett.

The overcrowding, he went on, made it impossible to separate those with temporary conditions, needing quietness and rest, from the noisy, the aggressive and the congenitally unwell.

The asylum was no longer able to accept the private patients whose fees had once helped to ease the financial strain on the asylum's budget. Now, the relatives of those who could afford to pay took them to asylums in other colonies, or even overseas. But even the less well-off couldn't always be admitted. Potential patients sometimes found themselves in a cell in the police lock-up for lack of a bed at the asylum.

To supplement his government stipend of three hundred pounds annually as colonial surgeon and one hundred pounds as superintendent of the asylum, Dr Barnett also ran a private general practice in Fremantle.[69] But that left him with far less time than he felt he required to supervise the asylum. In his annual reports, he regularly called on the government to increase his stipend as superintendent and appoint someone else as colonial surgeon, so that he could devote his time to the care of the mentally ill. The government seemed blind and deaf to his requests.

His visitor, in the report published by the *Daily News* newspaper, compared what he had seen in Fremantle to the asylum he had visited at Callan Park in New South Wales. While his picture of Callan Park might have been overly rosy, his description of the light, airy buildings of that institution, cheerfully decorated and surrounded by landscaped gardens, sounded heavenly in comparison to the Fremantle asylum.

FIVE: An inquiry into the asylum – 1891

'When men or women have the misfortune to lose their reason, they...are put into the Asylum by a process of law, in the hope that with care and proper treatment they might receive some benefit. But, once there, it seems to me that we do our very best to prevent their ever coming out again.'

Dr Edward Scott was addressing the members of the Legislative Assembly, gathered in their dimly lit chamber behind the Perth Town Hall on 2 February, 1891. Most of the thirty members of the Assembly were businessmen or landowners, elected by men of similar backgrounds. It suited them to meet in the evening so that they could go about their own business during the day. Dr Scott, an athletic, square-jawed man approaching forty, was member for Perth and also its mayor.

'I have visited the asylum many times,' Dr Scott continued, 'and I don't know that I have ever come away without feeling more disgusted than upon previous occasions. It seems that the accommodation is becoming gradually more and more inadequate, and the demand upon it... is getting greater every year.'

He picked up a sheaf of papers from the desk in front of him and read aloud from Dr Barnett's asylum reports from 1886 and 1888. 'Dr Barnett's last report was even more forcible' he continued, as he began reading from the 1889 report:

> *'However wearisome my reiterated complaints may be, I feel compelled to continue to advocate and press for those changes which I know are required. The correctness of my assertions as to the advisability of sep-*

> *arating curable from incurable patients has never been questioned, yet I have been left year after year to get on as best I could with unsuitable buildings and overworked attendants; my urgent representations have almost been ignored, and no practical action taken to give effect to that which everyone acknowledges should be done.*[70]

'That,' said Dr Scott, looking up, 'is what I am complaining of in this matter. The Government and everybody acknowledge the necessity for these reforms, but the difficulty is to get them to take any active part in dealing with this dreadful subject.'

He returned his gaze to the paper in his hand and continued quoting from the 1889 report.

> *'My aim is to do away with, as far as may be possible, the sad, gloomy, and poverty-stricken surroundings of the patients, and in some degree make the place a cheerful home for those unfortunates who suffer from this worst of all human calamities; but in order to do this, I must be treated liberally and have a free hand.'*

'Words such as these coming from a gentleman who has had the superintendence of this Asylum for the last twenty years certainly ought to carry more than ordinary weight,' said Dr Scott. 'The gentleman uttering them is well known to us all, and would not make them, unless he was quite prepared to give such evidence as would convince a committee from this House.'

John Forrest, as colonial treasurer, was non-committal. The government had nothing against the proposal to form a select committee, he said, but it was incorrect to say that the asylum had been neglected.

'I think there has been a great deal of money spent on that building by the Government,' Forrest said, in a voice that commanded attention. 'Year after year money has been voted for it. Even some of the loan money raised for harbor works was, some years ago, re-voted, and diverted for improving the condition of the building; and a good many additions have been made during the last year or two.

'I have no doubt that great improvements are necessary in these buildings, but members must be aware that we are a struggling colony,' he went on. 'It appears to me that to do all that is required by the Surgeon Superintendent would cost a very large amount of money—I should say £20,000 at any rate, perhaps more. However, if members think they are prepared to find that money out of loan—for I do not think we could spare it at present out of current revenue—that is a matter for the House to consider.'

Forrest, known for his long speeches, went on without pausing.

'I was formerly, for some years, one of the official visitors to this asylum,' he reflected, 'and I used to go and look at the Visitors' Book... I never saw an entry made in that book reflecting in any way adversely upon the management or the state of the institution.

'I have not been there since I ceased to be one of the official visitors, but I believe there is room for improvement.'

At any rate, Forrest concluded, the committee could do no harm, though he could not promise to act on its recommendations.[71]

Treasurer Forrest knew the members of the Legislative Assembly were unlikely to consider raising another loan to finance improvements to the asylum. He had recently introduced a bill to raise loans in London for the extraordinary sum of 1.386 million pounds, to carry out an ambitious program of public works. This was more than three times the colony's annual revenue.[72]

If the bill passed in the lower house (which seemed likely) it would still have to be approved by the Legislative Council, the unelected and conservative upper house.

Already, in the short time since the Legislative Assembly had been elected, it had become clear that the fifteen-member upper house would seek to maintain their control over the colony's activities and finances. The relationship between the two houses of parliament can be gauged by a ditty sung during the Perth Amateur Operatic Company's performance of *Iolanthe* on 28 January:

The Upper House was never meant
To stay the people's will;
To sneer at public sentiment,
Or to refuse to give assent
To every little Bill;
'Twas meant to interpose delay,
But 'twas not meant to bar the way.[73]

Any attempt to persuade the Council to approve a further loan for the purpose of improving the asylum would almost certainly be futile.

Despite the treasurer's lukewarm response, the Assembly agreed to Dr Scott's motion and a committee of five, headed by Dr Scott, was appointed to investigate, and report back to parliament.

* * *

The select committee visited the asylum on Wednesday, 11 February, in stiflingly hot conditions.[74] Accompanying Dr Scott were Messrs Venn, Traylen, Randell and Sholl. The colonial architect, George Temple Poole, also came along. Harry Venn, as Minister for Public Works, was responsible for the construction and maintenance of all public buildings, including hospitals and the asylum.

The committee interviewed Dr Barnett in his poorly ventilated office. The doctor was well prepared to make the most of this parliamentary visit. He described for them, in detail, the overcrowding and lack of staff at the asylum. The current staff of six warders and five matrons was quite inadequate for the number of patients, he said.

'What number of additional warders, matrons, and attendants are necessary?' asked Dr Scott.

'What I have calculated… is four probation warders (I shall call them probation warders so as to have them in the service on trial…) and four probation matrons. That is the smallest number it would be practicable to do what I want with,' Dr Barnett replied.

Dr Scott asked if he had ever had to refuse admission to patients.

'I have refused several cases that have been sent down,' Dr Barnett said.

On one occasion in the previous year, he continued, he'd had to refuse admission to a young woman because there simply wasn't a bed available. When the colonial secretary had questioned this refusal, he had explained, by letter, that the overcrowding was so bad that he already had three women sleeping in the dining room. The colonial secretary had written back saying, 'The Surgeon Superintendent should make some arrangement without delay for the reception of this girl; surely one more can be crammed in.'

'The Colonial Secretary wrote that?' asked Dr Scott.

'Yes; Sir Malcolm Fraser; he was then Administrator.'

Dr Barnett stressed the need to be able to segregate patients. At present, those who might quickly recover if placed in suitable surroundings were forced to endure 'the screaming and crying, and the horrible sights and sounds from other patients.' The committee members had been startled by some of these disturbing noises from outside the room while Dr Barnett was speaking.

'I think I might give you some idea of what some of these patients are like, in their habits, if I were to read their entrance papers, from the certificates of the Resident Magistrates and medical officers who send them here,' Dr Barnett said. 'I will not ask to have these particulars recorded, as they are simply disgusting and abominable. But they will give you some idea of the horrible sights and associations to which other patients are perforce submitted.'

From a pile of folders, he extracted several reports and read them aloud. He was an excellent and expressive reader, and he watched to see what impact his words were making on his audience.

'I have no means of separating the foulest and most dangerous from the quiet and curable patients—those who are here perhaps for a month or six weeks—patients whose reason is only under a temporary cloud,' Dr Barnett went on. 'To me it is most distressing, and it is not difficult to imagine the effect it must have upon the patients to have to associate with unfortunate creatures of the class I have just described.'

Even providing patients with what was required 'to keep them alive, and to cover their nakedness' was difficult. He compared the forty-five pounds per head, per annum, allowed by the government for patients in Fremantle with the 200 pounds per head spent, on average, in British asylums.

Dr Scott, knowing Dr Barnett's wish to travel, asked him what his objective would be if he were to visit asylums elsewhere.

'One would imagine that, with the number of years' experience you have had here, Dr. Barnett, you would be perfectly competent to suggest what was necessary. Personally, and speaking professionally, I can easily imagine what your object and your desire is, but perhaps the other members of the Committee would like you to explain?'

'My wish is to reorganise this Asylum, to replan it altogether, and, as far as possible, to make the new Asylum of the future something like one of the best county Asylums at Home,' Dr Barnett replied. 'I have been 23 years in the medical service of this colony, and during that time great improvements have been made in Asylums…I want to see for myself all the latest improvements, both as regards management and treatment.'

One of the commissioners, Mr Venn, mentioned complaints from local residents about the dreadful noises coming from the asylum. The town was growing, more houses were being built. Did Dr Barnett not think that it would be unwise to spend a lot of money redeveloping the present site?

'No doubt there are objections to having a Lunatic Asylum in the town,' Dr Barnett replied, 'but, on the other hand, there are great disadvantages in having such an institution out of town, especially as regards taking patients to and from the place, and also supplies.'

'You don't think, then, that the unpleasant noises—these horrible screams that we hear—would militate much against the extension of the town in this direction?' asked Mr Venn.

'I think the proof of that is before us in the fact that, immediately outside the walls, houses are going up at a surprising rate,' replied Dr Barnett.

Mr Sholl asked about the number of foreign patients, particularly Malays and Chinese, occupying beds in the asylum. Were they increasing in number? He was quickly reminded by Mr Venn that his question wasn't within the scope of the enquiry, but Dr Barnett responded anyway.

'Very much on the increase.'

'How do you account for this?'

'I can only imagine that they have got rid of them at Singapore, Batavia, and other ports. I presume they find they can ship them here, and get clear of them,' Dr Barnett replied. The cost of looking after these patients, who were mostly young men with chronic illness, was a burden on the colony, he went on, but they couldn't be sent back.

After answering all their questions, Dr Barnett led the committee members on an inspection of the asylum. For some, this was the first time they had been inside the asylum walls, and they later admitted they found the experience unnerving.

The following day, the committee formally interviewed the colonial architect, George Temple Poole, in one of the rooms attached to the Legislative Assembly chamber. Poole, an amiable, polite and immaculately dressed man, who was trained both in architecture and civil engineering, had been in the colony since 1885. He shared Dr Barnett's view that an asylum should be a hospital where the mentally unwell could be cared for and cured, not just a place to keep them incarcerated.[75]

After showing the committee plans for the extensions to the current building, with the men's quarters coloured yellow, the women's quarters in red and the administrative area in green, he described what he believed were the essential conditions for a hospital for the insane.

'If you had a free hand, or had your own way...would you make still more radical changes?' asked Dr Scott.

'Most certainly,' said Poole. The alterations being contemplated were designed to entail the expenditure of as little money as possible. In his opinion, to make the asylum worthy of the name of a hospital rather than a prison, an entirely new building was needed.

He brought out plans of the Callan Park asylum in Sydney to show the committee what might be achieved, on a smaller scale, in Fremantle. To complete a new building, including furnishings and fittings for two hundred beds, would cost £30,000, he estimated. He thought the present site of thirteen acres would be large enough for that purpose.

'If you had your own way, then, you would have a new building erected, rather than attempt any very large expenditure on the present building?' Dr Scott surmised.

'If I had my own way I certainly would,' said Poole. 'It is simply a question of expenditure, of what the colony is prepared to spend.'[76]

The Select Committee was scheduled to present their report on the asylum to the Legislative Assembly on the evening of Thursday, 19 February 1891. But before the report could be discussed, treasurer Forrest received a message from the Legislative Council. The Council had returned the Loans Bill and was requesting that each item on the bill be made the subject of a separate loans estimate.[77]

Standing orders in the Assembly were suspended while the matter was discussed, at length.

A committee of three (the treasurer, the attorney-general and Dr Scott) was set up. After withdrawing for a short while, they returned with a resolution listing reasons for rejecting the Legislative Council's recommendations. It concluded:

> *'The House of Assembly will at all times endeavor to meet the views of the Legislative Council wherever circumstances permit; but this House is convinced that the Legislative Council will recognise that it would be impossible for the representatives of the people to abandon their constitutional right to group such public undertakings in one set of Estimates as the interests of the country, and the convenience of Parliament, may require.'*[78]

In other words, we're doing what most lower house governments in the British Empire do. We're submitting just one bill to the upper house for approval of the loans we propose to raise.

The resolution was put to the vote and accepted. Both it and the Loans Bill were returned to the Council.[79]

All this commotion took up most of the evening. The Select Committee's report on the Lunatic Asylum was almost the last item on the agenda to be discussed by the weary parliamentarians.

Their visit to the asylum, Dr Scott said, had convinced the members of the Select Committee that nothing in Dr Barnett's reports was exaggerated. The asylum, though well situated, was understaffed, overcrowded and detrimental to the patients' wellbeing.

He also raised the matter of the asylum superintendent's salary of one hundred pounds, which was out of all proportion to Dr Barnett's responsibilities. Dr Scott, in summarising the report, appealed to the government's pride as well as their sense of humanity.

'Insanity is no longer regarded as incurable, and hospitals for its treatment are looked upon as entitled to as much consideration as hospitals for the treatment of bodily ailments,' he said. 'In this colony, however, the subject has received very little consideration, and the day has come when this, our only institution for the insane, should be placed on a more satisfactory basis.'

He produced a letter from Walter Padbury, a well-known local businessman and philanthropist. Padbury had offered a hundred pounds in support of the project, 'if the good work could be done as recommended by the Government doctor.'

It went to show that the subject was attracting attention outside, said Dr Scott. He didn't add that it should be embarrassing to the government that members of the public were offering to pay for what was required.

'What I wish is that the Government should pledge themselves to take some steps towards making this institution what it ought to be—a credit to the colony, instead of a disgrace to it,' Dr Scott concluded.

Other members of the Select Committee added their voices to Dr Scott's. John Forrest listened attentively, but as treasurer he was unmoved by what he heard. Unless the members of the house were willing to vote for more money to be added to the Estimates, the Government was limited to spending the £1,500 already allocated for the asylum from current revenue.

'Having been a Visitor myself,' he went on, 'I can well understand the feelings of the Honourable Members of the committee when they visited the asylum the other day.

'I do not mean to say for a moment that there is no room for improvement, and many improvements. No doubt we could spend 100,000 pounds, if we had it ... and I should be very pleased if the circumstances of the colony admitted of such expenditure. But, after all, we must be contented with what we can do with the means at our command.'

'Of course, if Dr Scott's resolution is carried,' he concluded, 'the Government will be glad to read it. But as for doing anything more, I do not see how we can do it. I very much regret having to say it, but such is the case.'

George Randell agreed with the colonial treasurer that 'it would not have looked well to have included 30,000 pounds in the Loan Bill to provide the colony with a Lunatic Asylum.'

He moved an amendment to Dr Scott's resolution, to replace the phrase 'the Government should...' with 'the Government shall, at the earliest possible moment'.

Dr Scott raised no objection to the amendment, and his motion was eventually carried.

'I know it is not within the range of possibility for the Government to do much at present,' he said. 'But I am sorry to hear the Premier speak as he did. It is simply because the honorable gentleman does not understand or does not appreciate the necessities of the case.

'As to the complimentary remarks in the Visitors' Book...all they go to show is that, under existing circumstances, the management of my friend Dr. Barnett is worthy of all praise.'

If the Government could not afford to put up a new building, Dr Scott continued, it was imperative that some additions should be made to the present building.

'The population of the colony is increasing, and the percentage of lunatics must also increase, and an asylum will not expand and stretch like an India-rubber ball.'

Dr Scott might have marvelled if he had known just how many more patients would be crammed into the asylum over the next few years.

* * *

During the week that the Select Committee was carrying out its inquiries and writing its report, Emily Barnett's niece, Lilian Hart, spent several evenings listening to debates in the Legislative Assembly. The vivacious and talented Lilian had recently begun writing a ladies' column for the *West Australian* newspaper and its weekend edition, the *Western Mail*, under the pen name 'Cora'. Having visited the Legislative Council in their chambers in St Georges Terrace a few weeks earlier, she was curious to see the new Assembly in action.

She sat in 'the bird cage', the name popularly given to the narrow space behind the Speaker's chair set aside as a ladies' gallery. A wooden latticework partition screened it from the members of the Assembly.[80] The gallery, which could hold about thirty ladies, felt overcrowded on the warm summer evenings Lilian spent there. It was 'one of the most stuffy and uncomfortable places I have ever had to spend an evening in,' she wrote in her ladies' column. 'Whoever it may be we have to thank to "crush the ladies out," I trust that he may feel as uncomfortable as we do in the bird-cage.'

From where she sat, Lilian could see the members seated on benches around the central table, with John Forrest, his ministers and other supporters on one side, the opposition on the other. She didn't have a good view of the Speaker, Sir James Lee Steere, enthroned on a high mahogany chair in his ceremonial robes and long horsehair wig.[81]

The debate itself was rather dull, she thought, except for a heated exchange between William Marmion, the member for Fremantle who was also Commissioner for Lands, and Stephen Parker, the unofficial leader of the opposition at the time. (Parker would become Forrest's colonial secretary in October 1892).

'Mr Parker', wrote 'Cora', 'is the best speaker in the house and makes the narstiest (sic) remarks in the nicest possible way.'[82]

She was probably referring to a debate on the Loans Bill on 11 February, in which Parker questioned the accuracy of the government estimates on how much the harbour plan for Fremantle, put forward several years earlier by

British marine engineer, Sir John Coode, would cost. Parker even suggested that John Coode's schemes were not always successful.

Mr Marmion was shocked that Mr Parker would doubt the abilities of the greatest marine engineer living. If the government didn't act on the advice of Sir John Coode, on what basis should they act?

Parker responded that he thought it would be a disgrace to the Legislature if they passed this item, which really committed the colony to the expenditure of half a million pounds, after just half-an-hour's debate.

John Forrest, speaking in his role as colonial treasurer, offered no objection to the item being postponed.[83] It could wait for the arrival of a new chief engineer. He was actively looking for someone to fill the role and had been disappointed that Henry Mais, the former chief engineer of South Australia, had rejected the offered position after he visited the colony in January. Mais preferred to stay in private practice. But no doubt, with a salary of 1,500 pounds on offer, a really good man would soon be found.[84]

SIX: Dr Barnett takes leave – 1891

The West Australian government's reluctance to spend money on the asylum had not gone unnoticed by the press. On 24 February, in its report on the Select Committee's findings, the *Daily News* asked why it was that the government could find funds to raise the salaries of well-to-do public officials, and even pay four thousand pounds a year 'for a brass band and a few redcoats to march up and down playing the "British Grenadier".'

Wouldn't the government immediately find fifty thousand pounds to rebuild the Governor's residence if it burned down? Why was the asylum left to lie, 'like Lazarus before the rich man's palace, pleading in vain for accommodation of the simplest kind,' the paper asked.

Such appeals were nothing new. Newspaper editors had been deploring the government's lack of attention to the asylum for the past decade, to no effect. The new government was just as unresponsive as the previous one. But perhaps the Select Committee's report had some influence in one respect. The government announced in mid-March that it had granted Dr Barnett's application for leave of absence for twelve months.[85]

His intention was to go to England, where he hoped to visit some of the more famous and innovative asylums. In April, he wrote to the colonial secretary requesting a letter of commendation to take with him, to facilitate his inspections of such places.[86] He also planned to visit family in Ireland.

But there was much to be done before he and his wife Emily could leave. Apart from anything else, he would have to wait until the government appointed someone to replace him as colonial surgeon and superintendent of the asylum.

Problems at the asylum did not wait for a new doctor to be appointed. Two weeks after Dr Barnett's leave was announced, the Burmese patient, Sue Long, tore his shirt into strips, tied them to the bars of his window and used them to hang himself. His lifeless body was found by a warder early in the morning.[87]

At the inquest held later the same day, the warder said he hadn't checked on Sue Long during the night because the patient in the next room became violent and troublesome if disturbed. Dr Barnett, with the insight of someone who had suffered, and perhaps still suffered, bone pain himself, said that he believed Sue Long had ended his life to escape his unending and agonising pain.

The jury accepted this. They added a rider to their verdict, that sick patients should be isolated so that the night warden could visit them.[88] They did not need Dr Barnett to point out that this was impossible unless the overcrowding at the asylum was addressed.

In reporting the inquest, *The Daily News* added wryly that there was now room at the asylum for one new male patient to be admitted.

Dr Barnett took a break from his medical duties one Wednesday afternoon in April, to accompany his younger daughter, Olive Barnett, to the altar for her wedding to Francis Saunderson McCoy, a solicitor from South Australia. The simple private ceremony was held in St John's church in Fremantle.

Though the description of the wedding in the *West Australian* didn't carry her 'Cora' by-line, it was likely written by Lilian Hart, with her eye for fashion detail. Olive, the newspaper reported, was 'becomingly attired' in a dress of pale blue silk trimmed with white lace and wore a large white feather hat. Lilian and Francis Hart's four-year-old daughter, Geraldine, was one of the three bridesmaids.

After the wedding, the Barnetts entertained the small group of guests with light refreshments at their home, Park Bungalow. Among the wedding gifts received by the couple was a piano, given to them by Olive's father, Henry Barnett.[89] Music played an important part in Henry's life, and he anticipated that the same would be true for his daughter and her husband.

* * *

Apart from booking their passage to England, the Barnetts had other preparations to make before they could leave Fremantle. From the end of March, auctioneers W. Hepburn Gale and Co. advertised that they would soon be auctioning Park Bungalow and all its contents on behalf of Dr Barnett: 'the whole of his elegant Furniture, Pictures, Plate, Glass, China, Linen, &c'.[90]

The coming auction was still being advertised when Dr Barnett himself placed an advertisement, on 28 April, announcing that Park Bungalow, a 'commodious and admirably situated residence' was now 'To Let or Sale'.

> *'The house has an entrance to Fremantle Park, and is situated about three minutes' walk from East Fremantle Station, and, with stables and outbuildings, occupies Fremantle Town Lots 933, 936, and 937, commanding a splendid view of Rottnest and the Swan River. Also for sale, a CELLAR of WINE. Apply to Dr. Barnett.'*[91]

Gale and Co.'s advertisements provide an insight into the life and interests of Dr Barnett. As well as pictures, bric-a-brac, plate and linen, the goods to be auctioned included 'a splendid collection of valuable shells and curiosities and about 400 volumes of choice and expensive books, Medical Works, &c'.[92]

On 27 May, the auctioneers issued a comprehensive list of items to be sold from Park Bungalow, detailing the furniture room by room, and highlighting the quality of the paintings and books being offered. The potted plants and flowers used to decorate the verandahs for the musical 'at home' were now for sale. Gale and Co. clearly expected interest in the auction to be brisk. They offered refreshments, and even buses to take people from the railway station to the house if it was raining.[93]

The *Daily News* described the coming auction as 'by far the most important and attractive sale of its kind that has been held in this colony. Dr. Barnett is a man of great taste and has collected at his beautiful home a quantity of rare and costly articles of furniture and adornment.'[94] The *West Australian* added that the wine cellar of West Australian wines being offered contained vintages from as early as 1884.[95]

Neither newspaper questioned why a man who was ostensibly planning to return to his post in Fremantle after twelve months away was selling not only his lifetime collection of goods, but also his medical books and supply of medications. The fact that the government provided nothing towards his travelling costs or expenses during the year might explain why he needed to raise funds for his trip.[96] He would be paid his full salary for three months, but then he would be reduced to half pay.[97]

On 9 June, the day the auction was to begin, the auctioneers announced that some of the light fittings, the blinds, the windmill and the water tank were being withdrawn from sale. Park Bungalow had just been let. The new tenant was a man who would forever change Fremantle.

SEVEN: C. Y. O'Connor arrives in Fremantle – 1891

When John Forrest, the West Australian Premier, approached C. Y. O'Connor in April 1891 (by telegram, through O'Connor's old friend Malcolm Fraser) with an offer for the post of chief engineer in Western Australia, it piqued O'Connor's interest. At the time, New Zealand was well ahead of Western Australia as a colony, socially and economically. But the position in Western Australia offered O'Connor the possibility of being in charge of his own department and would remove him from the irritation of having to answer to someone he believed less qualified and experienced than himself.

He expressed an interest in Forrest's offer. Even so, he did not accept the job until he had negotiated the pay and conditions to his satisfaction with the West Australian government, as well as negotiating with the New Zealand government for his retirement entitlements. John Forrest had set aside 1,500 pounds in the budget for the Engineer-in-Chief's salary, but, ever careful with public money, he initially offered O'Connor only 1,000 pounds. He and O'Connor eventually settled on a salary of 1,200 pounds. It was a big undertaking to move a family from New Zealand to Western Australia, and O'Connor wanted to ensure that they would have financial security. He also had a clear sense of what his skills and experience were worth.

On 13 May 1891, O'Connor left New Zealand after more than a quarter of a century of living and working there. He travelled first to Melbourne, where he would make a brief stopover to advise the government of Victoria on their railway system. From there he boarded the mail ship Massalia, on its way to London via the West Australian coast.

Three of his seven children accompanied him. Seventeen-year-old Aileen would act as supervisor to sixteen-year-old Frank and seven-year-old Bridget until their mother, Susan, joined them several weeks later with the rest of the family. It was a practical arrangement, since they would be depending on friends and acquaintances to host them until they could find their own place to live. But it's also likely that Susan and the children were not entirely eager to relocate from New Zealand to this distant colony, widely known for its harsh climate, lack of services and limited social life.

In an editorial on 14 May, the *Timaru Herald* regretted C. Y. O'Connor's departure, remarking that in his long years of service in New Zealand, O'Connor had 'given abundant proofs of great ability in his profession, of sterling honesty, and of an unlimited and untiring capacity for hard work'. Those same qualities would soon become apparent to the residents of Western Australia.

The *Herald* was taking a dig at the New Zealand government when it claimed O'Connor was going 'to a quarter where Ministries and Parliaments have not yet come to regard it as one of the most important parts of their duty to tear the public service to pieces and treat their officials with injustice and contempt.'[98] In time, both C. Y. O'Connor and Dr Henry Barnett would have reason to question this claim.

Like most newcomers to the colony, Charles Yelverton O'Connor first set foot on West Australian soil at Albany, on the south coast. He and the three children arrived aboard the Massilia on 30 May 1891. Ocean-going mail ships from Britain and Europe refused to call at Fremantle. They delivered and collected mail for the West Australian colony at Albany, which had a superior harbour. The mail then had to be transported three hundred miles north to Perth by train, an arrangement good for the economy of Albany, but inconvenient for most of the colony's population.

The sun had already set when the ship docked in Princess Royal Harbour and the weather was cold and unusually wet. O'Connor and the children found their way, past dark stacks of sandalwood logs waiting for export, to the customs shed. A customs officer looked over their luggage and told them what the jetty fees would be. He was reputed to charge double for 'after hours' arrivals and would pocket the difference.[99]

Albany was crowded and the hotels were full. The small coastal town, with its great natural harbour, was the main entrance to Western Australia for those travelling by ship. The discovery of gold in the Murchison to the north, and more recently in the Yilgarn region around Southern Cross to the east of Perth, had brought a steady stream of prospectors and people looking for work. Many of them came through the Albany port.

Fortunately, the O'Connors had friends in the town. John Arthur Wright, the general manager of the privately-owned Great Southern Railway Company, had learned his engineering skills on the Welsh railways, in much the same way as O'Connor had done in Ireland. Although there is no evidence that the two had met previously, Wright had been chief inspecting Engineer in Northern Ireland during the 1870s. From 1885 to 1888 he had been Director of Works, engineer-in-chief and Commissioner of Railways for Western Australia, as well as being a member of the Legislative Council, so there was much that he and O'Connor could discuss.[100]

Wright and his wife owned a magnificent home, 'The Mount', on Brunswick Road, overlooking the harbour. They would provide hospitality to Mrs O'Connor and her children when she arrived a few weeks later, so it's likely they did the same for this first contingent of the O'Connor family.[101]

If O'Connor and his children had hoped to do any sight-seeing around Albany, they would have been disappointed. The weather on Sunday was, if anything, worse than Saturday. A storm front hit the coast and the rain continued to fall heavily all day, flooding the streets and causing damage to the roads.[102]

The O'Connors left Albany on Sunday evening. On weekdays, passengers arriving by ship in Albany would take the train to Perth at 7.00 am the next morning. After travelling northwards all day, through what many considered monotonous countryside, with frequent scheduled and unscheduled stops along the way, they would arrive in Beverley late in the evening. The travellers would then have no option but to spend the night in this small wheatbelt town, with its two churches and three pubs. They would join the west-bound train on the government-owned Avon Valley line to Perth early the following morning. The total journey from Albany to Perth could take up to seventy hours.

But on Sunday evening, an overnight 'express' mail train ran from Albany.[103] It arrived in Beverley the next morning in time to transfer passengers to the Perth train, thus avoiding the overnight stay. The O'Connors took this option.

Beverley is only 100 kilometres (64 miles) from Perth, but that part of the journey still took a further six hours. When the train arrived at the station in York for a scheduled stop, it was met by the mayor and a group of influential York citizens. They persuaded O'Connor to join them at the nearby Castle hotel, where they drank his health with champagne. He was then allowed to return to the train.[104]

The fact that York and Northam were in competition for the route of the proposed Perth to Yilgarn railway line may have had something to do with this show of hospitality. The York newspaper would report a few days later that the new Engineer-in-Chief was 'much impressed' with York and its surrounding countryside.

The O'Connor family arrived, at last, at Perth's central railway station on Monday afternoon, after a twenty-hour journey from Albany. Whatever C. Y. O'Connor's impressions of the countryside and the people between Albany and Perth, he was surely not 'much impressed' by his introduction to Western Australia's harbour and rail system. As the colony's new Engineer-in-Chief and acting general manager of railways, he would have been left in no doubt about how much work he had ahead of him.

The family were met at the station by the colonial secretary, George Shenton; the Commissioner of Railways and Minister for Public Works, Harry Venn; and various other gentlemen.[105] After being formally greeted and welcomed, the O'Connors rejoined the train to travel to Claremont. There they would stay at the home of George Temple Poole, the colonial architect, until they took up residence at Park Bungalow.[106]

After the two weeks at sea with little to do, C. Y. O'Connor wasted no time in getting to work in Perth. The Monday that he arrived in Western Australia was a public holiday for Foundation Day. On Tuesday, 2 June, he turned up at his office, located in the Public Works Office in the Treasury building on Perth's St Georges Terrace, to find it newly painted.[107] But there was little else to cheer about. The Department of Works barely existed. He had few trained staff to work with, apart from George Temple Poole, who had been acting chief engineer before O'Connor's arrival. The list of tasks awaiting his attention was alarmingly long.

As well as being responsible for engineering works in progress, designing and building railways, maintaining and upgrading ports and jetties, and providing water supplies for steam trains and settlements, he was also expected to manage the actual running of the railways. The government-owned lines had been making a loss and he was tasked with reversing this. The *West Australian* was not exaggerating when it described his duties as being 'of an equally multifarious and pressing character.'[108]

But it was the need for a new harbour at Fremantle that had led to O'Connor being head-hunted by John Forrest (now Sir John, after the announcement of his being made a Knight Commander of the order of St Michael and St George a few days earlier). His tasks might be multifarious, but building a harbour was the most important.

By Saturday, 6 June, Sir John, the colonial secretary and other prominent citizens had taken their new Engineer-in-Chief on a cruise down the Swan River, to see the geography of the banks and inspect the rocky bar across the river mouth.

The question of where to build a harbour had been raised almost as soon as Captain Charles Horatio Fremantle planted a British flag in the sand at the mouth of the Swan River, in May 1829, and claimed the whole west coast of Australia in the name of his distant monarch, George IV.

He would later inform the admiralty in a letter that:

> *'The landing took place in a little bay close to the mouth of the river, to the southward of it, being the only landing in that neighbourhood where boats could go with security, the bar at the entrance of the river generally being impassable'.*[109]

To the Whadjuk Noongar people who had lived in the area for tens of thousands of years, the limestone bar across the river mouth had sacred and cultural significance. It divided the salt water of the ocean from the fresh water of the river and provided a sheltered place where they could spear abundant fish. They knew the area north and south of the river mouth, to which Fremantle's name later became attached, as Walyalup.

But for the Europeans who followed Captain Fremantle, the rocky bar across the river was always and only a problem to be overcome. When the first governor of the Swan River Colony, James Stirling, established his capital at Perth, twelve miles upstream, the river became the main transport route from the coast. The bar across the river mouth meant that people and cargo arriving by ship at Fremantle had to be off-loaded at a jetty on the coast, carried over land to a jetty in the river beyond the bar, then transferred to small boats for the rest of the journey. It was a cumbersome process.

A new and much longer sea jetty was constructed in 1873 from Anglesea Point, on the southern side of the river mouth. This jetty eventually provided mooring for six vessels of up to 20 feet in depth, but only during fine weather. In rough seas, larger vessels had to moor off the coast in Gage Roads. Even small vessels had to stay away from the jetty in a gale. And the difficulty of off-loading and transferring goods remained. As the colony and its trade grew, calls from frustrated shipping owners and businessmen for a sheltered harbour to be built at Fremantle increased.

Some who accompanied O'Connor aboard the little steamship for a tour of inspection in 1891 saw the bar as an obstacle to be removed, as soon as possible, so that a port could be built in the safety of the river mouth. Others, including Sir John Forrest, thought removing the bar was unfeasible, both in terms of the engineering required and financially. In fact, Sir John was so convinced of this that when, a few months later, he asked O'Connor to investigate the costing for a harbour scheme, the only plan he asked him to consider was a port south of the river mouth at Owen Anchorage.

It was probably during this first weekend in Western Australia that O'Connor agreed to lease Park Bungalow from Dr Barnett. The trip down the river had helped to convince him that if he was going to be involved in building such a major project at the port town, he should be based somewhere close. But it was left to seventeen-year-old Aileen to set up house while waiting for her mother and siblings to arrive.

The house was ideal for the O'Connors, with its many bedrooms, dining room, library, wine cellar and room beneath for a servant's accommodation. It also had stables, which made it appealing to O'Connor, whose chief relaxation was horse-riding.

One of O'Connor's first tasks as Chief Engineer and acting General Manager of Railways was to upgrade the colony's railway system. Over the next three months, he inspected the existing lines and drew up plans for improvements and new lines. Extending the rail system was vital to the government's agenda to open up new land for agriculture and establish new population centres.

In the middle of June, he was included in discussions between the Commissioner for Railways, Harry Venn, and a delegation from the Perth City Council, about the railway crossings near the centre of the city. The councillors complained that these were inconvenient and dangerous.[110]

A few weeks later, O'Connor travelled with Commissioner Venn to Bunbury to inspect the route for the South Western line.[111] In mid-August he and Venn travelled to Geraldton by coastal steamer, to assess the port and railway facilities in that region. The tall, trim figure of the Chief Engineer, one hand in the pocket of his distinctive grey trousers, surveying the scene with bright eyes from under his specially made felt hat, soon became familiar all over the colony.

During this time, he was also busy trying to fit out a department capable of carrying out the many works that he could see would be required. In July, the government appointed one of his former colleagues from New Zealand, Frank Martin, to oversee the construction of harbour works throughout the colony, under his supervision.[112] Martin later took on the role of supervising the construction and running of the railway system. Tenders were called for projects such as the construction of the Pinjarrah (sic) section of the South Western line.[113] O'Connor's name began appearing on newspaper advertisements looking for draughtsmen and other professions.[114]

It didn't take long for sympathy with him over his onerous workload to wane. After the discussion with the Perth City Council about railway crossings, the gates were removed from several crossings and replaced with warning signs. This included the gate at the Stirling Street crossing, although the council had requested in a letter that it be left in place. Some thought the lack of a gate was an accident waiting to happen.

On 12 October, the *Daily News* quoted 'a correspondent' who accused O'Connor of failing to answer two letters sent to him by the City Council. The Chief Engineer should be reminded that 'although civility costs nothing, he is nevertheless paid such a considerable salary (more than any other officer save the Governor) that he can afford to be civil to the public, and that it would be an unpleasant duty when next his salary is voted to have to tell him that amongst other things expected in return for his salary is the article mentioned.'

The newspaper didn't reveal the name of the correspondent, although the threatening tone of the letter suggested it was someone with a vote in parliament. O'Connor was stung. He responded by restoring the gates, then sent a letter to the council explaining that they had been removed in error.

He added a postscript, worded in a way that was perhaps unwise in someone so recently arrived in the colony:

> *'While admitting that I am indebted to the gentleman who wrote to the Daily News on this subject, for having been the means of informing me of the removal of the gates a few hours before I should otherwise*

> *have discovered about it, I may say that I can scarcely realise that this gentleman's style of correspondence can be considered as an example of the courtesy and politeness which apparently it is his ambition to teach. It might, however, be a good example to follow, if anyone wanted to be deliberately very personal and discourteous.'*[115]

His letter and its postscript were reported in the newspapers. Far from garnering sympathy, it provoked a backlash. Within days, the *Daily News* published an editorial criticising the government for the number of highly paid and unnecessary new appointments being made within the Railways Department. It also drew attention to the number of New Zealanders that had been employed by the Chief Engineer for the Works Department, his attempt to change the accounting system to one used in New Zealand, and even the purchase of engines, described as 'obsolete', from New Zealand.[116]

All of this must have wafted like the first hint of an unpleasant smell around O'Connor. He was being marked out as an outsider, not 'one of us', by the colony's elite. But his straight-forward approach to business and his fairness as a supervisor was winning him admiration amongst those who worked with him. He got along well with his minister, Harry Venn, and the Premier, John Forrest.

And, as one of the government's most senior officers, he was a sought-after guest at social events. Both he and his wife were invited to the Mayoral Ball in July, although Susan and the rest of the children had not yet arrived in Western Australia.[117] He attended the lavish event in the Perth Town Hall, accompanied by Aileen, who was reported to have worn a dress of 'granite-coloured silk'.[118]

The first mention of Susan's presence in Fremantle came in a report about a 'water party' held by Captain Scott, an influential Fremantle businessman, on 12 September. After steaming up the river aboard the steam launch *Cleopatra,* the party landed for an evening picnic before returning by moonlight to Fremantle.[119] Such picnic excursions were a popular form of entertainment in the colony.

On 9 October, O'Connor was elected to the committee appointed to oversee the celebrations for the first anniversary of Proclamation Day, the day when the colony gained self-government.[120] The previous year, Dr Barnett had suggested that the occasion should be celebrated with a floral festival, taking advantage of the abundance of wildflowers at that time of year. His suggestion had been supported by Lady Forrest, who was known for the skill of her wildflower paintings.[121] Dr Barnett would almost certainly have joined O'Connor on the committee this year, had he been in Fremantle. But by October he and Mrs Barnett were in London.

EIGHT: Dr Barnett's travels - 1891-1892

Dr Barnett's leave of absence officially began on 1 June 1891, after the government appointed Dr James Hope acting superintendent in his place.[122] Henry and Mrs Barnett were busy saying their goodbyes to friends and family and preparing for their trip, when another tragedy occurred at the asylum.

On 12 June, an elderly patient, George Burden, was badly burned after he was left unattended in the asylum bath house by an inexperienced orderly. Dr Hope was called, but he was out of his rooms and another doctor attended. Burden was seen by Dr Hope the following day. He died two days later.

The jury at the inquest found that his death was due to shock caused by the burns. They added a rider: the deceased had not been properly supervised. Prisoners should not be employed as orderlies, and the staff of the asylum should be increased.[123] Dr Barnett no doubt agreed wholeheartedly with their recommendations. But it was an inauspicious start to his long-awaited leave.

He and Emily left Perth for Albany on 24 June. Among the well-wishers who saw them off from the Perth railway station were Lady Forrest, Justice Stone and Dr Hope. Three days later, after the long and tedious train journey to the south coast, the Barnetts boarded the P & O Company's *RMS Victoria* in Albany. The vessel was bound for London carrying the colonial mail, along with other cargo destined for England and ports along the way.[124]

Life at sea aboard a ship must have posed some difficulties for a man on crutches. But as the land receded, the smell of sea spray and the throbbing of the engines brought back many happy memories for Henry Barnett.

* * *

The four-masted, twin funnelled *RMS Victoria,* which Henry and Emily boarded in Albany in 1891, was a very different ship to the *Bengal* of his early years. Almost five hundred feet long and fifty feet wide, she was one of four steamships commissioned by the P&O company in 1887 to celebrate its jubilee.[125]

While she was designed to carry mail and cargo as swiftly as possible between London and the colonies, powered by six double-ended steel boilers, her passenger facilities were the epitome of luxury and comfort. This was the class of ship that Sir John Forrest longed to see berthing in Fremantle.

The Barnett's cabin was roomy and well-lit by skylights during the day and electric lights at night. The whole ship was mechanically ventilated, so that passengers no longer had to swelter in stifling heat as they crossed through the tropics.

Renaissance-themed carvings, described by the company as 'chaste', decorated the ship throughout its hallways and staircases, the lounges, smoking rooms, ladies drawing rooms and dining saloons. Henry and Emily could spend time in the library or walk on the promenade deck which ran the whole length of the ship.[126] If Henry looked in on the ship's hospital, he would have noted with satisfaction the many ways that the ship had been fitted out for maximum health and safety.

Always curious, he might also have taken an interest in the livestock stowed safely on one of the lower decks. Among them was a consignment of live hares, destined for the markets in England. The cargo also included frozen meat, stored in huge, refrigerated chambers. The ship's extensive wine cellar, along with stores of fresh fruit and vegetables for the kitchens, was also kept well-chilled.

Being on board ship, with all the memories it evoked, must have brought home to Henry Barnett how much his life had changed as a result of the loss of his leg and the passage of time. He could no longer paddle a kayak, ride on horseback across the plains or take part in a game of cricket. He was a great patron of sports in Fremantle, especially the rowing club, but he was not a participant.

He never expressed any bitterness about his loss publicly. But at a farewell function in his honour at the Fremantle rowing club, before he left for England, he had jokingly responded to a toast by saying his only regret that evening was his physical inability to dance with every lady in the room. He added, rather ruefully, that 'there was a time when he could pull a good oar, handle a cricket bat, play with the foils and singlesticks, take a turn with the gloves and without them if necessary. Though his time had gone by, he took as great an interest as ever in manly exercises and was greatly gratified by the success achieved by the Fremantle Rowing Club.'[127]

He would have found the stories that sprang up about how he'd lost his leg amusing. One version said that he'd injured his knee while hunting big game in India.[128] Another story, possibly posthumous, reckoned that not only had he amputated the leg himself, without anaesthetic, but he kept the bones in a box on his desk. He was said to display them for the delectation of his friends, with the remark: 'These carried me about for 36 years, and I have carried them ever since!'[129]

The journey to London took just over five weeks. Out in the Indian Ocean, the passengers watched, enthralled, as two swordfish fought a life-and-death battle with a whale. The swordfish emerged the victors.[130]

By 7 July, the *Victoria* had reached Colombo in Ceylon (Sri Lanka). The Suez Canal came into sight on 21 July. After calling at Brindisi in Italy, the RMS *Victoria* finally arrived, on 2 August, at her destination in Plymouth docks on England's south coast. From there, the Barnetts travelled by train to London.

The *Inquirer and Commercial News* in Perth would report that Dr Barnett had attended the Congress of Hygiene and Demography, at St James Hall in London in August, though his name didn't appear in the published list of delegates.[131] Henry Barnett had a keen professional interest in sanitation and public health.[132] As colonial surgeon for Fremantle he was responsible for quarantine and vaccinations in the port city. Much in the Congress programme would be relevant to him in this role.

While he was in Britain, Dr Barnett also visited his family in Ireland. His father had died many years earlier and his mother in January the previous year, at the age of eighty-one. But his two older brothers, Richard and John, and his sisters, Isabella (Carson) and Margaret, lived in Belfast. Richard and John both had medical practices there.

During his time in Belfast, Henry's experience dealing with the mentally ill was put to good use in a conversation with his twenty-six-year-old nephew, George Whytock Barnett, the younger son of Richard. George had been showing evidence of paranoia since his early twenties and was convinced that his father, his brother and his sister Mary were against him. He had written letters to friends telling them that he was being followed by strangers.

George described to Henry Barnett how, at night, servants came up through the floorboards into his bedroom and 'bothered' him. Henry's advice on George's condition went unrecorded, but a few years later he would recount the conversation in a deposition for a court case when family members contested the validity of George's will. George died in 1896 in Peckham Asylum, a private hospital in Surrey, only a year after he was admitted.[133]

Henry Barnett may also have spent time with his youngest brother, William, while he was in Britain. His two younger brothers, William and Albert, were both businessmen in Argentina, and visited England only intermittently. Whether by co-incidence or intentionally, William arrived in England just a few months before Henry and Emily and remained until about the time they left.

But Dr Barnett's chief reason for coming to Britain was to visit some of the best-known asylums in the country, to learn more about how they were organised and how they cared for their patients.[134] He soon realised that for this he would need more time. In December 1891, he wrote to the colonial secretary from London, requesting a six-month extension of his leave, which was due to expire in the following June. After gaining Dr Hope's agreement to continue filling his positions in Fremantle, the colonial secretary granted the extension.[135]

Dr Barnett's travels took him to asylums in London, Edinburgh, Portsmouth, Belfast, Sussex, and Surrey.[136] His experience in Britain may well have been far from what he expected. For years he had been endeavouring to run the Fremantle asylum along the lines of so-called 'moral treatment' or 'moral therapy', a system developed in the early nineteenth century by doctors and asylum superintendents working in Britain, Europe and the United States.[137] The term *'traitement moral'*, coined by French doctor Phillipe Pinel, might be better translated as 'morale therapy'. It involved encouraging the patients' physical, mental and emotional wellbeing.

Under this system, the asylum was no longer seen as just a warehouse for restraining those too violent or chaotic to be cared for at home. The old 'mad house' was gradually replaced in many places by a therapeutic environment where people might be cured.

Freedom of movement within the asylum largely replaced restraint. Patients were provided with as much occupation and social activity as they were capable of, and unwanted behaviours were ignored as much as possible, with restraint and isolation used as a last resort. The list of rules drawn up by Dr Barnett for the Fremantle asylum staff in 1872 were closely modelled on moral therapy.

But by the end of the nineteenth century, when Dr Barnett made his study-tour, moral therapy had already passed its heyday. He would have been disappointed to find that the conditions he was struggling to overcome in Fremantle were certainly not unknown in Britain. Many asylums in England and elsewhere had become too overcrowded to put such ideals into practice. The number of people being admitted had grown out of all proportion to the increase in population over the previous half century.

One reason for this was the change in family dynamics that came with the industrial revolution and the growth of Victorian ideals of 'family'. People no longer lived in tight-knit rural communities with extended family around them. The average urban nuclear family found it hard to deal with a family member whose behaviour was difficult or bizarre. It was preferable, or even unavoidable, to have them admitted to a public or private asylum.

An unprecedented increase in the number of people suffering from the end stages of syphilis also contributed to overcrowding of the asylums. Syphilis cases burgeoned as people moved out of close-knit communities into cities. It was an insidious disease affecting all classes.

Often it became dormant after the initial symptoms had settled, only to reappear in mid-life, at the height of a person's career and family life. In this tertiary stage, as the syphilitic organisms invaded the brain and nervous system, the sufferer would become irritable or grandiose, spending money they didn't have, starting schemes that were doomed to fail, and beginning extra-marital affairs that were quite uncharacteristic. Eventually their desperate families would bring them to the asylum.[138]

Yet another cause of overcrowding in asylums throughout the industrialised world was a huge increase in alcohol-related illness. Consumption of alcohol had increased markedly as the standard of living increased. At the Royal Edinburgh asylum in the years 1874 to 1894, twenty percent of admissions among men were due to alcohol related conditions.[139] These included the acute delirium produced by alcohol withdrawal and more permanent forms of psychosis caused by chronic heavy drinking.

It was all most disheartening. Yet Dr Barnett was still able to glean some ideas from his tour. He sent a friend a copy of a literary journal, *The Morningside Mirror*, written, edited and published by the inmates of the Royal Edinburgh Asylum.[140] It was exactly the sort of activity that Dr Barnett would have liked to provide for his patients in Fremantle.

Meanwhile, his tenant in Fremantle was dealing with a workload that might well be described as insane.

NINE: O'Connor plans a harbour – 1892

Harry Passmore pulled gently on his oars, so as not to disturb the glassy surface of the water beneath the little rowing boat. The day was fine, the ocean calm, ideal for proving his point. His companion, C. Y. O'Connor, gazed down through water so clear that he could see the rocky seabed twenty or thirty feet below them. It was just as Passmore had said it would be. There were limpets attached to the rocks, and holes with seaweed growing in them nearby. If there really was sand drift along the shore at Fremantle, they should not be there.

O'Connor raised his head and said, 'Where were you when Sir John Coode visited the state?'

'At Albany' replied Passmore. 'Who gave him his information I could not say.'[141]

The story is anecdotal, told by Henry Passmore twenty years after it allegedly took place. But it might well be true. Passmore, an old soldier, had lived in Fremantle for many years and worked as a foreman for the Public Works Department. He knew the river and the coast well.

True story or not, C. Y. O'Connor was convinced, from what he'd seen, heard and measured since his arrival in Western Australia, that sand travel (i.e. sand being carried by ocean currents) would not be a problem if a harbour was built in the river mouth at Fremantle. And he would spend many months trying to convince people that in saying this, he was not criticising or contradicting the great Sir John Coode, who had said sand travel would make such a harbour impossible. Coode, O'Connor said, had simply been ill-informed.

In 1876, the colonial government had asked Coode to survey the west coast and offer a solution for building a harbour. At the time, Coode was unable to visit Fremantle. Instead he relied on reports of soundings and other measurements sent to him from Western Australia.[142]

He eventually submitted his report to the West Australian government in March 1878. He had concluded from the information he had received that a port inside the river mouth was impossible because, after removing the bar, sand drift from the ocean would necessitate constant and expensive dredging.[143]

Instead, he offered two plans. Design A was based on a concrete and rubble viaduct, running north of the river mouth from Rous Head, at a cost of 638,000 pounds.

Design B involved a wooden viaduct running southwest from the southern Arthur Head, with a concrete breakwater angled south of this, for a cost of 242,000 pounds.[144] Both of these plans were well outside the 100,000 pound limit the government had set for itself.

Discussion about Sir John Coode's schemes continued over the following decade. Meanwhile, the existing jetties were extended to cope with increased shipping.

Early in 1885, the government decided to go ahead with 'Design B' and invited Sir John Coode to visit Fremantle to give further advice on his plan. When Coode's report finally arrived, almost two years later, on 19 May 1887, the *West Australian* newspaper described it as 'a disappointing document'.[145] Having dismissed the idea of building a port either in the river mouth or at Cockburn Sound, Coode opined that a decent harbour, capable of attracting the P&O mail ships, couldn't be had for less than one million pounds. This was a staggering sum at a time when the colony's total annual revenue was less than four hundred thousand pounds.[146]

Instead, he advised adopting a modified version of his original Design B, with a solid breakwater parallel to the shore, attached to Arthur Head by a wooden viaduct. This, at a cost of four hundred and forty-eight thousand pounds, would be 'adequate' for the present generation's needs and provide shelter for ships with a draught of up to twenty-three feet. Sometime in the future this could be extended, for another five hundred thousand pounds, to accommodate the mail ships, which required a depth of thirty-four to thirty-six feet.[147]

None of this fell within the government's budget plans, although some commentators thought it would be worth borrowing the amount required for the initial work to get the job done.[148] The issue was put on hold until renewed discussion was prompted by the granting of responsible government, the election of the Forrest government in 1890, and the expectation that a new engineer-in-chief with harbour-building experience would soon be appointed.

In September 1891, while O'Connor was working to upgrade the railway system and establish a viable Public Works Department, he was formally asked by John Forrest to draw up plans for a harbour at Owen Anchorage. The plans to be produced by O'Connor were to include an estimate of what the harbour would cost.

Owen Anchorage, a shallow bay located south of Fremantle, lay between the river mouth and Woodman Point. From the ocean, the approach to the bay was flanked by two long sandbanks, the Success and the Parmelia Banks, which ran perpendicular to the shore. Both were ominously named after ships which had run aground on them.

The Owen Anchorage site had received some influential support in June 1891, soon after O'Connor's arrival, when members of the government and the Chamber of Commerce had met with Mr Yuill, manager of the Orient Steamship company, and Mr Turnbull of the Adelaide Steamship company, to discuss what was required for the mail ships and other large steamers to visit Fremantle.[149] Though not engineers, the two gentlemen offered their opinion that a harbour adequate for this purpose could be built at Owen Anchorage.

This convinced John Forrest that here was a better option than either of Sir John Coode's earlier plans. He instructed Septimus Burt, the Acting Agent General in London, to write to Coode and ask for his views on the practicability of opening a channel through the sandy bed of Success

Bank into Owen Anchorage 'with the object of berthing the mail steamers of the Orient and P & O Companies.'[150] O'Connor was aware of this communication.

Coode hadn't considered Owen Anchorage suitable as a possible harbour in either of his previous reports. In fact, in his 1887 report he wrote:

The borings through the Success and Parmelia Banks have shown, as before stated, that they consist almost entirely of sand. Any channel which might be formed through these shoals would inevitably necessitate frequent dredging for maintenance, and, as I pointed out in my Report of 1877, such an approach would be impracticable and dangerous in a gale from the West when the wind would be directly across the line of channel, and it would be impossible to confine vessels to the deep water track.[151]

Nevertheless, Coode now went ahead and calculated the engineering work required, and what it would cost, to cut a channel through the Success Bank and give ships access to Owen Anchorage from Gage Roads to the north. This would allow them to reach the shelter of the harbour without having to navigate between the treacherous Parmelia and Success sandbanks.

John Coode's response arrived in September 1891, three months after C. Y. O'Connor began work as Chief Engineer. The elderly British engineer's opinion was that the proposal to cut through the sandbank, construct a harbour at Owen Anchorage and build a railway to service it, could be done for a cost of one hundred and fifty thousand pounds.[152] This seemed a bargain compared to either of his two previous harbour schemes. It was widely supported in the press, though some questioned why the marine engineer had changed his mind so readily about the feasibility of the scheme.[153]

Since the Premier had specifically asked O'Connor to assess plans to build a port at Owen Anchorage, that is what he did. In a memorandum on 25 September to his minister, Harry Venn, O'Connor critiqued and essentially agreed with the details of John Coode's report. The newspapers took this to mean that the Chief Engineer was in support of building a harbour at Owen Anchorage.[154]

Yet his support for John Coode's plan certainly wasn't unequivocal. He concluded his report by saying that the question of a harbour for Fremantle, capable of berthing ships the size of the mail steamers or larger, had now been narrowed down to *two* possibilities: either dredging a channel into Owen Anchorage, as detailed in Sir John Coode's report, or constructing a harbour at the river mouth. Harry Venn had asked him to report separately on this second possibility, which O'Connor promised to do shortly if he had sufficient measurements.[155]

By December, preparations had already begun for the harbour works, with dredgers purchased but not yet delivered.[156] Meanwhile, O'Connor produced plans and charts, tabled in parliament, to show that, while Sir John Coode's proposal 'might' be completed for one hundred and fifty thousand pounds, it would cost more like three hundred and seventy-five thousand pounds to produce a fully working port at Owen Anchorage. This included the cost of building a rail link to Fremantle.[157]

He also provided Minister Venn with two charts and an itemised estimate of costs, showing how a harbour could be constructed at the mouth of the river. The initial cost of his scheme would be five hundred and sixty thousand pounds. Significantly, it would provide a harbour adequate in all weathers for the mail ships and other large vessels. The Owen Anchorage harbour, on the other hand, would still be difficult for mail ships to access in heavy weather.

At a later date his proposal could be extended, for a total cost of eight hundred thousand pounds. Some of the expense of the scheme could be recouped by selling the land that would be reclaimed along the river. O'Connor was convinced, from his own and others' measurements, that Sir John Coode had been ill-informed when he concluded that a river mouth scheme would run into problems with sand drift.[158]

Harry Venn was convinced by O'Connor's reasoning. He was aware that other members of parliament had their own doubts about the Owen Anchorage scheme, which seemed, at best, only a short-term solution to the problem of providing a harbour. Even Forrest himself admitted as much. Venn tried to warn Forrest that his proposal for Owen Anchorage didn't have the support of parliament. In a note included with O'Connor's plans, he wrote that while Forrest was showing 'resolution and a fixed purpose, we have the Upper House absolutely against us, almost to a man; and in the Assembly it will probably be difficult to command a majority.'[159]

Undeterred, on the evening of 6 January 1892, Sir John Forrest moved in the Legislative Assembly that the Owen Anchorage scheme be adopted. It was, he said, approved by both Sir John Coode and the Chief Engineer.

In a long speech, which roamed over the whole history of the harbour, he acknowledged that the government would have preferred a harbour closer to Fremantle. The Chief Engineer's alternative plan, now on the table, for a harbour in the river mouth was attractive. He respected Mr O'Connor's experience in building similar works elsewhere, he said. But the colony simply couldn't afford to spend half a million pounds on a scheme which had no certainty of succeeding.

With an apparent lack of confidence in O'Connor's abilities, he reminded everyone that Sir John Coode, an experienced marine engineer, had predicted that a harbour in the river would soon silt up. He quoted extensively from Coode's 1877 and 1887 reports on this issue.

'We have Sir John Coode, who says it would not be a success, and Mr. O'Connor, who says it would; and I, as a reasonable man, say that there is a doubt about it,' he concluded.

If, as some believed, the cut through Success bank into Owen Anchorage would silt up as quickly as it could be dredged, it would soon be discovered, and the scheme abandoned before much money had been spent. On the other hand, he said, they could spend half a million pounds on a river mouth harbour before finding it unsuccessful.

'In the future, when this country becomes far more developed than it is, it may be possible to open up the Swan River at Fremantle. It may be possible to construct a great harbor inside the mouth and to open the river up to Perth. I see no reason why anyone should not look forward to that time as not very far distant. But the time is not yet.'

His speech was the last, and by far the longest, of the session. It was already 9.15 pm when he finished. At the request of those who wanted time to consider the matter, debate was adjourned until the following week.[160]

Neither the members of Parliament nor the press were content to wait a week to discuss the matter. On 8 January, the *Daily News* published an article in favour of C. Y. O'Connor's river mouth scheme.[161] That same day, the *West Australian* argued that a joint committee of the two houses of parliament (the Legislative Assembly and the Legislative Council) should be set up, to look at the relative merits of the two schemes, Coode's and O'Connor's.[162] The editor of the *West Australian,* Winthrop Hackett, was a member of the Legislative Council and an associate of John Forrest.

Another member of Parliament, William S. Pearce, set up a meeting in Fremantle for the 12 January so that his constituents could be made aware of, and discuss, the two schemes.[163] Plans were displayed for the public to examine at Myerscough's circulating library in High Street.

Pearce, David Symon (member for South Fremantle) and William Marmion (member for Fremantle) addressed the meeting, held in the ornate Town Hall at the centre of Fremantle. Eight hundred people attended, and the gathering grew noisy at times. The old fear that if the river mouth was opened, ships would by-pass Fremantle and continue upstream to Perth was raised but was quickly dismissed. Countering that was the fear that moving the port south to Owen Anchorage would also leave Fremantle high and dry.

Marmion, a balding man in his forties with luxuriant mutton-chop whiskers, argued that if the Owen Anchorage site was rejected, the government could not afford to build anywhere else and there would be no harbour works. He asked if the public were more willing to trust the 'pretty pictures' of the 'shining new engineering prophet', or the advice of the London engineer of world-wide reputation.

'I would like to ask whether the Government has any confidence in their Engineer-in-Chief,' someone shouted.

'I do not think that is a proper question to put to me,' Marmion said evasively.

'If the Government do not recognise him, why pay him?' asked the elector.

Marmion reluctantly replied that he supposed they did have confidence in him, but they had preferred to refer the question to the most eminent maritime engineer in the world and they should accept his advice.

Eventually the alternative schemes were put to the vote. A harbour at, or near, the river mouth was preferred to the Owen Anchorage scheme by a majority of at least four to one.[164] The vote had no legal force, and did not specifically support O'Connor's proposal, but it made clear the feelings of the Fremantle electors about a port at Owen Anchorage.

The Legislative Assembly discussed the harbour works again at length, on 13 January, but again the debate was adjourned. Much of the discussion in the days that followed revolved around whether a parliamentary committee should be set up to examine the matter, whether this should be a select committee or a joint committee of both houses, and how to go about it. With only a year of self-government behind it, the parliament was still feeling its way on such issues.[165]

Sir John Forrest insisted that the government wasn't advocating the Owen Anchorage scheme because they were firmly attached to it. Rather, it was the only scheme which seemed affordable, given the limitations on how much money the government could borrow, set by the parliament itself. He was happy for a select committee to be appointed, if it helped to resolve the issues and get the harbour built.[166]

* * *

Forrest had more than just the debate over the location of the harbour works to contend with in January. There was also the question of who would be allowed to work as labourers in building and running the harbour and other projects.

On 15 January, in the midst of the harbour debate, the Fremantle Lumpers Union held a 'monster meeting' to discuss 'the Chinese Question'. The meeting, open to the public, had widespread support. The last evening train out of Fremantle was delayed until 10.30 pm to allow Perth people to attend.

The phrase 'The Chinese question' was first used in the British parliament in the 1830s, during discussions about Britain's trading rights with China.[167] It had been adopted in Australia as a shorthand description for the resentment and hostility of white Australian miners towards Chinese miners, who began arriving in tens of thousands during the 1850s gold rush in Victoria.

By the 1870's 'the Chinese Question' had come to refer to resistance among Australian workers to employers bringing in Chinese and other Asian labourers. These workers generally accepted much lower wages than their Australian counterparts and would work long hours with little concern for health and safety issues. But a strong streak of racism also under-girded the protests against Chinese and other non-white labour.

The colonial governments, including that of Western Australia, all agreed in 1888 to a uniform policy on non-white immigration, known as the *Chinese Restriction Bill.* However, the West Australian government had already introduced its own *Imported Labour Act*, which allowed employers to import Chinese and other non-white labour in areas of need, such as the pearling industry and sheep stations in the North-West. This was not over-ridden by the national bill.

In late 1891, the South Australian Premier, Thomas Playford, wrote to Sir John Forrest, protesting that many Chinese workers were entering his and other colonies from Western Australia. He asked for details of how many had arrived in Western Australia that year, and for an assurance that the numbers would be restricted. Sir John replied (after some prodding) that only 512 'aliens' had entered the colony during the year, and all but 128 had gone to remote areas.[168]

Newspapers in other colonies began commenting on Western Australia's failure to keep in step with her sister colonies. This was a significant accusation at a time when the colonies were discussing federation. Sir John Forrest, a supporter of federation, had attended the first meeting of the Federal Convention in 1891 and was keen to negotiate the best possible arrangements for Western Australia to join.

The meeting at Fremantle on 15 January attracted about 700 people. They called on the government to abolish the *Imported Labour Registry Act* (mistakenly referred to by some newspapers as the 'Chinese Labour Registration Act') 'so as to place the working men of West Australia on the same terms of competition with Chinese labour as the labouring classes in the Eastern colonies of Australia.'[169]

A copy of the resolution was forwarded to the Premier, who merely acknowledged that he had received it.[170] By 2 March, a petition containing over two thousand signatures had been presented to parliament, calling for the repeal of the *Imported Labour Registry Act*.[171] A motion to that effect was debated in Parliament on 10 March.

Both the Premier and his younger brother, Alexander Forrest, who was the member for Kimberley, in the far north, argued that the motion was too sweeping and ignored the needs of the population in the north of Western Australia for labourers. If the numbers of Chinese and other aliens in Fremantle increased substantially, then it would be time to modify the act.[172] The motion failed to carry but 'the Chinese Question' would continue to raise its head in the colony for many years to come.

Four days after the 'monster meeting in Fremantle, on Tuesday 19 January, John Forrest's original motion on adopting the Owen Anchorage harbour scheme was amended in the Legislative Assembly, to refer the harbour issue to a joint committee of both houses of parliament. The committee was to report on 'what plan would be the best to secure accommodation to the largest class of ocean-going steamers.'[173]

O'Connor was being given the opportunity to convince parliament of the benefits of his river mouth scheme. But it would be no easy task.

TEN: O'Connor grilled – 1892

Chief Engineer O'Connor was known for his patience in public, but today he was struggling to stifle his irritation. He had never had to face an inquisition like this before starting any of his New Zealand projects. With so many other tasks still to be done, the process was both time-consuming and annoying. And now he was being baited by the member for Fremantle, William Marmion, who seemed more intent on scoring points than finding facts. Even the newspaper reporters, scribbling away at their notes, looked aghast at the ferocity and rudeness of Mr Marmion's questioning.[174]

The Joint Parliamentary Committee to examine the harbour scheme began meeting on 22 January in the committee room of the Legislative Council.[175] When a request had reached the Legislative Council for five members to join the committee, John Wright, MLC, described the proposal as 'a parachute by which to enable the Government to descend gracefully from the position they have taken up with regard to Owen Anchorage.'[176] But after some debate, the Council had agreed to the proposition and added five members.[177] Harry Venn, the Minister for Public Works, chaired the committee.

As Chief Engineer and designer of the river mouth harbour scheme, O'Connor was the main expert witness. He was questioned intensively over several days. The committee also interviewed John Wright, as former Chief Engineer; Frank Martin, with his experience in harbour building; and Captain Russell, the Chief Harbour Master.[178]

With great patience, O'Connor answered questions that arose out of ignorance or misunderstanding of what his harbour scheme involved. He also confidently responded to 'what if' suggestions about alternative schemes that had already been dismissed as impractical.

Several times he referred to his experience in building harbors on the west coast of New Zealand—Westport, Greymouth, Hokitika—to show how the potential problems faced in Fremantle could be readily overcome. Most of his answers he supported convincingly with details of measurements and estimated costs.

But his patient demeanour began to show cracks when his competence or his integrity was questioned, or when the questions became irrelevant or impertinent. William Marmion seemed especially keen to portray him as incompetent and to trap him into denigrating the eminent Sir John Coode.

In response to a series of questions from other committee members about sand travel, O'Connor said that if it did occur, dredging would be required, but he had found no evidence for its existence.

'There seems so little evidence to base it upon. I myself cannot see any tangible evidence of it on the ground, and I cannot find anybody that can show it or prove it,' he explained.

Marmion was quick to pick up on this.

'Would you mind telling us the names of these local authorities that you pit against the evidence of Sir John Coode?'

After offering names, O'Connor expressed his frustration.

'I think that is hardly a fair way of putting that question. I did not say that I pitted anybody's evidence against Sir John Coode's. I do not think I ought to answer the question at all in that form.

'First of all, I never pitted anybody's evidence against Sir John Coode's, and, in the next place, I am not aware that Sir John Coode has given any evidence as to the existence of sand travel. He simply cites certain statements made to him that there was sand travel, and other statements that there was no sand travel, and, if I judge rightly, taking the whole of his reports, he has shown that the weight of evidence is against there being any serious sand-travel. So that I think I am coinciding with Sir John Coode rather than opposing him.'[179]

O'Connor alluded to a breakwater successfully built from limestone rubble at Westport in New Zealand and suggested that it would be cheaper and easier to build a similar structure at Fremantle. Marmion immediately saw his chance to score a point.

'Might I ask who designed that breakwater you are speaking of?'

'Sir John Coode designed the general arrangement of it,' O'Connor conceded. 'I may say I gave Sir John Coode the estimate of the cost of the stone before he started with his estimate of the cost of the work.'

After more discussion about measurements of sand travel and costs, Charles Harper gave O'Connor an opportunity to clarify his relationship with John Coode.

'You have a great deal of experience in working under Sir John Coode?' asked Harper.

'Yes, I have,' O'Connor responded.'

'Do you think if Sir John Coode were of the same opinion as you are now, that this sand travel is infinitesimal, he would be prepared to recommend a solid structure from the mains?' Harper asked, referring to O'Connor's proposal to build solid breakwaters, or moles, extending from Rous Head and Arthur Head.

'I really could not say as to that, but I have come prepared to show you what he recommended under similar conditions elsewhere,' O'Connor replied.[180]

Marmion asked if he was prepared to recommend the river mouth scheme to the government, to which O'Connor replied that he was.

'Are you prepared to take responsibility for recommending this in the face of so great an authority as Sir John Coode?' asked Marmion.

O'Connor was visibly annoyed by this.

'I really do not think it is fair to put the question in that way,' he said. 'I say it with all due respect. If you ask me my opinion I will give it to you, but why endeavour to drive me continually into a controversy with Sir John Coode?' Without waiting for Marmion to answer, O'Connor went on venting his indignation.

'I have no wish to come into conflict with Sir John Coode nor anybody else. I am Engineer-in-Chief of the colony, as you say, and as such am prepared to express my own opinion, though I feel the responsibility of the position as much as anyone can do. I do not admit that I am in conflict with Sir John Coode's present views on this subject. I think the probability is that if the matter were referred to him he would say there was no conflict between us at all, and that is what I say.'

Again, he went on before Marmion could interrupt.

'When you ask me continually whether, in the face of Sir John Coode saying this and Sir John Coode saying that, am I prepared to recommend this and to recommend that, I do not think it's fair to put it in that way. If you ask me what my own professional opinion is, I will answer you. But I do not think the question, in the form you have put it, is a fair one. I think I have a right to take a stand upon my professional reputation, and I do not think I am called upon to reconcile my opinion with Sir John Coode's opinion, or anybody else's.'

His response was vehement enough to startle those listening. But he still wasn't finished with putting the annoying Mr Marmion in his place.

'If you will pardon me, I do not think you are capable of forming an opinion as to whether our opinions, on a technical question, are in conflict or not, as you are not a professional engineer…

'I think it is unreasonable that you should harp upon this, that I and Sir John Coode are in conflict. You may think so, and no doubt you honestly think so. But if you had more experience in marine engineering you would probably come to the conclusion that we are not at issue at all. I certainly am not more at issue with Sir John Coode than Sir John Coode is with himself,' he concluded.

John Wright, in his time as chief engineer, had done some preliminary work assessing the feasibility of a river mouth harbour. When called before the committee, he too found himself under attack by William Marmion, in an attempt to discredit O'Connor.

'From your experience as an engineer, does the fact of a gentleman having "C.E." (i.e., Civil Engineer) after his name give him the right to give an opinion on a subject of this kind?' began Marmion.

'In the first place, men of any standing in the profession are not C.E.'s. They are members of the Institute of Civil Engineers,' Wright corrected. 'I have the honor of belonging to that Institute, as such. So has Mr. O'Connor, and so has Sir John Coode.'

'Then is a gentleman who has " M.I.C.E." after his name always competent to give an opinion on harbor works?' Marmion asked.

'I say that when a man occupies the position of Engineer-in-Chief to a colony he does the best he can for that colony,' replied Wright.

'I ask, does the fact of your having M.I.C.E. or C.E. after your name give you the right to express an opinion on a subject of this character necessarily?' Marmion persisted.

'Surely as so many people who have neither M.I.C.E., or C.E., or anything after their names may and do express an opinion, the Engineer-in-Chief of the colony may, even if he has not a duty to,' countered Wright in exasperation.

Marmion came to the point. 'Do you think that after the country has decided to refer the matter to an eminent marine engineer, his opinion should be totally ignored in favour of the opinion of others—civil engineers and amateur engineers?'

John Wright knew where this was leading.

'That is a question you have often put to me, both inside the House and outside.'

'I suppose there is no harm in putting it?' said Marmion.

'Oh no, but it does not follow that I shall answer it, and I object to answer it,' Wright responded. 'To follow your question to its logical conclusion simply means that no engineer may state his opinion against another engineer because you have chosen to place the latter on a pinnacle.

'Sir John Coode is one of the highest men in his profession as a marine engineer,' he continued. 'But that is no reason why another engineer, under particular circumstances, should not also give his opinion, as to what he considers a proper work to undertake, notwithstanding that Sir John Coode may not agree with it.

'I did this,' he said, referring to his own previous work assessing the river mouth, 'and have had a great deal of discredit attached to me for having the presumption to do it.'

Marmion continued to prod, until John Wright refused to answer any further questions on what he considered a matter of engineering etiquette. Harry Venn, as chairman, stepped in and warned Mr Marmion that he should not ask any further questions which pitted the opinion of one engineer against another. Even then, Marmion continued to ask Wright if he thought his opinion should prevail against that of Sir John Coode, but Wright declined to answer.

After seven meetings, the committee completed their report on 15 February. Despite what the newspapers referred to as Mr Marmion's 'gratuitous discourtesy' towards O'Connor, the committee unanimously agreed that the Engineer-in-Chief's harbour scheme should be adopted.'[181,182] They urged that the work should be undertaken 'without further delay'.

ELEVEN: Progress – 1892

Even after the parliamentary committee made its recommendations on the harbour scheme, there were still those who wanted to seek the opinion of Sir John Coode. But as if to make clear that an era had ended, Sir John Coode died on 2 March 1892, at his home in Brighton, Sussex, at the age of seventy-five.[183]

By 5 April that year, workers had begun constructing a tramline along the river from Rocky Bay to Rous Head, at the northern tip of the river mouth. Stone from Rocky Bay, a few miles upriver from Fremantle, had long been used for buildings in both Perth and Fremantle. It was hoped that much of the limestone needed to build the north mole could come from the cliffs at the site, and a team of men had begun test quarrying at various places, with promising results.[184]

A few weeks later, blasting began on a section of the bar across the river near Rous Head, under the supervision of foreman Harry Passmore. The large stones dislodged from the surface were deposited at the end of Rous Head where the north mole was to be built. Over 200 men were now working on the harbour project.[185]

By June, the work being done at the harbour, together with ongoing upgrades and extensions to the colony's rail system had resulted in a shortage of rolling stock—wagons and locomotives—and delays getting goods away from the jetty. This had been partially overcome by importing railway trucks from New Zealand, though it became another focus for criticism of O'Connor. Materials for building more trucks locally was on order.[186] The chaos was soon over, but it foreshadowed a much worse crisis in future.

Those working on the harbour were employed directly by the Public Works Department rather than the work being let out to contractors.[187] This was O'Connor's preference, though it raised the ire of the contractors, who in many cases were used to preferential treatment by their colleagues and relatives in parliament.

Most of the men employed worked nine hours per day, but they soon organised themselves into a branch of the 'eight-hour day' movement. On 3 July, they wrote a petition to Sir John Forrest urging that they should have the same conditions as men working in similar conditions in other colonies. They pointed out that the work they were doing was more continuous and more dangerous than that of other labourers employed by the government. But by the beginning of August, they had heard nothing.[188]

Thomas Molloy, MLA, took up their cause, and by September Minister Venn had agreed to their request.[189] This was despite there being no shortage of men seeking employment, due to a deep recession in the eastern colonies.

Years later, O'Connor, speaking at the annual picnic at Bicton for harbour work employees, told of his support for their campaign for an eight-hour day. As he often did, he stressed the importance of facts over feelings in his coming to a conclusion.

'When that proposal was first made it received my cordial sympathy,' he said. 'It was not a sentimental sympathy, but one based on experience.' He said he felt sure that if they, the employers, got an honest eight-hour day's work, they got as much out of the men as if they kept them going for twelve hours.[190]

O'Connor might have shown a progressive concern for his workers, but his vision was still that of the Victorian civil engineer, helping the colony to reshape the natural environment in the name of progress and prosperity. In the planning and construction of the harbour neither he nor anyone else considered the environmental impact of removing the limestone bar across the river and allowing salt water to flow upstream.

Nor did anyone consult those who had lived in the area for a thousand generations. The local Whadjuk Noongar people had an intimate knowledge of the land and its finely balanced environment. But the idea that they might have an opinion on the matter, a stake in the land, or information to contribute, didn't have a place in colonial thinking.[191] What mattered was economic progress and bringing the colony into line with the rest of the world, particularly other parts of the British empire.

The government's emphasis on economic prosperity was the main reason for a deputation of fifty-five women from the Women's Christian Temperance Union (WCTU) visiting John Forrest in his office on 16 August 1892. They asked that the Premier, on behalf of the whole Government, should publicly state that 'the moral welfare of the people would receive the same careful attention that it now gave to their material prosperity.'

The delegation wanted restrictions on the sale of alcohol to children, and more say over where public houses were built. They also advocated raising the age of sexual consent for girls, from fourteen to sixteen, providing support for women being released from prison, and building a place for sailors to go while on shore as an alternative to the hotel bars. All this they explained to the Premier.

John Forrest, after hearing their requests, said their presence was 'as unexpected as it was agreeable to him'. He would make no commitment to issuing a declaration that the government took an interest in the moral welfare of the colony. They knew it did, he said.

There was some truth in the statement that you couldn't make people moral and good by act of parliament, he went on. Churches and schools taught people how to live morally good lives. The government couldn't be expected to do everything. But it would work hand in hand with those concerned with the moral welfare of society.

The ladies listened attentively to his response and murmured 'hear, hear' at some points. But when the Premier said he thought it would be a good thing if people could be taught to give up drinking altogether, and prohibition would do no-one harm, they asked 'Why has this not been done?'

People liked drinking and didn't like to give up a luxury, he replied.

'Governments live by popular suffrages,' he added, 'and members of Parliament are elected by the community, and if people will do that which is detrimental to their interests, how is the Government to prevent them? It is the majority of people who send members to Parliament.' The implications of his words were not lost on the women listening.[192]

* * *

On an overcast day at the end of August, Chief Engineer O'Connor hosted a select group of gentlemen in an inspection of the progress being made on the harbour works. They included the colonial secretary, O'Connor's minister, Harry Venn, several other members of parliament, the harbour master, and a reporter from the *Daily News*.

After providing generous refreshments, O'Connor led the party to a waiting 'special' train at East Fremantle station. The train, consisting only of a locomotive and an ambulance wagon, produced some humorous comments. They travelled first to North Fremantle and from there to Rous Head, at the end of the narrow peninsula at the northern side of the river mouth. A small settlement of tents and wooden houses belonging to the workmen had already grown up on the site, and there was even a vegetable garden with cabbages, peas and lettuces.

With threatening skies overhead and a dark, choppy sea behind him, O'Connor described to his visitors the work going on and how the mole would be constructed. He explained how, from a narrow base at the river mouth, it would gradually become broader and flatter as it extended into deeper water. Inside the estuary, land would be reclaimed for wharves.

He mentioned that he had been waiting for longer than he would have liked for twenty-seven tipping trucks to be delivered from New Zealand, as well as wood, iron and imported English wheels and axle boxes. These would be used for the construction of another forty trucks locally. Some would be equipped with cranes.

The rain had begun to fall as the party hastily returned to the train and travelled the two miles to the start of the quarries on a curve in the river at Rocky Bay. Here, oblivious to the attractiveness of the natural bushland setting, dozens of men were busy extending the rail line along the face of the quarry, which ran along a steep limestone bluff above the water.[193]

As the visiting party approached, they heard the dull boom of an explosion from 'shots' placed in the stone face. The quarry was already yielding large, good quality stones, while the softer, more crumbly material from the surface was being put to good use for road building. O'Connor explained that when exposed to salt water, the outside of the quarried stones would naturally harden.

Rounding the hill, away from the river, the group came to where another short railway line was to be built. This would allow quarrying on both sides of the hill as well as at nearby Buckland Hill. The area was still largely unpopulated government land, which, as O'Connor was quick to mention, meant that it cost the government very little to use. The astute reporter immediately saw its future value as real-estate.[194]

In charge of the Rocky Bay quarry site was one of O'Connor's New Zealand recruits, engineer John Irvine, who had worked with him at Hokitika. Irvine and his wife and family had been living in Clarence in New South Wales for several years before being invited to come to Western Australia to become a superintendent of harbour works.[195]

As work continued on the harbour and the quarry at Rocky Bay, O'Connor endeavoured to spend as much time as he could in Fremantle, where he had set up an office in an old wooden customs building. Sometimes he worked from home, accompanied by Frank Stevens, another New Zealander employed as his private secretary.[196] But as Chief Engineer, his other responsibilities didn't stop while the harbour work went on.

TWELVE: The Cross and the indignant – 1892

Five days after taking the party to inspect the harbour works, O'Connor travelled to the Yilgarn, at the eastern edge of the colony's pastoral district. He went to inspect the route for the proposed railway line running east from Northam to the Yilgarn's main settlement, the mining town of Southern Cross. At the time, the line from Perth extended no further east than the Avon valley, while the Great Southern line from Albany ended at Beverley. From there, travellers either hired a cart or walked the remaining 270km to 'the Cross'.

After visiting Newcastle (later renamed Toodyay) to decide on a site for a new railway station, O'Connor went on to Northam, where it seems likely he hired a horse-drawn trap to take him the rest of the way.[197] This was his first exploration of the vast and sparsely settled area to the east of Northam. He stayed overnight in some of the isolated settlements along the unpaved road—Tammin, Merredin, Burracopin—where he used the opportunity to gather information about local rainfall.[198]

On his way, he would have seen what was, at that time, still a novelty in the colony; 'Afghan' cameleers, with their camels laden with goods and equipment, headed to the goldfields. Camels had been used sporadically in Western Australia in the past, by explorers and surveyors. There had been a failed attempt to set up a camel transport business in 1887. But in 1892, brothers Faiz and Tagh Mahomet, previously of Adelaide, saw an opportunity and imported dozens of camels to work the routes to the goldfields, first to the Murchison and then, in August, to the Yilgarn. They also opened stores in many remote settlements. Others joined them and soon there were hundreds of camels in service across the West Australian outback.

The cameleers recruited by businessmen like the Mahomets were generally referred to as 'Afghans', though they came from across southern Asia and even Turkey and Egypt, sometimes via South Australia. Most were Muslims. While some locals appreciated the economical service they provided, their colourful costumes and their polite, sober habits, they were unpopular with the teamsters who had previously transported goods at much higher prices.[199] The cameleers would play a vital role in the construction of the railway line to Southern Cross and beyond.

O'Connor arrived in Southern Cross on 14 September.[200] The township comprised a collection of thrown-together shacks of corrugated iron, wood and canvas, interspersed with a few more permanent structures such as banks and hotels. It was set down on a plain in the middle of nowhere. Here and there, a spindly eucalyptus had been left to provide shelter. But most of the trees not already removed by the earlier sandalwood cutters had been cleared, either for building or for fuelling the condensers that provided the town's water. No-one came to Southern Cross for the scenery. Gold was what drew the town's white population.

The landscape was very different to the rain-soaked forests and icy mountain passes through which O'Connor had built the roads, bridges and railways that helped open up the goldfields of New Zealand's west coast.

His time in that rugged landscape, working among the mining communities, had been a positive and maturing experience. The miners, coming as they did from many different nationalities and backgrounds, had taught him that people could live together in harmony, despite their differences.[201]

Harmony was a commodity in short supply when O'Connor arrived in Southern Cross. Six weeks earlier, miners employed by four mining companies had gone on strike after the directors tried to reduce their pay. The government Warden, who had jurisdiction over local matters, endeavoured to remain impartial. The government, many of whose members were businessmen with an interest in the mines, supported the companies.

As the conflict dragged on, the companies hired new workers in Perth, telling them that the strike was over. When the men got to Southern Cross, they found this was not the case, and most of them joined the strikers. On 16 September, four men were sent to prison for failing to fulfil their contracts and refusing to pay fines.[202]

Amidst these tensions, the Southern Cross town council and ratepayers entertained O'Connor liberally at the Club Hotel, a solid two-storey brick-and-iron building. O'Connor, in an impromptu speech, took responsibility for the delay in the construction of the eagerly awaited railway line. The surveying work had been done and calls for tenders issued. He estimated that it would take a couple of years to see it completed. Reflecting on the dead-flat and sparsely wooded landscape that he'd seen all around him since leaving Northam, he said it would be one of the easiest railways to construct that he'd ever seen.

The gathering drank his health, and that of the Premier, followed by the surveying staff and the press. A correspondent for the *West Australian* reported that the Chief Engineer 'left a very pleasing impression on those who had the privilege of meeting him.'[203]

On his return to Perth, O'Connor found a different dispute simmering, one in which those involved were less pleased with the impression he was leaving. His plans for the harbour included removing the railway workshops from their current location near the river at Fremantle and relocating them to Midland. This would provide necessary space at the harbour for wharves, and room at the new site for badly needed expansion of the workshops themselves. While Midland was twelve miles from Fremantle, it was close to the intersection of the eastern and northern railway lines, and land there was cheap. O'Connor had received support for this move from Mr Allison Smith, a locomotive superintendent from Victoria, who had been invited to Western Australia in July to report on the railway system.[204]

During O'Connor's absence in Southern Cross, the residents of Fremantle had held an 'indignation meeting' to discuss this proposal. Several politicians and councillors attended the rowdy meeting in the crowded Town Hall on 19 September. Daniel Congdon, a Legislative Council member and former mayor of Fremantle, moved:

'That this meeting views with alarm the suggested removal of the railway workshops from Fremantle, and would ask the Government to pause before committing an act which would paralyse the commercial interests of the port of the colony, and prove a lasting misfortune and injustice to its inhabitants.'[205]

A deputation of men with commercial, industrial and shipping interests, led by the member for Fremantle, William Marmion, called on the Premier John Forrest, a few days later. Each in turn expressed their concerns about the effect the relocation of the workshops would have on the economy and well-being of Fremantle. Sir John responded that 'they could rest assured that nothing adverse to the good of Fremantle would be done unless the interests of the colony demanded it.'[206] The deputation shook his hand and left, but they and the other residents of Fremantle didn't rest assured. The dispute would go on for years.

The same morning that O'Connor left Southern Cross, a prospector named Arthur Bayley strolled into town.[207] He quietly showed the 554 ounces (15.7 kg) of gold in his pack to Warden Finnerty and registered his claim to the site where he and his partner, William Ford, had found it, at Fly Flat, near the native well known as Coolgardie. Bayley had already had some success as a prospector both in the Murchison and the Yilgarn fields, but this was an unheard-of amount of gold from one site. By the end of the week, Southern Cross lay deserted as everyone rushed to stake their own claims on the new field.

Even before construction began on the Southern Cross rail line, miners were calling for the new line to be extended to Coolgardie. And as the news of the find was telegraphed around the world, people began pouring into Western Australia, hoping to unearth their own riches, or exploit those who succeeded. The need for a functioning harbour in Fremantle had never been greater.

THIRTEEN: Heartaches and hospitality – 1892

While Charles O'Connor was occupied in carrying out his many roles, the rest of the O'Connor family were settling into their new home and the Fremantle community. Susan assisted with the catering and decorations for the Fremantle Rowing Club annual ball on 3 August, a major social event in Fremantle. The following evening, Kate, Bridget, Roderick and Frank O'Connor all went in costume to the Rowing Club's popular juvenile fancy dress ball. Aileen, the eldest daughter, was on the team that represented Fremantle at a tennis tournament early in September.[208]

Although O'Connor was quite reserved and didn't much enjoy large formal gatherings, he attended the many government and social functions to which he was invited with good grace, and he was widely liked by many. Late in August, he and Susan were invited to a musical 'at home' at Government House, hosted by Sir William and Lady Robinson.[209]

The O'Connors were also generous hosts themselves, though usually for smaller and more informal parties. Not long after Susan arrived in Fremantle, they provided refreshments 'in the kindest manner and in ample degree' for a party of about thirty equestrians who met at a point known as 'the halfway tree' on the Fremantle to Perth road in Claremont. Everyone pronounced this social gathering a great success.[210]

O'Connor, with his own great love of equestrian activities, encouraged all his children to learn to ride. But on a Sunday afternoon in October this would lead, indirectly, to a terrible accident near the same halfway tree.

As one of the O'Connor boys was riding alone on the scrubby hillside above the Fremantle road, his horse was startled by a group of cyclists on the road ahead.[211] He was thrown to the ground close to the horse's hind legs. The frightened animal, prancing about, accidentally struck him hard in the head with one of its hooves, causing serious injury.

A cart provided by the owner of the nearby Halfway House hotel took the bleeding, unconscious boy to the hotel and a doctor was brought from Cottesloe. Charles O'Connor, who was also out riding, was found and informed of what had happened. On hearing the news, he rode to Fremantle to bring his own physician, Dr Birmingham. Once the doctors had done what they could for the boy, he was carried home to Park Bungalow. There his anxious parents watched over him, unsure what damage might have been done or even if he would recover.[212]

Fortunately, the boy survived his horse-riding accident near the halfway tree and recovered, apparently without any lasting effect. But the experience must have been haunting for Charles, Susan and the children old enough to remember the tragic accident at Hokitika.

***

Just over a month later, O'Connor, Minister Venn and other staff of the Public Works Department were responsible for organising a major social event in Fremantle. Although work on the harbour had been progressing steadily since April, the harbour works were officially inaugurated on the afternoon of Wednesday, 16 November, in a ceremony hailed as 'impressive'.

A train, brightly decorated with flags, flowers and greenery, left Perth station at 2.00 pm, carrying five hundred passengers. Among them were the Governor and Lady Robinson. On reaching Fremantle, further carriages were added, bringing the total to eighteen. This unusually long train, powered by three engines, steamed to Rous Head, where eight rail tip trucks, bearing huge stones, stood waiting.[213]

After disembarking from the train, the crowd gathered along the water's edge in the early summer sunshine, the men in sombre suits, the women in colourful summer dresses. Lady Robinson, swathed in claret-coloured silk with a white corduroy waistcoat, gave the signal from the locomotive. The first truck ran down to the end of the line and tipped its four massive stones into the ocean, with a mighty splash and a great cheer from the onlookers.

Once the other trucks had off-loaded the sixty tons of stone they carried, the crowd of about seven hundred people headed for a huge marquee set up near the end of the railway line. Here they enjoyed a champagne luncheon, served by fifty waiters and waitresses hired especially for the occasion.[214] A number of uninvited guests joined the party, but no-one seemed to mind.

C. Y. O'Connor was seated at a table with Governor Robinson and Lady Robinson, Sir John and Lady Forrest, Mr Venn, Mr Marmion and other distinguished guests. Susan O'Connor attended the luncheon, but neither she nor the two ministers' wives were seated with the guests at the top table.

Inevitably there were speeches and toasts. While most may have seemed long-winded and predictable to a casual observer, they were full of pointed remarks and innuendos, attempts at self-aggrandisement and shifting responsibility.

Harry Venn, who oversaw proceedings, opened with a toast to the Governor and Lady Robinson, in which he praised O'Connor's work. The Governor had attended many inauguration ceremonies in his time in the colony, Venn said, but this was the most important of all. The effect of a good harbour couldn't be overestimated.

'This is now about to be undertaken by the Engineer-in-Chief, Mr. O'Connor, upon whom, I am assured, rests the eye of the colony this day. The Government has freely entrusted this work to that gentleman and has every reason to be assured that that confidence would not be misplaced...'

Governor Robinson, in responding to the toast, also praised the Chief Engineer.

Sir John Forrest had been given the task of proposing a toast to the Engineer-in-Chief. He rose and waited for the applause to die away following the governor's speech.

'On some occasions I feel a difficulty in expressing what I want to say,' he began coyly, 'but I hope today I will have no such difficulty because the subject is to me an easy one. I think it not only a courtesy on the part of the Commissioner of Railways to ask me to propose this toast, but that it is right that it should be trusted to me, and for this reason. I am responsible for bringing to this colony the Engineer-in-Chief.'

Forrest told how he had employed O'Connor without even meeting him, based on the recommendations he had received. He continued, 'I think—and I speak now after two years' experience of him—the colony and the Government ought to be congratulated in having a gentleman of the energy, capacity and honour of the Engineer-in-Chief. I say there is no act of mine since I formed this Government, up to the present time, that I look to with more satisfaction than the appointment of Mr. O'Connor.'

Harry Venn had referred in his speech to two well-known Fremantle residents who had taken a keen interest in the harbour but had not lived to see it completed. John Forrest picked up on this.

'I cannot allow the opportunity to pass without referring to one present, who for 20 years and more has advocated the creation of a commodious harbour in Fremantle—that is my friend Mr. Marmion,' he said, turning to his left to where Marmion sat. The member for Fremantle's name produced a loud cheer from the audience.

'The scheme which we are inaugurating is not exactly that of my honourable friend,' Forrest continued, in a wry reference to Marmion's conflict with the chief engineer, 'but for all that, there is no one more anxious and more desirous for the success of this undertaking than Mr. Marmion. All he wants is that a first-class harbour should be provided.'

'Hear, hear!' said Marmion, to more cheers.

Forrest returned to his designated task, recounting the history of the scheme, and his hopes for the harbour and the colony.

'I can only, in conclusion, say that with my whole heart I wish this work success' Forrest said. 'I do not want any credit for it. I give all credit to the Engineer-in-Chief. I believe that in him we have an able and energetic, a brave and self-reliant man, and I only hope in this great work he has undertaken that he will be successful, and in a few years we will be here to join with the people of the colony in congratulating him on the completion of the scheme he has propounded.'

After the toast had been made and drunk, O'Connor stood to an enthusiastic welcome from the gathering.

He acknowledged the praise given him by the governor and the ministers of the crown, then taking up a theme he would reiterate many times in future, he went on:

'I have been put today into a position of rather more prominence than I am entitled to enjoy. As a matter of fact, although I recommended this work in a constitutional colony it must be understood... that the Government of the day are responsible for every act that is done, and if these harbour works are a success and an immense benefit to the colony...it is to the Ministry of the day who had the courage to support them in the House the credit is due. As an expert it is my duty to recommend what I believe is the right thing from an expert's point of view, but to take the responsibility...that is for the Government to do. The Government has done that, and I believe they will earn the everlasting gratitude of the colony for having done so.'

The harbour, he said, was absolutely essential to the progress of a large colony like this, but it was only part of a larger scheme that would see the harbour connected to the other colonies by an interstate railway. After describing, in detail, the cost of the harbour, the quality of stone from Rocky Bay, the equipment already bought and on order, and the unprecedented rate of railway construction in the colony, he expressed his indebtedness to the Minister of Public Works, Harry Venn, for the kindness with which he had been treated ever since he came to the colony. He made no direct mention in his speech of John Forrest.

Although the speeches were formally over, Governor Robinson rose to propose a toast to Mr Venn, who had so ably presided over that afternoon's arrangements. He had been pleased, the governor said, to see Mr Venn's name on the list of ministers submitted to him by Sir John Forrest when he formed his government. Being a colonial minister was a position of great responsibility, but he had no doubt, knowing the man, that Mr. Venn would carry out the expenditure with which he had been entrusted faithfully and well.[215]

Perhaps he was already aware of a growing rift between Forrest and his minister. His words would take on even greater significance a few years later, though by then a different man would be installed as governor.

* * *

The harbour inauguration came at a time of upheaval for the O'Connor family. A few days earlier, Charles and Susan had attended a garden party in the leafy grounds of Government House, in honour of Lady Robinson who was soon to leave on a trip to 'the old country'. Among their fellow guests were Henry and Emily Barnett, fresh from their overseas travels.[216] The O'Connor family's time at Park Bungalow was coming to an end, for now.

FOURTEEN: Dr Barnett's return – 1892-1893

A large group of friends were waiting on the platform when the train carrying Dr and Mrs Barnett steamed into the Perth railway station on 4 November 1892. As the Barnetts excitedly exchanged greetings and news, and recovered their baggage, a reporter from the *West Australian* came over to ask how their trip had been. And how was Dr Barnett feeling?

The holiday had been very enjoyable, Dr Barnett replied, and the change had left him feeling thoroughly renovated. After basking in this warm welcome, the Barnetts went to stay with Francis and Lilian Hart at their home in Hay Street, Perth for a few weeks.[217] The O'Connor's lease on their house in Fremantle would expire at the end of December.

After nearly eighteen months away, it was inevitable that Dr Barnett would notice changes when he returned to Fremantle. Some were minor – the house now had a telephone, installed by the government at O'Connor's request.[218] Others were more remarkable. New buildings had sprung up in the town centre. Across the river, a constant stream of railway trucks could be seen delivering stone to the end of Rous Head, where the north mole already protruded several hundred feet into the ocean.[219]

Observing the river with the eyes of a traveller, Dr Barnett wondered why there was no steamboat service between Fremantle and Perth, as he'd seen elsewhere. He wrote a letter on the issue to the *West Australian*. 'There are few matters which cause more surprise to a newcomer in West Australia, than the absence of any steam communication for passengers on the Swan between the city and the port', his letter began.[220]

When he returned to work in January 1893, he found little had changed at the asylum, and those changes that had occurred were mostly not to his liking. Dr Hope had struggled, just as Dr Barnett always had, to find places for all those who needed to be admitted. The thirty-one admissions in 1892 had far outnumbered the nine patients discharged and the twelve who had died, all by natural causes.[221] Among the deaths were two of the most long-standing patients. Mary Gilmour, who died in January 1892 at the age of eighty-two, had first been admitted soon after her arrival in the colony, before the current building was completed.[222] Mary Taylor had been a constant resident for 20 years when she died in May, aged seventy-four.[223] Their places had soon been filled.

During Dr Barnett's absence, the *Daily News* had printed a seven-part series of articles about the Fremantle asylum and its problems.

'Insanity is admittedly the worst affliction that can befall suffering humanity,' began the author, 'Lex', who had recently penned a similar series on the Fremantle prison. Asylums, he wrote, were usually constructed to afford 'the very best medical treatment possible', and to lessen 'the burden of so terrible an affliction.'

Not so in Western Australia, where 'free men and women are treated in similar manner to our convicts and criminals—a solitary instance of an institution for lunatics, conducted on the lines of prison life and rule, and where the daily routine of existence is but too closely allied with discomfort, dejection, and misery.'

The series went on to discuss the history of the building and its structure ('a marvel of inconvenience and stupidity') staffing, expenditure and the daily life of patients, including their plain diet and inadequate clothing. Many of the facts and figures quoted came from the government 'Blue Books', the annual accounts of various government departments and institutions. But 'Lex' also appears to have visited the asylum and was familiar with its layout and management.[224]

While not critical of Dr Barnett, 'Lex' deplored the fact that there was no resident medical officer at the asylum, and patients received only cursory medical attention. Due to the doctor's other duties, he was only able to visit the asylum four times per week, for half an hour at a time, claimed Lex. He noted Dr Barnett had urged the government, year after year, to make changes to the way the asylum was staffed and managed. The Select Committee of the previous year had recommended the same, without effect.

'It is to be hoped, however, that as soon as Dr. Barnett returns from his visit to the mother country, and can lay the result of his investigations in the matter of Asylum management before the Government, no time will be lost in giving effect to his recommendations, and this serious blot upon the control and efficiency of our only institution for the insane promptly removed,' Lex added.[225]

If Dr Barnett ever wrote a report of what he had learned on his visit to asylums in Britain, it was never acknowledged in parliament or in the press.

The government had not entirely neglected the needs of the asylum while Dr Barnett was away. In February 1892, it had set aside a sum of three thousand pounds for repairs and extensions to the asylum, although at the time many people, including some members of parliament, objected that this would be wasted expenditure. What was really needed was a new building altogether.[226]

By July 1892, perhaps spurred to action by Lex's newspaper articles, the government decided to spend the three thousand pounds on renovating 'The Knowle', on Fremantle's South Terrace. It would be used to house some of the 'imbecile' and other harmless male patients and free up places in the main asylum building.[227]

The two-storey Knowle had been built in 1853 as a home for Lieutenant-Colonel Edmund Henderson, Comptroller-General of Convicts, and his family. It had later been used to house invalids from the prison. By 3 December 1892, even before the improvements were completed, eighteen patients from the asylum had been transferred to the Knowle, and others were ready to be moved.[228] It was a makeshift measure that took some pressure off the asylum, but it meant that Dr Barnett, when he returned, would now have to visit two establishments to attend to patients.

The government's use of the Knowle was not popular with the residents of Fremantle. They had been wanting a hospital in the town for years, and many had hoped that the Knowle might be used for this purpose. What other town of 8,000 people didn't have its own hospital, they asked.[229]

Fremantle's City councillors had already offered the government a plot of land adjacent to the existing asylum for an extension and objected to having what they saw as two asylums in the heart of the town. The government assured them that this was a temporary measure, and when money was available the asylum would be moved to a location in the countryside.[230]

This resentment fed into another change that Dr Barnett experienced on his return. Although stories and rumours about his colourful past life abounded, he had always been respected in the Fremantle community and his professional acumen had never been questioned.

But at a meeting of three hundred ratepayers on 10 March, which Dr Barnett didn't attend, he came in for harsh criticism during discussion on the need for suitable hospital accommodation in Fremantle.

A few days earlier, reported Councillor Marshall, Dr Barnett had ordered a severely injured man to be taken to the casualty ward (a building which was really little more than a shed near the railway yards, also used for storing dynamite). Then, deciding there was no bed available, Dr Barnett had abruptly told those carrying the patient to take him instead to the train and have him conveyed to the hospital in Perth. The dying man was shaken about, and his treatment delayed. He wouldn't even have had water to drink on the train, if those carrying him had not provided it, Councillor Marshall reported.

'Was that the way to treat human beings?' asked the Councillor. And yet, he added, Dr Barnett was their Colonial Surgeon.

'He ought not to be,' and 'Shame!' responded some in the crowd.

Only Dr Hope defended his colleague, pointing out that the government did not supply what was needed for such situations.[231]

Three months later, on 12 June, a letter appeared in the West Australian, which described how a patient from Geraldton had been sent by ship to Fremantle so that he could receive medical care. On arrival, he was so weak that he had to be carried. Dr Barnett, it was reported, refused to admit him to the casualty ward while he was waiting to be transferred to the Perth Hospital. Even after the mayor of Fremantle had telephoned Dr Barnett, he refused to admit the man to the casualty ward.[232]

The ward had no attendant, which might explain Dr Barnett's reluctance to admit the patient. But a certain intransigence had begun to creep into his interactions with the public, and especially with public officials, which would increase over time.

The weight of being colonial surgeon as well as superintendent of the asylum, pressed heavily on Henry Barnett, who had celebrated his sixtieth birthday during his overseas trip. Apart from visiting the asylum and the Knowle, tending to accident victims and acting as JP in the local magistrates' court, he still had his private practice to run.

Help arrived in March 1893 in the form of Dr Louis Wheeler, a twenty-four-year-old graduate from the medical school at Queens College Belfast, who came to the colony as doctor in charge on the *Gulf of Taranto*. The ship arrived in port on 12 March, carrying forty-seven female migrants recruited to work as domestic servants. Dr Wheeler announced on arrival that he would be joining Dr Barnett in his practice.[233]

Young, trim and handsome, Louis Wheeler was a welcome addition to the social life of Fremantle. He had trained with Henry's nephew, Kennett Barnett, and may well have been recruited by Dr Barnett during the Barnetts' time in Britain.[234] He would prove a great support to the older doctor, both professionally and personally.

But almost as soon as he arrived, Dr Wheeler was temporarily seconded to another role. In the last week of February 1893, a Singhalese man, who had arrived in Fremantle aboard the *Saladin*, became unwell with a rash. He was quickly isolated at the hospital in Perth, but it took some time for the doctors who saw him to come to a firm diagnosis. He had smallpox.[235]

By the beginning of April, the infected man was recovering. But despite all the precautions taken, a nurse had developed symptoms. She was diagnosed and isolated.[236] Soon more cases appeared.

Fremantle council sent a letter of protest to the colonial secretary when it was suggested that the infected patients should be moved to the quarantine station at Woodman Point near Fremantle.[237] Despite the council's caution, by 13 April the outbreak had reached Fremantle and suspected cases were also being reported elsewhere in the colony.[238]

Initially, supplies of vaccine were low, but stocks were brought in from Melbourne, and a vaccination campaign began. On 21 April, the mayor of Fremantle announced that Dr Barnett would be performing free vaccinations at the Town Hall, three evenings per week, and at any time for Aboriginal people.[239] Within a week, Dr Barnett had vaccinated 350 people and stocks were running low again. Meanwhile, Dr Wheeler had been appointed to act as health officer at the collection of tents that formed the quarantine station in Subiaco, on Perth's outskirts.[240]

The outbreak had subsided by early June, after fifty cases and seven deaths.[241] The quarantine station was disbanded, and Dr Wheeler returned to Fremantle. By this time Dr Barnett had vaccinated 665 people, about eight per cent of the Fremantle population and more than any other doctor in Fremantle. He was at least commended for this.[242] But it must have added to his feelings of exhaustion.

One thing that hadn't changed in Dr Barnett's time overseas was the rampant anti-Chinese, anti-foreigner sentiment of the population. During the smallpox outbreak, a prankster wrote 'Smallpox' on official-looking yellow streamers and attached them to the window of a laundry run by a Chinese man, Sam Lee. The guilty party was reprimanded, not for maligning the Chinese owner, but for frightening the public.[243]

When Dr Hope, in his role as acting superintendent, submitted the annual report on the asylum for the year 1892, his comments echoed those of Dr Barnett over many years. Despite the added accommodation at The Knowle, the asylum was overcrowded, and the building inadequate and unfit for purpose.

As was Dr Barnett's practice in previous years, Dr Hope also noted the number of 'coloured' and 'foreign' patients being admitted, without making any comment. The *Daily News* picked up on these figures. In an article on 'colored cheap labour', the paper questioned why the government was allowing these people into the colony, to be treated at the public's expense. The article blatantly misquoted Dr Hope, adding the words, 'it is alarming to contemplate the number of dark-blooded men who get admitted', to the text of his report.[244]

Also unchanged during Dr Barnett's time away was the Forrest brothers' dominance over West Australian politics. During the Barnetts' absence, Alexander Forrest, the Premier's brother and member for the far northern seat of Kimberley, had accepted nomination for election as the Mayor of Perth.[245] Alexander shared his older brother John's fame as a surveyor and explorer but lacked both his rotundity and his equable nature. He was close to John Forrest and although never officially a minister in his government, he was often referred to as 'the sixth minister'.

His two opponents in the mayoral election, Messrs Randall and Traylen, were also both sitting members of Parliament. Forrest was elected on 26 November 1892. Dr Barnett attended his swearing-in ceremony at the Perth Town Hall on 1 December, soon after his return from overseas.[246]

Returning to Western Australia meant the Barnetts once more joined the endless stream of social events, musical evenings, garden parties, dances, and dinners. In mid-June, Dr Barnett and Emily attended the Governor's Ball at Government House, an elegant building set in well-tended gardens, with porticoed entrance and a sweeping staircase. So many attended the ball that dancing was almost out of the question. But despite the crush, and the smell of kerosene from the lamps used to light the rooms, the guests were soothed by the lavish supper and popping of champagne corks, and the ball was deemed a great success.

The O'Connors were also there, with their daughter Aileen among the seven debutantes presented to the governor that night. Lilian Hart, writing as 'Cora' for the *West Australian*, lovingly described what all the most notable ladies, and even some of the gentlemen, were wearing. Emily Barnett's pink brocade dress came in for special attention. It was a gown, she wrote, 'in which one quickly detected the Parisian modiste', and she went on to describe it with a precision suggesting she had seen and admired the dress before the ball.[247]

Henry and Emily Barnett hosted their own small party at Park Bungalow on 6 July, to farewell Mr Thomas John, the retiring chief warder of the asylum. All the asylum staff who were not on duty attended. After a speech thanking Mr John for his long service, Dr Barnett presented him with an armchair as a farewell gift, then invited 'all those whose teetotal principles did not preclude them from doing so' to join him in a glass of wine.[248]

Less than two weeks later, both the Barnetts became seriously unwell with influenza, which had reached epidemic proportions that winter in Fremantle.[249] Newspapers from Geraldton to Bunbury reported the severity of their illness and expressed fears that Dr Barnett might 'take a turn for the worse'. Although he and Mrs Barnett both recovered, Dr Barnett's health remained fragile in the following weeks.

As a result of his illness, Dr Barnett missed the Fremantle Rowing Club ball on 2 August. This was a blow to the club, as Henry was its patron. In his absence, he donated a five-guinea prize, for a competition to be open to all club members.

The O'Connor family were also enthusiastic members of the rowing club. Susan O'Connor helped with the catering and the decoration of the hall for the event. Frank O'Connor won prizes for the junior fours and for swimming, while Aileen O'Connor and her ladies' team were awarded gold bangles for their win at the recent regatta.[250]

In mid-October, Dr Barnett was still struggling with his health. He was granted leave so that he and Mrs Barnett could visit Singapore for recuperation. They sailed from Fremantle aboard the *Saladin* on 29 October. Dr Wheeler became acting colonial surgeon and superintendent of the asylum while Dr Barnett was away.[251]

Just before Dr Barnett left, the *West Australian* printed an article he had written aboard ship, on his way home to Fremantle the previous year. Titled *A Peep at Ceylon*, it described the Barnetts' visit to Ceylon (Sri Lanka) during their outward voyage to England. The timing of its publication was probably not random. Henry Barnett was offering a peep not only at Ceylon, but also at his reasons for thinking a trip to Singapore would be good for his health. The article began:

'No man knows the value of water until he has felt the want of it. So it is with sleep, and many other blessings which, when constantly enjoyed, we think little of.'

This reference to sleep, slipped in among a list of blessings taken for granted, suggests that the doctor was already suffering from the insomnia that would wrack his life in the years ahead. The cause of his sleeplessness at this time was never made known. It may have been the neuralgia from which he later suffered but might also have been due to the mental strain he was under or even a consequence of his recent influenza infection.

The article continued, with more than a hint of weariness and nostalgia:

'Similarly, after residing two dozen years in one colony how thoroughly delightful it is to roam over the world once more, and resume the almost forgotten joys of globe-trotting.'

He went on to marvel at how the man-made breakwater at Colombo provided a safe haven from the 'angry ocean' for the large ships that came and went each day. This, he noted, was one of the great works of Sir John Coode. Dr Barnett had been out of the country during the debate over the harbour at Fremantle, so he probably had no ulterior motive in mentioning John Coode's achievement.

The *RMS Victoria* had spent some time berthed in port at Colombo. Henry described a carriage ride he and Mrs Barnett had taken through the town and suburbs of the city, followed by a daytrip by train through the mountains to Kandy. Everything he saw in this country, 'more beautiful than I can express', filled him with delight. The tropical vegetation, the fruit, the flowers, the mountain vistas, the 'people occupied in a hundred ways', seemed intoxicating, and reminded him of his time in the tropics thirty years before.[252] A trip to Singapore would refresh his soul as well as his body.

FIFTEEN: The omnipotent Chief Engineer – 1893

Chief Engineer O'Connor had no time for a break, though after two years in the colony, working at an obsessive pace, he surely needed one. He spent much of his time travelling about the country, inspecting projects that the public works department was working on. Having others to share the load with him was becoming a necessity. At his request, the government employed Arthur Dillon Bell, a New Zealander, as Inspecting Engineer, to take on some of O'Connor's role in supervising public works.

Work on the Fremantle harbour project was going well. By March 1893, powerful steam-driven cranes had arrived from overseas and were being used to handle the massive stones being excavated at Rocky Bay. A second railway line had been extended to the end of Rous Head, which allowed the tipping trucks carrying the stone to be emptied and return to the quarry more efficiently.[253] By the time the Governor gave his speech at the opening of parliament for the year on 5 July, he was able to report that the breakwater now extended 1200 feet.[254] It had already proved effective in sheltering the river mouth during winter storms.

But storms of another kind were brewing over O'Connor. In the Legislative Assembly on 19 July, the member for Perth, Thomas Molloy, moved that a report be provided on the number of people being employed by the Public Works and Railways Department.

'It is complained, especially in the Works Department,' said Molloy, 'that there is most reckless extravagance; that the supervision in regard to the

Loan works is too costly; that there are too many officers employed for the purpose.

'It is also complained, in this department, that the Engineer-in-Chief seems to have complete control; that he seems to have the management of the affair as though it was his own concern, and as though he was not a public servant; that he seems to be omnipotent, to have entire control, and to employ whom he thinks fit.'

Molloy rehashed the claim that O'Connor favoured New Zealanders when employing staff and had imported equipment from New Zealand, to the detriment of the local workers.

'I do not wish to say this officer is not competent, but I do say he has proved himself, since he has been here, to have a thorough disregard of economy,' said Molloy.

He specifically queried the recent employment of Dillon Bell. It seemed to Molloy an unnecessary expense.

The Director of Public Works, Harry Venn, rose to defend his Chief Engineer. He accused Molloy of an unwarrantable (sic) attack on a government officer. A report on the appointments and expenditure in the Public Works Department had already been requested and had been tabled that evening. Mr Molloy should refer to that rather than request another, he said.

Molloy objected to the term 'unwarrantable attack'. Mr Venn offered no apology for using it.

'Some time ago a noise was made about the preference alleged to be given to New Zealanders in the harbour works at Fremantle,' said Venn, 'and when I heard of it, I sent down there at once to have a return prepared showing every individual employed and what places they came from. The Engineer-in-Chief knew nothing about the inquiry I was making.

'That information, when obtained, was published in the newspapers, and it showed, what was a notorious fact, that the New Zealanders, who were said to be so numerous, because of the preference shown to them, were really in a minority to an enormous extent.'

Venn was likely referring to figures which the newspapers had published as far back as May. These showed that, of 169 men employed on the harbour works project (other than ordinary workmen) only eleven were New Zealanders. Seventy were West Australians, with the rest made up of men from other Australian colonies.[255]

The Chief Engineer had nothing to do with most appointments, other than making recommendations on a couple of occasions, continued Venn. Was it surprising if he recommended people he knew and could trust? All expenditure was the responsibility of the government. Mr Molloy was doing the Chief Engineer an injustice.

'It is impossible for Mr. O'Connor to attend to the important duties in his office, and at the same time go travelling all over the colony to inspect works in progress and give directions in particular cases,' said Venn. The Chief Engineer was under great strain because of his enormous workload. He had asked for an Inspecting Engineer to be employed to take some of the strain.

Alexander Forrest, the Premier's brother, came to the support of Molloy.

'I think the honorable member did not intend to cast reflections upon Mr. O'Connor. Far from it,' he said. 'What he intended to convey was that the Works and Railways Department is carried on at an extravagant rate that will ruin the country.'

He offered examples of what he considered wasted expenditure on the South-western railway line.

'I am a supporter of the Government in their general policy, but when I see the way in which the works are carried on, it makes one say there must be a shingle short somewhere,' he said.

'We know that in Mr. O'Connor we have an able man, but we know also that the rate of expenditure now going on is astonishing. As to the appointments made, it is notorious that men from New Zealand have been put into all the good billets in the colony.'

Other members of the Assembly joined the discussion, many arguing that it was inappropriate and 'unmanly' to be attacking the Engineer-in-Chief in his absence. Responsibility for the Public Works Department and its expenditure rested with the Director of Public Works, Mr Venn, who was there in the house to defend himself.

The debate went back and forth, until the Premier, John Forrest, brought it to a close. The government had been pushing ahead with construction projects at a great speed, he said, and this had created the need to employ more men in public works.

'These preliminary labours are over,' he went on, 'and the Director of Public Works will now tell you I have latterly been urging him just as strongly to reduce the temporary men on the professional staff, because the principal works have been let for construction, and we can dispense with a great many of the employees. In fact, during the next two or three months the Director of Public Works will dispense with the services of a great number.'

Mr Venn, the Director in question, made no comment. Sir John Forrest concluded by expressing his support of O'Connor's work.

'I know he wants to do things well, that he is a man of great integrity and ability, and I do not think he is extravagant,' said the Premier. 'It is fortunate we have such a man, because it is on his professional recommendation we have to act, and we cannot, to a great extent, go against his recommendations, because he has a practical knowledge of what is exactly required.'

This refrain of 'we have no choice but to trust him because only he has the necessary knowledge' was one that Forrest would return to more than once when discussing the Engineer-in-Chief.

C. Y. O'Connor was well aware of the rumours and accusations being made both inside and outside of parliament. They were reported daily in the newspapers. But he was occupied with more pressing problems.

As early as January 1893, reports had come from the goldfields, and along the route to Coolgardie, that water was in short supply. The influx of people that followed the rich gold find in September had put immense pressure on the existing water supplies, which came mainly from soaks and seasonal clay pans.

These had served the local indigenous people for countless generations but were being sucked dry by the hundreds of men now living on the goldfields. Clear-felling of trees for fuel and building material only made things worse.

Water at Gnarlbine Rock near Coolgardie was exhausted, and the authorities were warning that people going to Coolgardie did so at risk to their own lives.[256]

Rainfall late in January eased the situation slightly, although water was still being sold at two shillings per gallon.[257] Men who had been holding off going to the goldfields because of the water shortage now headed out, creating more pressure on the limited supplies.

In March the government appointed Frederick G. Renon as Superintendent of Water Supply for the whole colony, including the routes to the goldfields, under the direction of the Lands and Mines Department.[258] An expert in water boring was sent to the goldfields, but the result of his first drill in Coolgardie was disappointing.[259]

Paddy Hannan's discovery of gold thirty-five miles northeast of Coolgardie, in June 1893, led to an exodus of miners from Coolgardie to 'Hannan's' (later Kalgoorlie) and a new rush of miners from Perth, the northern goldfields and interstate.[260] By July there were an estimated 1,200 men on the field. Winter rainfall provided temporary water for this new influx but couldn't be relied upon long term.

Despite Renon's best efforts in conserving and regulating water supplies, the situation remained dire, and by November, responsibility had been handed back to the Public Works Department.[261]

O'Connor, tasked with extending the railway line from Northam to Southern Cross and beyond, could not ignore the problems created by lack of water along the route. Not only the miners, but the construction teams and the steam trains themselves needed water. Although it would be another two years before plans to build a pipeline from the coast to the goldfields became open to public discussion, O'Connor was certainly gathering information and considering the problem long before that.

When the colony's budget was discussed in parliament late in August 1893, John Forrest, in his role as treasurer, noted with satisfaction that not only was the work on the harbour progressing as planned, but the cost of constructing the north mole had worked out at only ten pounds per foot.

This was four pounds per foot less than the Chief Engineer had estimated initially.[262]

Not everyone was impressed. The expense of the project still caused concern to some. Public servants' salaries had also been criticised in the press several times over the year. The Chief Engineer came in for particularly harsh criticism.

In August, a letter sent to the *Daily News* and the *West Australian* under the pseudonym 'Jarrah', argued that the 'enormous salaries' of civil servants should be reduced and the money saved used to employ more men in public works.[263] This was not the first time that 'Jarrah' had used the newspapers to express his views on the high salaries paid to public servants, especially those from New Zealand.[264]

On 6 September a letter writer calling himself 'Honor' responded to 'Jarrah'.

> *'Sir_*
>
> *if you would be good enough to give publicity to the following, you would confer a benefit on, and perhaps secure fair play for some of our civil servants.*
>
> *For some time letters have appeared in the papers about fat salaried civil servants and the Engineer-in-Chief's large salary. A correspondent signing himself Jarrah (in whose character I see no resemblance to that fine timber, unless in a wooden-headed disregard for facts) speaks of draughtsmen in the public works receiving over four hundred a year for three or four hours work per day.*
>
> *Now I would remind "Jarrah" that the Chief Draughtsman only gets 400 per annum; while draughtsmen receive £180, £150 and less, down to about half the wages of a bricklayer. They are kept in constant fear of retrenchment, have to dress well, be well educated, active, energetic, and able at their profession, and must put in at least six good hours work a day; and any overtime, which pressure of work may require, without receiving any additional pay. Their occupation is trying to the constitution and very hard on the eyes.'*

'Honor' evidently had personal insight into the training, duties and salaries of draughtsmen. He went on:

> *'As to the Engineer-in-Chief's salary, if it be compared with that of bank managers, merchants, insurance agents or of other men who have not a tenth of the responsibility, it will be found very small, a smallness only excusable on account of our limited means in this colony, and the general depression in other parts of the world, forcing able men to take low rates of remuneration for their services.'*

The writer pointed out that even a slight error by a less skilled engineer could result in far more than the cost of his yearly salary being wasted on one single mile of railway or harbour works.

> *'Our railways are the cheapest constructed in the world, and the salaries of our professional staff are about the lowest. Men work often almost night and day, real hard work at school and college and in articles spending hundreds of pounds, and the best years of their lives to acquire a profession, and are then very frequently paid less than a labourer.'*

Despite 'Jarrah' having argued his case from the working man's point of view, 'Honor' apparently believed 'Jarrah' to be a wealthy man and seems to have known, or at least suspected, his identity. He concluded his letter:

> *'Would it not be better to raise a tax on unused land and absentee landlords, and from the revenue thus obtained raise the pay of the workers, who are doing their best to open up our country instead of diminishing those already small, in some cases almost starvation wages, in the manner wished by one of Perth's wealthy citizens.*
>
> *Yours truly,*
>
> HONOR'.[265]

'Honor's concern for truth and fairness, his disdain for absentee landlords and the general tone of the letter all suggest that this could have been written by C. Y. O'Connor. He was known for his support of workers' demands for fairer conditions. Absentee landlords had been one of the factors behind the Irish famine of his childhood, which had so disrupted his own family life.

Having learned his lesson from the response to his published comments about the railway crossings the previous year, he would have known better than to write under his own name. It would be unprofessional to do so. But the jibes about his salary surely goaded him. His honour and reputation were extremely important to him. And he would not stand by and see others unjustly criticised.[266]

O'Connor's reputation came under further harsh attack about this time from another quarter. The Auditor General, Frederick Spencer, in his annual report for the year ending December 1892, made comments critical of the Engineer-in-Chief's handling of goods and materials belonging to the Railways Department. A select committee was set up in July 1893 in response to the Auditor's comments. The committee reported back to parliament in September and the *West Australian* newspaper published the committee's findings.[267]

Essentially, the Auditor General accused O'Connor of not conforming to the procedures laid out for the department. He was said to have given orders verbally where they should have been in writing; he had lent stock to contractors without consulting anyone or being authorised; and he had tried to change the ways the department's accounts were kept.

While these changes might be desirable, the committee concluded, they had caused friction and made the job of the Auditor General more difficult. So long as the present Act and Regulations remained in force, it was the duty of every member of the department to carry out the requirements and regulations of the Audit Act.

The committee also noted 'with regret', that the minister, Harry Venn, had been guilty of providing evidence from a witness to the Engineer-in-Chief during the enquiry, something he was not entitled to do.[268]

The *West Australian* described the committee's report as 'feeble', failing to either accuse or exonerate the Engineer-in-Chief. Nor were the Auditor General's concerns addressed. It was a waste of time, the paper concluded, a sentiment that O'Connor surely agreed with.[269]

But O'Connor never suffered fools gladly, nor would he allow his reputation to be unfairly dishonoured. The criticism continued to ferment in his mind.

On 28 October, having failed to receive the public exoneration which he felt he was due, O'Connor wrote a memorandum to his minister, Harry Venn, for consideration by the cabinet:

> *'Having waited very anxiously, for a considerable time, in the hope that there would be some distinct and authoritative refutation of the very serious charge made against me in the above-mentioned report, I feel constrained, as a duty to myself, as well as to the profession to which I have the honor to belong, to ask the Government to make some distinct and public Announcement of the fact that this charge is entirely unwarranted by the facts of the case.'*

He wanted, he said, an acquittal by the government from the imputed impropriety with 'a publicity equal to the publicity given to the imputation itself.'

His memorandum continued for several pages. After restating the evidence he had given to the committee, which he felt had been misrepresented, he expressed concern about the government's proposal to move the custody of the railway stores to the Treasury. This would be seen as confirming the allegations made against him, in the 'violent and acrimonious attack' made on him in the Auditor General's report.

He concluded his memorandum:

> *'Failing this refutation, my career in Western Australia will be a truly remarkable one, consisting of two years' of the most trying and unremitting labour which I have ever had to undertake, with the result*

> *that I am met, at the end of it, by the most violent and personal attack which has, I think, ever been levelled, in a Report to Parliament, on an officer in my position, and that when I have conclusively shown this attack to have been entirely devoid of any foundation, I fail to get that distinct and public acquittance which truth and justice demand. I cannot, however, for a moment believe that such will be the eventual result.'*

Along with the memorandum he enclosed several documents, as evidence both of his innocence and of the damage to his reputation.

He would have to wait until the following February for a response from the government.

SIXTEEN: Mishaps, meetings and memorandums – 1893

Although work had been going according to plan on the harbour project, it had not been without a human cost. During the first twelve months, several workmen had been injured in minor and not-so-minor accidents. One had his leg broken by falling rocks, another crushed his hand while coupling railway trucks, while two others were concussed in an explosion at the quarry at Rocky Bay.[270]

On 2 October 1893, a thirty-two-year-old stone cutter named Henry Bennett became the project's first fatality. He had been shovelling rocks at the quarry face when he heard a noise above him. As he looked up, he was hit by a falling stone. He died instantly, his skull crushed.

At the inquest held two days later, witnesses said there had been no blasting going on nearby for several days. They thought the stone must have been loosened by the wind removing sand from around it.

John Irvine, the Harbour Works manager, corroborated their evidence and said that whenever blasting took place, all loose rock and debris was immediately removed. He estimated the rock that struck Bennett had fallen fifty feet and weighed sixty to seventy pounds.[271] The jury at the inquest gave a verdict of accidental death.

Henry Bennett had arrived in Western Australia from Victoria about eighteen months earlier. His death left his wife and child without an income and cast a shadow over the harbour works.

C. Y. O'Connor initiated a subscription fund to support Bennett's widow, which John Irvine administered. On 23 October, Irvine reported that Bennett's fellow workers at Rocky Bay had contributed twenty-eight pounds.[272] In total, the fund raised forty-six pounds, six shillings and sixpence.[273]

Early in November, another two men narrowly escaped death when a charge, which had apparently failed to detonate, exploded while they were investigating it. One received serious burns to his arm, face and right eye. They were taken to the casualty ward. Dr Barnett had already left on his trip to Singapore, so they were treated by Dr Wheeler.[274] The incident would be neither the last, nor the most serious, involving explosions.

Despite these accidents and tragedies, work continued. By the anniversary of the official inauguration of the works in November, the north mole had been extended almost a third of a mile (half a kilometre) from Rous Head, and its end stood in 24 feet of water. The quarry face at Rocky Bay measured almost a mile in length. Altogether, the harbour project was employing over 250 men.

Although their wages contributed to the well-being of Fremantle, and the harbour, when completed, would greatly benefit the port city, its residents were still concerned about what would be lost if the railway workshops were moved.

On 3 November, an estimated one thousand people gathered in a public meeting at Fremantle Town Hall, to discuss the removal of the workshops. The mayor, W. F. Samson, presided, and several members of parliament attended. Alexander Forrest sent a telegram expressing his sympathy with their objective and promised to do all he could to ensure the workshops remained in Fremantle.

Daniel Congdon, MLC, reported that he had telephoned Sir John Forrest and told him about the upcoming meeting. Sir John had apparently asked, 'Are the people of Fremantle in a hurry to get rid of the workshops?'

'No, we are not,' said Mr Congdon. To which John Forrest had reportedly replied, 'Neither are the government.'

Though the answer could be understood to mean merely that the workshops would not be moved immediately, the meeting took it that the

Government were against moving the workshops.

William Marmion, the member for Fremantle, told the crowd that he too had spoken to the Premier. He read out a letter in which John Forrest had assured him that 'the Government have all along been adverse to removing them (i.e., the workshops) from Fremantle unless under the most urgent necessity in the interest of the whole railway system.' The government had not yet had time, the letter continued, to consider the report of a commission set up to investigate the matter, so it was too soon to give an opinion.

The letter, Mr Marmion believed, 'was a sufficient indication of the position of the Government in regard to the workshops question, and they might rest assured that so long as they had a good friend in the ministry (i.e., himself) it would not be an easy matter to remove the Fremantle Workshops or to do anything else that would be adverse to the best interests of the town.'

A proposal to create a Vigilance Committee 'to watch events, and, if necessary, draw up a memorial to the Parliament to protest the removal of the workshops' was accepted and a number of nominations agreed to.

The meeting concluded by accepting a motion to oppose any person offering himself as a candidate for Parliament at the next general elections, who supported the removal of the Government workshops from Fremantle. With an election due the following year, it was not a meaningless threat.[275]

***

Elections were also on the minds of the women of the Women's Christian Temperance Union. They had not forgotten John Forrest's words about governments depending on suffrage, and they wanted a say in how the colony was governed. They visited him on 20 November and called on him to appoint a Royal Commission 'to enquire into the effects of the liquor traffic…upon the finances…the sobriety, crime, vice, insanity, health, disease, vital statistics, morality, religion and education of the people of this colony, with a view to initiating suitable legislation in the future'.

And they asked that the Commission should be partly composed of women.

Their resolution went further. The WCTU had concluded that the best way to have a say in how laws affecting women and children were discussed in parliament was for women to have the vote. They called on all members of parliament in Western Australia to unite with them to secure this right as soon as possible.

Women in Western Australia had been campaigning for the franchise to be extended to them for several years, petitioning parliamentarians, holding rallies and publishing pamphlets. By an odd quirk of politics, they had almost been granted the vote a few months earlier, in July 1893, when parliament was discussing the *Constitution Act Amendment* Act. The amendment was intended to increase the number of members of the Legislative Council from seventeen to twenty-one, and to have them elected by all males over the age of twenty-one, rather than members being appointed by the governor.[276]

On 26 July, during the discussion in the Assembly over what should be the qualification for voters, the member for Sussex electorate in the southwest, Joseph Cookworthy, moved that single women, widows and *femes soles* should also have the right to vote.

He thought it only right that women who maintained themselves and their families, women engaged in business and other occupations, and women who employed the very men who, under this law, would have a right to vote, should not be debarred from exercising the same privilege.[277]

His amendment evoked a keen, though sometimes jocular, debate. Some conservatives supported it and even wanted the vote extended to all married women, not just property owners. They could see the advantage of having local women's votes to balance the influence of the many young men who had recently arrived in the colony from outside, on the assumption that women would vote the same way as their husbands.

Others thought that if Cookworthy's amendment passed, it was likely the vote would soon be extended to all women. And that was precisely why the motion should be defeated. Granting the vote to women before any of the other British colonies did so could bring Western Australia's parliament into ridicule.

During the debate, John Forrest argued, somewhat spuriously, that since no-one had asked for suffrage to be extended to women, not even women themselves, the proposal should be postponed for further discussion of the principles involved. It could have implications that hadn't been thought through properly.

More than once, Joseph Cookworthy had to insist that his proposal wasn't a joke. Eventually, the motion was put to the vote. It was narrowly lost by thirteen votes to twelve.[278]

With all this as background, when the ladies of the WCTU met with the Western Australian Premier in November 1893, they had good reason to hope that women in Western Australia (by which they meant white, non-indigenous women) might be granted suffrage, if they just kept pressing for it.

In response to the women's proposals, John Forrest said he would lay their request for a Royal Commission before his colleagues. But perhaps they should wait for the result of a similar commission being conducted in South Australia, since the two colonies were similar.

As for extending the franchise to women, he was not against the concept, but he thought it needed more consideration. As it appeared such a reasonable thing that every intelligent woman should have a vote, how had it come to pass that no British community had as yet given the franchise to women, he asked. There must have been some reason, or the other Australian colonies, which had enjoyed responsible government for thirty years, would have granted it.

'Slow and sure' was not a bad motto, he suggested. He was 'very glad' that New Zealand had recently given the franchise to women.[279] The West Australian government would wait and see what the effect would be. If it were successful there, he had no hesitation in saying that in a very short time it would be adopted in Western Australia.[280]

It would, in fact, be another six years before women in Western Australia got to vote.[281]

***

'Slow and sure' might also have been John Forrest's motto when it came to satisfying C. Y. O'Connor's demand for an apology over the Auditor General's accusations earlier in the year. O'Connor had sent his memorandum to the cabinet, via Harry Venn, in October 1893. In February 1894, he finally received a response from John Forrest:

> *SIR,-With reference to paragraph 5 of the Auditor-General's report to Parliament, and to your letter on the subject, I have very great pleasure in recording, on behalf of the Government, that there were no grounds whatever in connection with the issue of the iron work, wheels and axles to Mr. Neil McNeil for any imputation of improper conduct on your part, and that you had full authority to issue them, and, indeed, had no choice in the matter, as it was an issue provided by the South-Western railway contract, and was in no way subject to your discretion.*
>
> *You are at liberty to make any use of this letter that you may care to.*

This brief response barely touched on O'Connor's complaints, but he made good use of it. His original memorandum, and the Premier's reply, were published, in full, in newspapers around the colony.[282]

In January 1894, O'Connor and his minister, Harry Venn, made a hot and exhausting visit to Southern Cross and Coolgardie to inspect the work being done to supply water to the two towns.[283] Lack of water was aggravating the insanitary conditions on the goldfields and there were fears that the sporadic cases of typhoid recently reported would soon become an epidemic.[284] The residents of Coolgardie were also keen to discuss the extension of the eastern railway line and the telegraph service to their part of the goldfields.

But back in Fremantle, the two most pressing concerns of its citizens were not water, sanitation or telegraph services, but the location of the railway workshops and the ongoing need for a hospital in the town. The workshop issue would dog O'Connor for years. Conflict over where to locate the hospital would draw in Dr Barnett and bring into question his physical ability to do his work.

SEVENTEEN: A Physical Drawback - 1894

The existing casualty ward in Fremantle satisfied no-one. Its location, close to the railway lines, made it unpleasantly noisy for patients and dangerous to access. It was cramped, and getting stretchers in and out was difficult. There was no room at the site for a much-needed dispensary. From Dr Barnett's point of view, it was an inconvenient distance from his home, the asylum buildings and the Knowle.

It had been suggested, back in July the previous year, that the old barracks in South Terrace could be converted into a casualty ward. The government had seemed prepared to go ahead with this. But Dr Barnett was not impressed with the idea, and his objections were partly the reason that nothing had been done to further the plan.

The long, two-story stone barracks, built during the convict era, had once housed the retired soldiers who acted as guards to the convicts. In Dr Barnett's opinion, the rooms were too small and poorly ventilated, and couldn't easily be modified. Besides that, the building was too far from the port and the railway yards, where most accidents occurred, and from the police station, from where help in such accidents often came.

After coming in for harsh criticism from some councillors, early in January 1894, for his role in delaying progress on the matter, Dr Barnett wrote a letter in support of a purpose-built cottage hospital of eight rooms, to be staffed full-time by a caretaker and his wife. It could, he thought, be constructed for the relatively small sum of one thousand pounds. He suggested it should be built at the corner of Fremantle Park, mid-way between the police quarters and East Fremantle station. Though he didn't mention it in his letter, his home, Park Bungalow, and the asylum both overlooked the park.

At the council meeting on 23 January, the councillors discussed Dr Barnett's letter and accepted a proposal to ask the Premier to set aside one thousand to fifteen hundred pounds in the next estimates to build a hospital in Fremantle.[285]

A few days later, in a letter published in the *West Australian,* a writer calling himself 'Pro Bono Publico' poured scorn on this idea. He accused Dr Barnett of wanting to build the hospital close to his own home, to reduce his workload (which the writer admitted was excessive).

> *'In view of the unfortunate physical disability under which Dr. Barnett labours—to say nothing of his advanced age—it would no doubt be a great convenience to him, while he retains his present official position, to have the hospital close to his own door, but if considerations for Dr. Barnett's past services influenced the Council in the decision they arrived at, I think it would be to the interest of the rate-payers if he were allowed to retire on a pension, equal to his full salary, and let a younger man take his place. His partner, Dr. Wheeler, is well qualified for the post, and there is no reason why he, or some other younger practitioner should not be appointed.'*[286]

Pro Bono's letter drew an immediate and furious response from Dr Wheeler. In a letter published the following day, he condemned the writer for his invidious comparisons between himself and Dr Barnett, and his rude and unfeeling references to Dr Barnett's age and physical drawback ('for I decline to call it, as does your correspondent, a disability').

> *'If the public, and more especially the Fremantle public, are interested in my opinions on this subject, common fairness and a sense of decency and right compel me to affirm that I have not found Dr. Barnett's age,*

which is by no means extreme, interfere with the performance of his public duties; that I consider his medical and surgical opinion deserves to rank high in the colony; and that his physical drawback, which I repeat is most cruelly referred to, cannot and does not interfere with his management of medical and surgical cases.'[287]

Over the years, Dr Wheeler's ongoing support for his mentor and partner came in many forms, including echoing Dr Barnett's complaints about conditions at the asylum. At an inquest earlier in January, he had described the facilities available at the asylum as most unsatisfactory for treating patients and a disgrace to the colony.[288]

The location of the asylum itself became a contentious issue in 1894, an election year. The growth in population due to the Coolgardie gold rush, and the promise of a fully functioning harbour, had provided an economic boost to Fremantle. New warehouses, offices and shops were appearing all around the town, many built in impressive style. Others were being extended.[289] Land values were increasing, and housing was in short supply. For the first time, newspaper editors and politicians began to question the effect of the asylum on land values in Fremantle.

In February that year, it came to light that James Morrison, MLC, had offered forty acres of land at Greenmount, a rural area on the edge of the Darling ranges east of Perth, as a site for a new asylum. But the government decided that the 30,000 pounds George Temple Poole estimated it would cost to build was still more than the colony could afford at present and declined the offer. Instead, they set aside five thousand pounds to extend the existing asylum once more.[290]

This disappointed many, including an editor at the *Daily News,* who wrote: 'It is much to be regretted that the Government should have decided to merely improve the existing Asylum instead of building a new one in a suitable locality. The buildings at present in use are situated in a populated, though not populous locality, and the value of property is seriously deteriorated by the fact, as the noises and the general surrounding are not such as people care for, as a rule…

'(T)he removal of the building will be absolutely essential as the population of Fremantle increases, and the Asylum becomes an additional public nuisance, as well as additionally unsuitable for its purpose.'[291]

Dr Barnett, it seems, expected the building extensions to be completed quite quickly, and to provide him, at last, with space to segregate patients. As early as 19 February, he wrote to the under-secretary, Octavius Burt, requesting to be relieved from his duties as colonial surgeon in order to focus on his work at the asylum.

'The alterations about to be made in buildings will necessitate a largely increased staff, to obtain which there will be much difficulty, and then I shall have to prepare them for their duties before the much-needed separation of classes of lunatics can be effected,' he wrote. 'All the arrangements have to be thought out and planned. This will greatly augment my duties.'

He received support for this proposal from a surprising source. Francis Hart, Lilian's husband, sent a type-written letter to John Forrest on 5 March.

'It seems to me quite impossible for one medical man, however youthful and alert, to attend to the asylum satisfactorily and at the same time perform the duties of Colonial Surgeon,' Hart wrote.

But on the same day that Hart sent his letter, 5 March, Dr Barnett wrote again to Burt, this time withdrawing his previous request. He said he had been concerned that he and Dr Wheeler would soon separate, and he would be left to do all the work himself. Now he had come to an agreement with Dr Wheeler which would enable him to carry on all his duties as before.

Given Dr Wheeler's strong defence of Dr Barnett just a few weeks earlier, it seems unlikely that there had been any personal rift between the two men. But Dr Wheeler, still a few years short of thirty, was ready for a new challenge after his two years' experience as an assistant in Fremantle. Evidently he had agreed to remain in partnership with Dr Barnett for the time being.

All the letters were forwarded to John Forrest, who suggested to cabinet that the matter should be brought up during the next estimates debate.[292]

Concern about the time and extra work required to employ and train new staff was not the only reason Dr Barnett wished to reduce his other duties. While his age and his 'physical drawback', as Dr Wheeler described it, may not have interfered with his ability to work, another health problem was beginning to affect his life and activities adversely– neuralgia.

In May 1894, he was unexpectedly absent from a concert given at the asylum by a visiting English opera company. Dr Wheeler entertained the visitors and showed them around the asylum afterwards.[293] In a note to the under-secretary, requesting reimbursement for the food provided, Dr Barnett said he had been unable to attend the concert 'owing to severe neuralgia'.[294] This may have been nerve pain related to his amputation stump, or possibly he had developed the facial condition known as trigeminal neuralgia.

Whatever the form of his neuralgia, it would have caused him intense pain, distress, and lack of sleep. The only pain relief available at the time, morphine, was seldom effective against neuralgia. Before better treatments became available, trigeminal neuralgia was often referred to as 'the suicide disease'.[295]

Despite his condition, Dr Barnett continued to keep up a remarkably busy life, both professionally and socially. On 10 August, he and Mrs Barnett attended a dinner at Government House to meet Dr Emily Brainerd Ryder, an American physician who had just arrived in Perth to give a series of lectures.[296] Dr Barnett's medical qualifications and his knowledge of India were probably what led to his inclusion on the guest list.

Emily Ryder was on a world-wide campaign to bring an end to child marriages in India. During the several months she stayed in Western Australia, she also gave talks on health-related issues to women in Perth, Fremantle and several country centres. Lilian Hart attended one of these. In her weekly social column as 'Cora', she wrote that after listening to Dr Ryder's 'very severe' lecture, she was almost afraid to mention the frivolities of fashion.[297]

Dr Barnett made sure Dr Ryder became acquainted with the ongoing difficulties he faced at the asylum and the changes he desired. And she took note. In November, towards the end of her tour of Western Australia, she addressed the women of the newly established Karrakatta club, set up to promote education and leadership opportunities amongst women. (The club would soon join forces with the Women's Christian Temperance Union in campaigning for the right of women to vote.)

Among her suggestions for the club, Dr Ryder included the need to bring about change at the asylum:

'One of the duties possibly of the club will be to send a committee to see the insane, and find out how your sisters are accommodated in your asylum, and I make no doubt but that you will be able to obtain the changes which the doctor in charge so earnestly desires. There ought to be a woman doctor for your insane women, as well as your sane women, and you will find that pretty nearly all the world over there is a woman doctor in all large insane asylums—at least assisting.'[298]

Dr Barnett's thoughts about Dr Ryder's suggestions were not recorded. But his concerns about the state of the asylum were widely publicised when his annual report for 1893 was tabled in parliament at the end of August 1894. Little had changed in the past ten years, apart from ever-increasing numbers of patients. With a note of despair, Dr Barnett wrote:

> *'Whilst in the United Kingdom I visited and inspected many asylums, and was pained to see how favourably they contrasted with our Asylum in Fremantle. Cheerful rooms, bright with flowers and lively with singing birds, and music, are very desirable, but utterly impracticable in a small unsuitable building, where maniacs and idiots (i.e. the congenitally mentally impaired) cannot be separated from the other patients from want of room and paucity of attendants—male and female.'*

He mentioned in his report that while in Singapore he had visited the asylum there, in the hope that he might arrange for some of the Chinese and Malaysian patients in Western Australia to be transferred. But the

Singaporean asylum was also full of cases from neighbouring states, and he came away disappointed.[299]

Dr Barnett's hopes that the asylum extensions would quickly be completed were also unmet when he wrote his report. The proposed extensions, designed by George Poole, included two blocks, extending east and west from the existing female quarters, with sixteen rooms in each, all 'light and airy' and built of stone to match the existing building.[300] The government had awarded the tender in July. So far only the foundations had been constructed.

But while the building remained unaltered, several changes were about to be made to the running of the asylum. A Royal Commission into all aspects of the civil service had been established by the government in April. The impending release of its preliminary report, which included a damning assessment of the condition of the asylum, prompted the government to act. Late in September, it announced that the permanent staff at the asylum would be increased from four to six, and the provisional staff from three to ten, with an additional nurse.[301] Prisoners would no longer be used as orderlies in the male section of the asylum.[302] This would fulfill at least some of Dr Barnett's wishes.

Another positive change was about to be made. During discussion of the budget and salaries on 1 October, John Forrest (still Premier and treasurer after the elections) announced that the government also planned to appoint Dr Barnett full time superintendent of the asylum and increase his salary for this position to five hundred pounds per year. Dr Hope would take over Dr Barnett's role as colonial surgeon.[303]

Most parliamentarians approved both the increase in staff at the asylum and the appointment of Dr Barnett as full-time superintendent. Some expressed regret that the government hadn't seen fit to build a new asylum on a better site. Sir John Forrest said the 30,000 pounds required to move the asylum 'could not be conveniently voted for that purpose at present, when there was no urgent necessity.'

'I remember visiting the asylum some years ago, and even if the condition of the place has continued the same now, I think that some of the remarks made in the present discussion are somewhat exaggerated,' Forrest said in parliament. 'I cannot think that an experienced man like Dr. Barnett would allow things to be in such a terrible state.'[304]

The news that Dr Barnett was to be replaced as colonial surgeon stirred Dr Wheeler into action. Even though Dr Hope's appointment had already been announced, he wrote to the colonial secretary on 3 October, offering himself as a better candidate for the position. He pointed to his experience in the role during Dr Barnett's absence, as well as his having done much of the work of colonial surgeon alongside Dr Barnett. Dr Hope, on the other hand, already had far too much work, with his three other government-funded positions. Dr Wheeler also wrote to John Forrest along the same lines, adding, 'I am a well-known social entity in Fremantle and my opinion carries some weight in most matters'.

The colonial secretary, unconvinced, advised under-secretary Burt to inform Dr Wheeler that the decision had already been made.[305]

Dr Wheeler nursed his disappointment during a trip to Melbourne with the Hart family. Francis Hart and the Governor, Sir William Robinson, had collaborated on a light opera, *Predatoros*. After testing it on a predictably enthusiastic audience in Perth, they planned to produce it for a larger audience in Melbourne.[306] Dr Wheeler, though he had no publicised role in producing the operetta, travelled with the Harts aboard the *Ophir* at the end of October, and returned with them in December. [307]

Dr Barnett was left alone to run the asylum. The absence of his friends and colleague seems to have left him in a pensive mood. On 13 October, the *West Australian* published a poem he had submitted. Titled 'An Elegy on an L. E. G.' it was said to have been written in 1870, which would have been the time when he was recovering after his amputation.

In mock serious tones, the poem parodied the classical elegiac form. It began by describing a quiet evening settling over Perth, then moved on to a grave site at Perth Cemetery:

Mark, on that hill, that mound of barren land,
Where scattered tombstones sentry human graves,
And where, on high, shading the arid sand,
One stately jarrah in the zephyr waves.

Here rests at last, beneath this dry, red earth,
A leg, to various countries well known,
Secure it walked through Calendoia's [Caledonia's?] Perth,
But West Australia marks it for its own.

The poem's focus shifted to a mother possum, who told her baby how the jarrah tree in which they were sitting had grown from the knee joint of a leg. She listed all the places where the leg's owner had once roamed—England, France, Spain, China, India, Manila, Canada and more.

The mother possum concluded her story:

Where 'ere it went it could not shirk its fate,
For fate, as Homer shows, rules gods and men:
So learn, young 'possum, ere it be too late
This moral true_____
(Here a gunshot kills the possum, stops her sermon upon legs,
and a sawmill cuts the jarrah into artificial pegs.)[308]

The timing of the publication of this darkly humorous poem was odd. It was the first time Dr Barnett had submitted any poem to the paper for over twenty years.[309] Those who knew him must have pondered what message he was trying to convey. Was he envying his friends' freedom to travel? Was he trying to remind the world, and himself, of his own creativity, now curtailed? There had been little time for writing anything other than reports in the past few years. Perhaps the year-long public focus on his ability to fulfill all his duties had left him reflecting on his 'physical drawback'. Certainly, if he hadn't lost his leg, it is unlikely he would have become superintendent of the asylum, with all its problems and stresses.

The compositor at the *Daily News* apparently struggled to make sense of the poem, with many spelling mistakes and substitutions, for which the paper later apologised.

Three weeks later, about the time that Dr Wheeler and the Harts arrived in Melbourne, another of Dr Barnett's poems, *Moonlight among the Bergs*, appeared in the *West Australian*. It was footnoted 'Ship Nourmahal, 1861'.[310]

This had none of the humour of the previous poem. It described, in solemn phrases, a voyage across the Southern Ocean, among the icebergs, and ended with homage to the moon for lighting the way:

Safely our noble ship speeds on, for tho'
The ice crags tower threat'ning in our way.
Thy light, dear Luna, shines on all below,
Changing the dark, drear night to brilliant day.

Again, the poem looked back to a period when Dr Barnett not only had time and inspiration to write poetry but was free to roam the world without a care and without the physical hardships he now had to endure.

EIGHTEEN: This gentleman from New Zealand – 1894

As far as is known, C. Y. O'Connor never published, or even wrote, any type of poetry or fiction. His creative talents went into imagining and building great engineering projects which others, with less skill and imagination, said were impossible.

The rest of the O'Connor family were not without their own creativity, which they frequently put to good use in the community. Susan helped superintend a concert and a series of 'tableaux' in the Town Hall in April 1894 on behalf of the St John's church building fund. She also helped run one of the stalls at the All Nations Fair in September.[311] Seventeen-year-old Kate O'Connor was on the team that arranged a maypole dance as part of the entertainment for the fair.

In October 1894, Kate entered two drawings in the Fremantle Music Festival, which, despite its name, showcased the arts, science and industry as well as musical items.[312] It was her first foray into the art world that would one day become her career.[313]

Even with his heavy workload, her father Charles O'Connor still found time to be involved in the community. He was invited to become the inaugural president of the Fremantle Yacht Club in February 1894 and the president of the Fremantle Chess club in April.[314] That same month he became patron of the Fremantle Rugby Club.[315]

But despite his popularity among the general public and the respect in which he was held by his workforce, the year would bring increasing tensions and conflict for C. Y. O'Connor. Accusations that he was autocratically taking over the colony surfaced again late in the year. His minister, Harry Venn, did his best to support him, but faced his own conflicts.

Things went well enough for the Chief Engineer in the first half of 1894. In January, a new two-storey central railway station in Perth, designed in neoclassical style by George Temple Poole, was close to completion. Stations were also being built at Bunbury and Geraldton.[316]

O'Connor had realised almost as soon as he arrived in Perth that the grades on the existing eastern railway line over the Darling scarp were too steep and this significantly increased the cost of transporting goods. The steep track was also dangerous, with accidents and derailments common. Something would need to be done before the line was extended from Northam to Southern Cross. By moving and levelling the line, building a tunnel through the granite rock, and straightening some of the curves between Guildford and Spencers Brook, near Northam, the line could be made much more efficient.[317]

In January 1894, the contract for building the tunnel and rerouting the line (a project known as the Mahogany Creek Deviation) was awarded to a South Australian company, Smeaton and Hedges.[318] Work began in February, and would continue until 1896.

Things were also going well at Fremantle harbour. By mid-April 1894, the *West Australian* was able to report that the north mole of the harbour had been extended to 2,000 feet, at a cost of twenty-eight thousand pounds. This was considerably less than the forty-nine thousand pounds originally estimated for this work, based on the cost per cubic foot.[319] The works manager, John Irvine, forecasted in May that, at the current rate of construction of thirty-five feet per week, the north mole would be completed by November.[320]

During the June-July election campaign, John Forrest focussed on his government's programme of public works. The loan for these works was about to blow out by another one-and-a-half million pounds. But the colony's population and its annual income had both increased markedly as a result of gold exports, supplemented by agricultural expansion.[321] By March 1894, the population had reached 71,000, a fifty per cent increase from 1891.[322] What would once have seemed an impossible sum to finance now seemed far less daunting. In an election speech in his home seat of Bunbury, John Forrest promised that his government would set aside money under public works for a museum, an observatory and a mint. He made no mention of hospitals or the asylum.[323]

Two-hundred-thousand pounds of the loan money was earmarked for the next stage of the harbour project. A much larger portion of it would be required for the railways, which were steadily expanding and improving under O'Connor's supervision. Few candidates in the election quibbled with the need for the harbour works to continue, though the candidates for seats in Fremantle were careful to again make known their opposition to the railway workshops being moved.

In February 1894, O'Connor had received his brief apology from the Premier for the allegations made in the Auditor General's report the previous year. What didn't come to light until the select committee's full report into the matter reached parliament in June 1894, was John Forrest's stinging ministerial minute to his minister, Harry Venn. Dated 2 July 1893, it read, in part:

> *'As Premier and Treasurer, I am most concerned in taking care that discredit does not come upon the Government and I am convinced that if your Department had worked with the Treasury in the loyal and proper manner it should have, the difficulties that have arisen, and which have culminated in the Auditor General reporting your Department to the Legislature, would not have arisen.*
>
> *'As head of the Government and as Treasurer I will not allow this obstruction to continue any longer; and I insist on your Department, and all other Departments, carrying out loyally and faithfully the wishes of the Treasury and Audit Departments.'*[324]

The once-cordial relationship between Forrest and his most important minister had begun to unravel.

The auditor general's next report was laid before the new parliament in July 1894. It covered only the six-month period up to June 30th, 1893, so it was well out of date. But it aroused the attention of the newspapers because, once again, the auditor was critical of the Engineer-in-Chief, for having made variations in a contract for building the Bunbury railway without being authorised.[325] However, this time even the newspapers felt that the auditor was being heavy handed.

During parliamentary debate in October, George T. Simpson, MLA, who had been on the committee looking into the previous complaints against O'Connor, accused the government of having 'smuggled' the committee's report through the last parliament just before it was prorogued. He said the Chief Engineer's criticisms of the way accounts were audited were warranted, and the committee's recommendations for changing the way auditing was carried out had been ignored. The treasurer, John Forrest, disagreed.[326] But it must have been encouraging for O'Connor to have this support of his views expressed in parliament.

By July, preparatory work had begun for construction of the south mole. Removal of much of the limestone outcrop known as Arthur Head, on the southern edge of the river mouth, would eventually leave only the portion containing the old gaol, the Roundhouse.[327] Everything else would be brought to street level, and a railway line constructed. The government assured the concerned Fremantle public that the aesthetic value of their favourite promenade along the Head would not be damaged by this process.[328] No such reassurance was given to the Whadjuk Noongar people, though the area, known as Manjaree or Manjarup, was also of great cultural significance to them, a place for meeting, trade and ceremony.[329]

If the residents of Fremantle were dubious about the work on Arthur Head, they had even more reason for concern when, on Saturday, 18 August 1894, two explosions shook the windows in buildings close to the harbour in Fremantle. Engineers were making experimental blasts on the rocky bar at the mouth of the Swan River. It became clear that any surface charge large enough to be effective in removing rock from the limestone bar was likely to cause damage to buildings nearby.[330]

Historically, this was not the first attempt to blast the bar from the river and open a channel for ships. As far back as January 1848, five years after C. Y. O'Connor was born, holes had been bored and test explosions successfully carried out on the Rous Head side of the bar.[331] But lack of government funds to continue the work, and unexplained delays in supplies of explosives to the colony, hampered the project.[332] Despite repeated calls by businessmen and newspaper editors in the years that followed for the work to recommence, it somehow never had the support of the governor. It seemed that the question of removing the bar across the river mouth had been settled as impractical.

O'Connor was intent on proving this wrong. His plan was to cut a preliminary channel through the bar, one hundred feet wide and ten feet deep, so that the dredges could take shelter in the river during rough weather. This channel would then be deepened and extended to a final width of seven hundred feet.

O'Connor was in Bunbury, inspecting work on the new railway station there, when the first test blasts were made.[333] On his return to Fremantle, he was informed of the unsettling results. He proposed instead to drill long pipes six feet into the rock and place charges at their base. After the rock had been broken up in this way, the debris could be removed by the bucket dredge.

Despite O'Connor's caution, Fremantle's residents soon became alarmed and then annoyed by all the blasting going on. Buildings shook, and the explosions could be felt in the ground beneath their feet. There were claims of damage to older buildings.[334]

Residents were also uneasy about the ten tons of dynamite and gunpowder, along with detonators, which were being stored in the Fremantle magazine and the old morgue nearby.[335] The member for South Fremantle, Elias Solomon, brought up the matter in the Legislative Assembly. He was assured by Sir John Forrest that the blasting posed no danger, but the explosives would be moved to Owen Anchorage.[336] However, by October the dynamite and powder hadn't been moved, and there were concerns that sparks from coal-fired, steam-driven equipment could ignite the lot.[337]

The arrival of the steam dredge *Fremantle* in Fremantle on 22 October 1894, after a difficult six-month journey by sea from Glasgow, provided a cause for celebration at the harbour works. One hundred and fifty feet long and twenty-seven feet wide, she had been constructed by William Simons and Co. Described as 'a peculiar vessel from a seaman's point of view', she was shaped rather like a huge tuning fork. Powerful steam-driven engines at the rear of the ship worked a chain of huge steel buckets that ran through the two 'prongs', forward of the bridge. A trial run had shown that she could move five hundred tons of silt and debris in thirty-five minutes.[338]

By the end of November, the work of setting up the heavy equipment on board the dredge had been completed and she was ready to start work in early December. She soon became a familiar sight in the harbour.[339]

In the meantime, O'Connor had once again to deal with the wisdom of amateur marine engineers. This time they proposed that the south mole was unnecessary and could be dispensed with. He and the minister countered their arguments in parliament and in the press. O'Connor also had a scale model built to demonstrate how the future harbour would work.[340]

Nor had he heard the last of the debate on the railway workshops. On 12 November, the member for Albany, George Leake, moved in parliament that the workshops should be moved from Fremantle to a site near Midland Junction. This inevitably stirred strong feelings among the parliamentary members, as was probably the intention of the member for Albany. It provoked all the same arguments that had been made so often already. It also provided an opportunity for Alexander Forrest to renew his personal attacks on O'Connor, under parliamentary privilege.

Those members of parliament in favour of moving the workshops pointed out that when Mr Allison Smith had been brought in from Victoria in 1892, at some expense, to examine the issue, he advised moving the workshops as soon as possible. The government had already bought land at Guildford, near Midland. Why not get on with it?

John Forrest, in his usual conciliatory way, said that while he thought it inevitable that the workshops would have to be moved eventually, it would be an expensive process and he would be glad to delay the move for as long as possible. He denied that the land in Guildford had already been purchased for railway workshops. The government wanted to do what was best for the colony, he said.

Alexander Forrest was impressed neither by the argument that the move was inevitable nor that it was in the colony's best interests. He had little regard for the expertise of Mr. Allison Smith.

'What character does this gentleman bear in Victoria at the present time?' he asked. 'I think he has been dismissed, or next door to being dismissed, from the public service. As to the Commission that reported on this question, I believe they called in no experts to give evidence.'

'The Engineer-in-Chief…' began George Randell, who since the election had taken on the role of leader of the opposition to the Forrest party.

'I don't take any more notice of what the Engineer-in-Chief says than that,' responded Alex Forrest with a snap of his fingers. 'He has no more idea of saving money for this colony than—I won't say what. He is well known to this House. He is a very able officer, no doubt, but he is inclined to be very extravagant. If the Engineer-in-Chief had his own sway, in ten years' time we might as well hand the colony over to him.'

After a long debate, the house voted for an amended motion that agreed only to move the workshops 'to a more advantageous site.'[341]

Most newspapers, when reporting the debate, omitted Alexander Forrest's comments about Mr Allison Smith and the Engineer-in-Chief, but the *Inquirer and Commercial News* printed his comments in full.[342] O'Connor could not have been unaware of them.

A week later, Alexander Forrest made a much longer verbal attack on the Engineer-in-Chief in Parliament. The assembly was debating a motion to disband the Civil Service Commission (whose preliminary report had been so critical of the lack of funding for the asylum) because it was becoming too expensive.

Some members of parliament wanted to amend the motion, to allow the Commission to finish its inquiry into the Works and Railways Department before it was disbanded. They were particularly concerned that the department was not extracting in full the agreed penalties on contractors who didn't complete their work on time.

Harry Venn, the Minister for Works and Railways, having explained at length why some penalties were not applied, concluded, 'Our actions were regulated by truth, and justice, and honor, and nothing else. And, under the circumstances, to have inflicted the full penalty, when the contract was honestly carried out, and the delay caused no loss to the Government, would in my opinion have been improper and uncalled for.'

In tone, it was a response that might have come from O'Connor himself. It was too much for Alexander Forrest. After suggesting that the minister had 'sneaked' the estimates for his department through parliament when things were quiet, he turned his attention to the minister's Chief Engineer.

'With all due deference to my friend the Commissioner, I think his department ought to be inquired into. We know that the Engineer-in-Chief represents and rules not only the Works and Railways but the whole colony. He not only rules my honourable friend's department, but every other department of the public service. And, as I stated the other day, in ten years' time we may as well hand over the whole colony to this gentleman from New Zealand, who will no doubt show us how to spend our money. We shall have had the pleasure of paying. I don't know what he will have had.'

'He's too clever for the honorable member,' quipped George Randell from across the chamber table.

'No doubt he is too clever for me,' Forrest responded. 'I am only an ordinary business man. I don't aspire to be an Engineer-in-Chief, nor to be a man who can rule the whole colony, and spend 99 per cent of the whole revenue. I think this Commission will not be going too far if it goes into this department thoroughly.'

Forrest said contractors complained to him that they could never get to see the Engineer-in-Chief to sort out their payment.

'Why should the colony be ruled by one man, however clever he may be? I do not say it is not to the advantage of the colony—far from that, because I have a very great opinion of his ability—to have a clever man like the Engineer-in-Chief, but we don't want him to be chief ruler of the colony.'

'I thought the Premier was the chief ruler,' Randell said. Given John Forrest's growing reputation as a one-man band, and Alexander Forrest's influence with his brother, it was a pointed remark.

'The Premier is nowhere,' Alex Forrest responded. 'Whatever the Engineer-in-Chief says is to be done, must be done. I have often wondered why a great colony like New Zealand should have let this man go. I never could understand it myself, because I believe he received a greater salary there than he does here.'

'No,' John Forrest interrupted.

'About the same, I think,' his brother corrected. 'I took the trouble while I was in Sydney a few years ago to inquire how it was that the New Zealand Government had let this great man go, and I was told that the fact of the matter was he ruled the ministers.

'I believe he does the same here, and I am very sorry to hear it. I do not want to say anything against him, but he seems to be so persistent and so overbearing, that he can overrule his own Minister, and I believe he even overrules the Premier himself. And if a stop is not put to this gentleman, all I can say is we had better hand over the colony to him.'

Alexander Forrest's tirade became increasingly personal as it continued. Under parliamentary privilege, he told of an occasion several months earlier, when he had described O'Connor's response to a parliamentary question about the purchase of railway sleepers as 'impudent'.

'Some four or five months afterwards I happened to meet this great man who rules this Country. I had not thought anything more about the matter myself, and I went up to him to speak to him, like one citizen might to another. And he told me, "Unless you apologise for your conduct in the House" (or words to that effect) "I do not wish to know you."'[343]

Forrest and O'Connor might both prefer not to know one another, but they could hardly avoid each other. In a colony with a population the size of a small market town in England, the two men would run into each other regularly at social gatherings and official functions. Such jealousy and belligerence on one side and wounded honor and pride on the other must have made their meetings highly unpleasant. Forrest certainly had no intention of apologising. And O'Connor seldom compromised in matters affecting his honor.

But Alexander Forrest wasn't the only one suggesting that the Chief Engineer had too much power and spent the public money too freely. After John Forrest reshuffled his ministry in December, following the resignation of both the colonial secretary, Stephen Parker, and William Marmion from Crown Lands and Mining, the editor of the *West Australian* bemoaned the fact that Mr Venn had not also been moved aside to another post. [344] He was too easily swayed by his subordinates, said the editorial.

> *'...it is safe to say it requires not only a strong man but a new man to make head against the ENGINEER-IN-CHIEF. This officer may be counted in many respects the most valuable acquisition which the Civil Service of this colony has yet received, and Western Australia is distinctly the better enabled to take advantage of its present good fortune through his presence and help. But ...Mr. O'CONNOR can, for the most part, give a better and more forcible reason for doing the wrong thing than other men are often able to give for doing the right thing.'*[345]

Two weeks later, O'Connor would find himself asked to give reasons for a dramatic incident at the harbour works.

NINETEEN: Fremantle rattled – 1895

New Year's Day was traditionally Cup Day at the races in Perth. Throngs of people braved the sultry weather on 1 January 1895 to watch the races, meet friends or just show off their new dresses and hats at the West Australian Turf Club's grounds at Belmont.

Just after midnight that night, while many revellers were still about, a loud explosion shook Fremantle. Windows shattered. One man's ceiling fell in on him as he was sleeping. A group standing on Mount Eliza in Perth reported that they felt the ground shake and saw the glow of the explosion.[346] People as far away as Rockingham, sixteen miles south of Fremantle, also felt the shock wave.

Residents all over Fremantle rushed into the streets to see what had happened. For a while confusion reigned. Some thought a ship must have exploded in the harbour. Others suspected that the powder magazine used by the harbour works on Arthur Head had gone up.[347] Only recently a fire had been discovered on a rail truck carrying dynamite, and disaster had been narrowly averted when the flames were extinguished.[348]

Policemen arrived and began investigating. They soon found the centre of the midnight explosion had been in a shed used to store dynamite charges at Rous Head, on the north side of the river mouth. The wood and iron building, which had once been used as a prison cell, was destroyed. Debris was strewn across the beach and the river mouth. Fortunately, two magazines tunnelled into the rock nearby, holding dynamite and torpedoes, had not been ignited, though their heavy wooden doors were blown off.

By another miracle, a labourer sleeping in a rough hut not far from the explosion escaped serious injury, though his accommodation shattered around him. He was taken to the casualty ward for treatment of bruising and a broken bone in his arm. The family of one of the foremen living next door were all unharmed, though their house was damaged.

Arthur Dillon Bell, one of the New Zealand engineers recruited by O'Connor, did his own investigation when daylight came. He quickly reported what he had found to the Chief Engineer.

All the explosives were stored within a fenced enclosure with a locked gate. Generally, only enough for one or two days' work was kept on-site, with the main magazine being at Rocky Bay. But on this occasion, because of the New Year holiday, about twice as much was stored in the rock tunnels than would usually be there.

The old convict building where the explosion had occurred had been carefully lined and locked to prevent anyone entering without authorisation. Dillon Bell estimated that between the cartridges and the primers housed there, a total of about 620 pounds of dynamite had been in store.

The whole site had been under the supervision of James Waddell, a man highly experienced in safeguarding explosives, and the men working under him were also experienced.

'I am unable to give any tangible cause for the accident, for which, of course, I assume all responsibility,' Arthur Dillon Bell concluded his report. 'The precautions taken throughout have been more complete than usual on works, and the magazine foreman was thoroughly experienced.

'The police are investigating the matter, and are being afforded every facility in doing so. I can only again express my deep regret that the accident should have occurred. There has hitherto been an unusual immunity, seeing the nature of the work.'

Saturday's *Western Mail*, reporting on the explosion, accepted Dillon Bell's conclusion that every precaution had been taken. But, the paper added, 'this fact only makes it the more difficult to understand how the explosion was caused. It may be hoped that the investigation which is being made will do something to elucidate the mystery. It is not pleasant for the people of Fremantle to think that the large quantities of dynamite stored within the vicinity of their town are liable to explode without any apparent reason.'[349]

The people of Fremantle were certainly not happy with this mystery. A delegation including the mayor, local MPs and councillors met with Sir John Forrest in his office a few days later. O'Connor and Dillon Bell were also present to listen to their concerns and their demand for reassurance that something would be done to protect the town.

The mayor, Daniel Congdon, MLC, suggested that explosives for the harbour works should be stored offshore, on Garden Island for instance. Councillor John felt that there should be a sworn investigation into the way explosives were handled in and around Fremantle, citing cases of people seen smoking near where explosives were being transported.

Premier John Forrest replied that he, too, was concerned about so much explosive being stored close to the town, in part because he didn't know much about explosives. He was pleased to tell them that arrangements were underway to remove most of the explosives to a ship, the *Laughing Wave*, anchored far offshore. But he had been pleasantly surprised to read in the papers how much care the Works Department had taken to safeguard the stores. The government would leave nothing undone to reduce the risk of explosion as much as possible.

At the Premier's request, O'Connor then spoke. Unlike Forrest, who liked to smooth the waters, O'Connor preferred to present the unvarnished facts. Three different departments were involved in receiving, transporting and using the explosives, he explained.

'I'm rather pleased that something has occurred to cause the matter to be brought up and fully investigated,' he went on. 'I think there have been somewhat slipshod arrangements in the past. No one has been particularly at fault, as no one has quite realised that the responsibility rested with him.'

The plan the Premier had told them about, to keep stores offshore, seemed a good one to him, he continued. Even with the best precautions, explosions could occur for no apparent reason, and keeping explosives at a distance from populated areas was a better protection than employing guards and security measures.

'With the greatest possible care there is no absolute safeguard from explosion. An explosion might occur at any time where there are explosives. But I would like people to recognise that with the small quantity which would in future be stored, it would not be a very serious matter.'

The councillors did not look convinced.

'The recent explosion did not do more damage than is sometimes done by the firing off of one of the big guns,' O'Connor said, referring to the cannons used by the local artillery volunteers. 'Although it was heard in Perth, no damage was done in Perth or Claremont, and in Fremantle only some windows were broken.'

'It was an intervention of Providence,' declared one of the councillors.

'It was not a special intervention on the part of Providence, but the action of physical laws,' O'Connor countered. 'I once exploded three tons of dynamite in a hill about 200 yards from the general post office of a town…and all that was felt by the townspeople was a rumble like thunder. The people did not know that an explosion had taken place, but I did this deliberately, knowing what the result would be.'

His confidence still didn't convince the councillors.

'You are looking incredulous, but I am telling you facts,' O'Connor said. 'Three hundred cases, each of 25lb., would give 3½ tons of dynamite, and if that amount exploded in the Rocky Bay magazine it would not do much damage.'

One of the councillors interrupted. 'Only a few weeks ago the people of Adelaide insisted on the magazine, containing six tons of dynamite, being taken away twenty miles at least from the city,' he protested.

'For the private consumers the cost of the dynamite would be very much more if the magazine were removed too far away from the town,' O'Connor replied, 'and the cost would be increased to the Government, which uses from 2 to 3 hundred-weight per day.'

Arthur Dillon Bell decided it was time to add his support to O'Connor's argument. In all the projects he had worked on, he said, in this country and elsewhere, he had never seen so many precautions taken. The department made up their own dynamite cartridges, at some risk to those involved, in order to reduce the risk to the town of storing ready-made cartridges.[350]

John Forrest brought the discussion to an end. 'An inquiry might be held if the people wish it, but I do not see that much good would be derived from it,' he said. 'I think the principal thing to do is to take every precaution that there should not be a repetition of the accident.' With that, the councillors thanked him for his courtesy and left, with the mayor commenting that he 'felt very much relieved in his mind'.

In the weeks that followed the explosion, outrage slowly settled, and a certain calm returned to the harbour works. O'Connor visited Garden Island on 7 January to select a site for a new magazine, well away from Fremantle. He was accompanied by Arthur Dillon Bell and John Irvine, as well as the harbour master, Captain Russell.[351]

Later that week, O'Connor and the minister, Harry Venn, took a party, including the Premier and the mayor of Fremantle, to inspect the dredge *Fremantle* at work. Despite a strong breeze and heavy seas preventing the dredge from working at full efficiency, they were impressed with what they saw.[352]

When Sir John Forrest attended the federal Postal Conference in Hobart early in February, he felt so confident in the progress already made that he told everyone that he intended to put a motion, 'That…provision should be made that, as safe and commodious harbour accommodation was now being provided at Fremantle, it be compulsory for the mailboat companies to have their steamers calling at that port.'[353]

The motion raised eyebrows in the other colonies, and the ire of the Albany Chamber of Commerce, who pointed out that it would be many years before mail ships could enter Fremantle harbour.[354] An 'indignation meeting' held in Albany a few days later drew a large crowd which condemned John Forrest's suggestion.[355]

Sir John modified his resolution slightly when he finally put it to the postal meeting: 'That as soon as safe and commodious harbor accommodation is provided at Fremantle, it shall be compulsory for the mail steamers to call at that port.'[356] The meeting accepted the motion.

By 7 February, the *West Australian* was able to announce that the north mole had now been extended to the length originally planned, but at a cost twenty thousand pounds less than estimated. O'Connor decided to use the money saved to continue extending the mole, to provide further protection to the harbour.[357]

It was encouraging news. But that same day, a disaster occurred that would cast a dark shadow over the harbour project. The constant push to save money may well have contributed to it.

TWENTY: Fallen in a noble struggle – 1895

By early 1895, Dr Barnett had formally dissolved his business partnership with Louis Wheeler, with the younger doctor taking over the general practice.[358] This left Dr Barnett free to devote his time to the asylum, in line with his new appointment as full-time superintendent.

Dr Wheeler was in his surgery on Thursday afternoon, 7 February, when the telephone rang. The quaver in the voice on the other end left him in no doubt about the urgency of the call. It belonged to Harry Horne, the clerk of harbour works. There had been an accident at Rocky Bay, an explosion. Three men had been injured, two of them badly. One of the injured was John Irvine, the supervisor.

When Dr Wheeler reached the North Fremantle railway crossing, he met rail trucks carrying the three men, accompanied by a crowd of workers from the quarry. Some were in tears. He quickly assessed the men's injuries. John Irvine lay groaning in pain. Half his jaw was shattered, and his face unrecognisably burned. But it was his back that was causing him the greatest agony. He managed to tell Dr Wheeler that he thought it was broken.

Another man, a quarryman named Timothy Yorke, had terrible facial injuries. The third man, Purkiss, who had been a visitor to the site, had some damage to his eyes and was dazed, but was able to walk.

Irvine and Yorke were transferred to stretchers and carried to the casualty ward, now located in a room rented from the recently opened Wesleyan Home in Cantonment Street. An injured Afghan camel driver, who had been the only occupant of the ward, left to make room for the new patients. Purkiss was able to board the train for Perth.

Other doctors arrived at the casualty ward. Dr Wheeler and Dr Birmingham performed surgery on Irvine's jaw and a wound on his neck. They confirmed Irvine's own assessment of his back injury. His lower limbs were paralysed and numb, and although he was talking coherently, he was clearly in shock. The doctors could do little for him except give him morphia for pain.

Meanwhile Doctors Lotz, White and Hope had anaesthetized Yorke with chloroform and removed his irreparably damaged left eye, then treated his other lacerations.[359]

By the time the newspapers had published the details, next morning, of what had happened, John Irvine was dead. Yorke remained in a serious condition.

It seemed Irvine had been testing a new explosive material named 'taipo'. Its inventor, John Oldfield McCardill, claimed that it was safer than dynamite and only required half as much powder to produce the same effect, thus saving expense. He and his brother-in-law Purkiss, a lawyer, had been present at the test but were not as close to the explosion as Irvine and Yorke.

After tipping a measure of the powder into a pre-drilled hole and inserting a fuse, Irvine had continued to add more measures of taipo. When he found that he couldn't tamp it down, he asked for a thin metal rod, called a pricker, so that he could break through the blockage.

As he jabbed the pricker down into the hole, the powder exploded, sending him and Timothy Yorke flying into the air. Irvine landed ten feet beneath the ledge where they had been standing, onto the rocks below. The fall had broken his back.

C. Y. O'Connor received news of the explosion from Harry Horne. He rushed to the quarry. He had been unaware of Irvine's intention to test the new explosive and knew nothing about it.

After looking over the site of the accident with the resident engineer, John McDonald, he appointed an explosives expert, Christian Henri Andre, to prepare a full report of what had happened. He then ordered Andre and

McDonald to destroy what was left of the taipo at the quarry.

Andre became a key witness at the inquest, opened on the day Irvine died and completed on 15 January. He explained that unlike dynamite, taipo could not be exploded by an impact or friction. It required a spark in a confined space. He speculated that the pricker must have scraped the hard rock wall of the hole, creating a spark that resulted in the explosion.

Andre was not a totally independent witness. He had worked with McCardill before and had received payment for his services. Nevertheless, his evidence was accepted. After hearing from McCardill, Dr Wheeler, and those who had witnessed the explosion, the coroner and jury gave a verdict of 'death by accidental means'.[360]

Irvine's funeral, held on Saturday, 9 February, attracted a crowd estimated to be fifteen hundred people. A thousand workers from the harbour works and Railways Department, who had been given the day off, lined the streets. Flags throughout Fremantle flew at half-mast. C. Y. O'Connor, John McDonald and Arthur Dillon Bell were among the pall bearers.

Irvine's fellow workers paid for his tombstone and set up a fund to support his widow and seven children.[361] Several entertainment companies put on shows in the days that followed to raise money for this fund.[362]

Timothy Yorke, who had permanently lost his sight, was not forgotten. Concerts and sports matches were held for his benefit during the year.[363] In November, the government announced that it had arranged for him to be accepted into the Industrial Institution of the Blind in Sydney. There he would be taught basketry or mat-making so that he could support himself.[364] The government later granted him an annuity of seventy-five pounds per year.[365]

Work soon resumed at Rocky Bay and on the harbour works. John McDonald oversaw the work on site, but O'Connor continued to supervise the overall project on a daily basis as he travelled to and from home in Fremantle. Whatever his personal feelings about the loss of John Irvine, O'Connor suffered no public criticism over his death. During the weeks that followed, the daily newspapers all published glowing reviews of the work already completed on the harbour. In an editorial on Monday 11 February, the West Australian went so far as to say that, while Irving's death was regrettable, 'the struggle to subdue nature and make it obedient to our purpose unhappily demands some victims, and all that can be said in the way of consolation is that they fall in a noble struggle'.[366]

To avoid annoying or alarming Fremantle's residents, blasting on the limestone bar across the river mouth was only undertaken during the day. Men scrambling over rough mobile jarrah trussels (trestles) drilled holes fifteen feet in depth, ten feet apart. They inserted pipes into the holes, dropped charges into them, then used fuses to fire two at a time. Dressed in their everyday shirts, waistcoats and trousers, their only safety equipment was their hats to keep off the sun—no harnesses, railings or lifejackets were provided.[367] Most workers were employed for eight hours a day, except for those on the dredges who worked twelve-hour shifts.

Up to forty charges were fired each day. This level of blasting was far from what could have been achieved in an engineering sense, but it represented a compromise between efficiency and good relations with the town.

The two dredges, one on either side of the bar, removed the pulverised rock and silt. Much of it was used to create the foundations for the south mole, as well as the retaining wall that would allow wharves to be constructed on reclaimed land along the river.[368]

The year 1895 proved to be the worst for fatalities associated with the project. With massive stones being extracted from Rocky Bay and transported by rail, to form the top of the moles, it was perhaps inevitable that accidents would occur.

In April, a thirty-four-year-old worker named John Doheny was badly injured when the rocks he was helping to offload from a tilt truck suddenly dislodged. He was taken to hospital, and seemed to be recovering, but he died from his injuries a few days later. He left a thirteen-year-old son.[369]

On 7 August a thirty-two-year-old man, Thomas McGovern, was crushed to death in an accident at Rocky Bay. He had been digging out the sand from around a massive boulder, in order to attach the chain from the steam crane that would lift it onto a rail truck. Without warning, the rock split in two and half of it toppled over, killing him. McGovern had come from Hokitika in New Zealand to work on the project.[370]

Non-fatal but serious injuries also occurred several times during the year. In December a man named Cornelius Flynn lost his right leg in an accident with a railway tip-truck.[371]

Work stopped temporarily after such accidents, and safety procedures were reviewed. But anyone working on the project must have had in the back of their mind the thought that they too might one day become the victim of an accident. Their families would be left with no support, apart from what might be provided by charity and their fellow workers. Without any form of social security available, anything which prevented a man from working would be devastating to all those who depended upon his income. Not surprising, then, that workers did what they could to protect their livelihoods.

TWENTY-ONE: Monster meetings – 1895

Antagonism towards Asian immigrant workers remained strong in the community, especially amongst labourers and miners. In March 1895, the Trades and Labour Council petitioned the Fremantle Municipal Council for the use of the Town Hall to hold a public meeting. Their purpose was to protest the continued importation of 'Chinese and Asiatics' into the colony as cheap labour.[372]

The meeting, which went ahead on 21 March, was well attended, with Fremantle councillor Doonan acting as chair. Several members of parliament who were present at the meeting spoke in support of the motions being discussed. Mr Marmion, Mr Wood and Mr Solomon, all members of parliament, sent their apologies.

The president of the Trades and Labour Council, James Ball, moved that the meeting 'emphatically protests against the increasing influx of Chinese, Afghans and other Asiatics and urges upon the Government to introduce such legislation as will prevent the continuance of such emigration.'

He referred to what he described as 'one of the meanest and most insignificant letters that had ever appeared in the daily press.' The letter in question had been published by the *West Australian* on 13 March.[373]

Using the pen name 'Fiat Justitia', the writer protested Fremantle council's allowing what he (or she) called 'faddists' to use a building constructed with public money. 'The idea of asking the mayor to officially preside at the meeting seems to me peculiarly impudent,' he wrote.

The Chinese, Afghans and Indians were hard-working people who would benefit the colony. Intemperate and improvident English working men could learn from them the virtues that made them successful.

James Ball felt sure the author must be 'a man with a retreating forehead, and a narrow-minded expression—one who also resembled that specimen of natural history known as the Weasel. In a subject such as that under discussion, I, as the representative of a large body of laborers, could honestly say that I represent a large proportion of honest industrious men.'

It was not prejudice that motivated the meeting, he insisted, but the self-preservation of English working men and women, from people who 'came to take advantage of that which our forefathers had worked for, and to undersell us in every shape and form.'

No-one contradicted him. Both workers and employers took it as a given that employers could, and would, negotiate with workers for the lowest possible wages. Shipping companies and pastoralists were notorious for the number of non-European labourers they employed, though often because no-one else would accept the working conditions offered. The only way to prevent immigrant workers from accepting subsistence level wages, and undercutting locals, was to keep them out. This meant preventing employers from recruiting them from overseas.

It would be another year before an amendment to the Victorian *Factories Act* introduced the first minimum wage in Australia, for a limited number of workers.[374] The idea of a minimum wage for all workers would have to wait until the Harvester Judgement in 1907.[375] By then the White Australia policy, which restricted non-white immigration, was also in place.

Frederick Illingworth, MLA, quoting from a Vatican paper on a living wage, argued at the Fremantle meeting that the working man needed three things; a full and complete supply of the necessaries of life; a sufficiency to maintain a comfortable home; and enough income to educate his children. 'But did the Asiatics who were coming to our shores propose to work under these conditions? Certainly not!' he said.

Without a hint of irony, this immigrant from Yorkshire continued: the Scriptures stated that the boundaries of the inhabitants of the earth had been fixed, and he had yet to learn that a Chinaman's allotment pegs extended to Australia. He supported the motion, because 'the presence of these aliens amongst us could only lead to national retrogression.'

James Ball's motion was carried. An eight-man deputation was formed to wait upon the Premier to discuss their concerns.[376]

They were not the only deputation wanting to wait on Sir John Forrest. The night after the Trades and Labour Council meeting, another 'monster indignation' meeting was held in the Fremantle Town Hall. Those who gathered were there to discuss, once again, their opposition to the removal of the railway workshops to Midland. The discussion was lively and almost unanimous.

A few days earlier the Vigilance Committee, established in November 1893, had met to discuss a letter received by William Marmion from the Premier. After prevaricating for so long, John Forrest put forth the reasons why the government had finally decided to move the workshops to Midland. The advice of the Engineer-in-Chief had been a deciding factor in their decision, he wrote. He assured the people of Fremantle that the opening of the port would do far more for Fremantle than the workshops ever would.

After reading the letter, the Vigilance Committee had called the indignation meeting.

Alexander Forrest, whose presence at the public gathering was greeted with enthusiastic cheers, took the opportunity once again to attack O'Connor. It was all very well for the Engineer-in-Chief or other experts to say the workshops would be better at the Midland Junction, he said, but he believed there was no need for them to go so far. They all had vested interests in Fremantle, and it was the duty of the government to protect those interests, not to drag people away who had homes, stores, and businesses of their own, to a spot twenty-two miles inland.

There was no common sense in it, he continued. It would be far better for the government to get rid of the Engineer-in-Chief than to ruin half of Fremantle. He concurred with other speakers that the workshops could be moved, if necessary, to a site nearby.

Cheers and applause frequently interrupted his speech. He concluded by offering the gathering help if they sent a delegation to Perth.

The meeting agreed to form a 'monster deputation' to visit the Premier the following Wednesday, 20 March. A special train would be laid on to allow people to get to Perth.[377] The Town Clerk of Fremantle, Mr Bland, wrote to Sir John Forrest on behalf of the mayor, to ask if he would receive the deputation at the Perth Town Hall.

Sir John's reply was blunt. The government had already discussed all the points brought up at the indignation meeting. The decision had been made, and the government deserved sympathy for having done in the public interest what was against their personal interests. If they wanted to discuss the issue, they could visit the Commissioner for Railways. He, the Premier, would not be meeting with the delegation.[378]

The members of the Vigilance committee were incensed by this. Marmion told them he had 'had a few words' with the Premier. Sir John would not agree to meet a large delegation at the Perth Town Hall, but he was open to meeting a smaller delegation of, say, twenty elected delegates in his office.

Marmion added that the feeling in Perth was that the people of Fremantle were planning a demonstration 'of a menacing character.' The committee denied this and agreed to ask Sir John Forrest to receive a representative deputation. The citizens of Fremantle would be invited to escort the deputation to Perth.[379]

Two days later, somewhere between four hundred and a thousand people from Fremantle accompanied the delegation to Perth and marched in procession from the railway station to the Town Hall. Some marched on to the Premier's office in the Treasury building, while the rest hung around at the Town Hall, which the mayor of Perth, Alexander Forrest, had made sure was open to them. Forrest accompanied the twenty-man delegation to visit his brother.

John Forrest greeted them with less than his usual cordiality. After listening to all the usual arguments being rehashed, including one that the government should call in another expert to give advice, Sir John rose to speak.

'I have a somewhat difficult task,' he began, 'inasmuch as I will have to defend the action of the Government before a deputation, every one of which I suppose is adverse to the line of argument that I would use. I do not think that I have ever been in such an unfortunate position before.

'But I would have been in a still more unfortunate position if I had met 1,000 men all imbued with the same sentiments,' he said. 'Everyone in the colony knows the feeling of the people of Fremantle in this matter. It was not necessary for a deputation of a thousand men to come to Perth to tell me what I already knew.'

However, he went on, he was very glad to see them, and he recognised that the deputation included the most influential men of Fremantle.

He said he had racked his brain for the past four years trying to find a way to avoid moving the workshops far from Fremantle. He had visited the alternative sites that the delegation was suggesting, and expert opinion had forced him into the position he was in that day.

As for wanting yet another expert opinion, they already had the opinion of Mr Allison Smith and their own Chief Engineer. They could dismiss Mr Smith's opinion if they wished, but he took his stand on Mr O'Connor's opinion. They had embarked on building a million-pound harbour on the advice of Mr O'Connor. The people of Fremantle were willing to take Mr O'Connor's advice on such a great question...

'That is as a marine engineer,' someone interjected.

'But would they not accept it on this matter?' continued the Premier. 'His knowledge as a marine engineer is not greater than his knowledge as a railway engineer.'

The delegates were not persuaded, and his patient and prolonged attempts to placate them with facts and figures went nowhere.[380]

The meeting lasted longer than anticipated, and those gathered in the Town Hall were becoming impatient by the time the delegates returned. Marmion did his best to present what had been said by the Premier in a positive way. Others felt Sir John had failed to answer their concerns. But the disappointed crowd remained well behaved and duly trooped back to the station to return to Fremantle.[381]

Sir John Forrest's arguments had relied heavily, once again, on the necessity of having to accept the expertise and advice of his Chief Engineer. Yet when a reporter from the *West Australian* interviewed O'Connor a week later, he was far from adamant in his views on where the workshops should be located. O'Connor quoted his own words to the 1893 commission:

'I do not really care, from an engineering point of view, where these workshops are to be, so long as we get what we want in the way of space to work in, etc. They may be in Perth, or Subiaco, or the Canning, or Bayswater; I don't in the least mind where they are, provided we get the class of shops we want, with a sufficient area of ground.'

He pointed out some of the advantages of the Midland site, including the fact that land was cheap and the workmen who would be uprooted from Fremantle could afford to build more comfortable and spacious homes for their families in Midland. 'That however is possibly only a sentimental advantage,' he added. 'A more materialistic advantage is the level character of the ground at this spot.' The other sites mentioned would not only be more expensive to purchase but would cost far more to level.

'As to the removal being desirable or necessary, I need only quote one fact. In May 1891, there were 362 vehicles in the colony including locomotives, wagons and carriages, and then the workshops were not adequate. Now there are 1,567 vehicles in the colony and 197 to arrive shortly.'[382]

If John Forrest's reluctance to be confronted by a thousand Fremantle residents in March had caused consternation, his refusal to meet with the delegates of the Trades and Labour Council in April produced outrage.

The TLC had joined forces with the Coolgardie-Southern Cross Anti Asiatic League, after a meeting on 12 April with one of its founders, Frederick Vosper. They agreed to set up a branch of the league in Perth and Vosper became part of a committee established to call a public meeting to deal with 'the Chinese and Asiatic question'.[383]

The pale and intense Vosper had migrated to Queensland from England in 1886. After working in a variety of occupations, he became a journalist and political activist. He was a strong advocate of workers' rights and republicanism, and a staunch opponent of Asian immigration. In 1893 he had arrived on the West Australian goldfields and became editor of the Coolgardie Miner in 1894.[384]

In December 1894, Vosper had been prominent at a meeting in Coolgardie where hundreds of angry residents discussed 'the Afghan problem'. Tensions between Afghan camel drivers and other residents over water had been rising as the number of Afghans (a term applied very loosely) grew, while the water supply became more precarious.

Those at the Coolgardie meeting expressed sympathy with a man named Knowles, who was in gaol in Albany facing trial for murder. He had shot and killed one Afghan and seriously injured another during a fight at a watering hole.

The meeting agreed to get up a petition on behalf of Knowles and to inaugurate the Anti Asiatic League. The provisional committee of the League determined at its first meeting to petition the government to do all in its power to prevent further immigration and deport 'such Asiatics as are already here'.[385]

The League had many aims in common with the Trades and Labour Council, and Vosper was invited to join the deputation to visit the Premier. Several members of Parliament were also included among the proposed delegates. However, on 26 April the Premier's under-secretary, Octavius Burt, wrote to one of these, Mr Walter James, MLA;

> *'...with reference to the deputation waiting upon the Premier in connection with the Asiatic Question...I am directed to inform you that the Government has for some time past had the question under consideration, and may be able to introduce legislation in regard to it next session. The Government is fully aware of the phases of the question, which require careful consideration, and see no reason for a deputation; but should it be so desired, the views held by you and others can be communicated in writing.'*

It was a snub. The Perth branch of the League called a hasty committee meeting, while Vosper telegraphed to Coolgardie to ask for instructions.[386]

But perhaps Sir John Forrest's response lacked his usual tact and diplomacy for personal reasons. On Saturday 27 April, the *Daily News* reported that the Premier had gone home the previous day with a severe chill, associated with rigors and a temperature of 104 degrees Fahrenheit. Lady Forrest, alarmed, had called a doctor. The following day, Sir John seemed to be improving.[387] But a week later he was still off work, though hoping to return to his office the following Monday.[388]

C. Y. O'Connor had little sympathy with the racist tones of the Anti Asiatic league. While his concern for the welfare of his workers was well known, he was also a believer in the benefits of the mingling of all nationalities and beliefs.

In his farewell speech at Hokitika in 1880, he had specifically mentioned both Jews and Mohammedans (ie Muslims) among those whose cultures and ideas enriched others in a mining community:

> *'(F)or if it is true that the admixture of races produces advancement and progress...how much more so is it the case when the inventive faculty of each race is called into requisition by engaging in pursuits previously foreign to them...*
>
> *...'we have here assembled the countrymen of David and of Solomon, the countrymen of Alexander, Socrates and Plato, the countrymen of Caesar and Galileo, the countrymen of the Ptolemies, the countrymen of Mohummed...all met together, and while each is preserving to some extent the* esprit de corps *and patriotism of the particular nationality from which he sprang, and carrying on with him the great thoughts and individual conceptions of his immortal progenitors, all are trying to outdo the others in a grand march towards the most stupendous goal of progress to which the opportunities of any country or nation have ever tended.'*[389]

Such sentiments were foreign to Vosper. The fiery journalist would become one of O'Connor's greatest antagonists in the years that followed.

But as the chilly autumn days of 1895 headed towards winter, the O'Connors were not thinking of Vosper. On Wednesday, 1 May, Aileen married one of her father's engineering protegees, Charles Young Simpson, in what was described in the papers as one of the largest and most fashionably attended weddings that had ever been witnessed in the colony. Charles O'Connor proudly escorted his eldest daughter down the aisle of the packed church of St John, Fremantle. Aileen's three sisters, Kate, Eva and Bridget, along with another young girl (whose name the newspapers could not agree on) followed as bridesmaids.

The sun shone on the young couple as they left the church to join their hundred and fifty invited guests at a reception of light refreshments, served at the O'Connor's rented home, Plympton House in Cantonment Road (now Queen Victoria Street).[390] Dr and Mrs Barnett and Dr Wheeler were among the guests. So were Francis and Lilian Hart. Lilian lovingly recorded every detail of the wedding and the female guest's attire for the readers of the *West Australian*, though she didn't use her 'Cora' by-line on this occasion.

Sir John and Lady Forrest were invited, although the lack of any mention of Lady Forrest's dress suggests they were unable to attend because of Sir John's illness. The Marmions and the Venns were there. The out-going mayor of Fremantle, Daniel Congdon, and his family were also on the guest list. The mayor of Perth was not.[391]

TWENTY-TWO: A question of accommodation - 1895

The two Irishmen—Doctor Barnett and Engineer O'Connor, the landlord and his former tenant—crossed paths frequently. Both attended St John's church on Sunday mornings and shared a friendship with its minister, Archdeacon Watkins. They both supported the Fremantle Rowing Club's events whenever they could. Both their names could be found on the guest list for social events, from balls to private dinner parties. But neither man left any record of their interactions or what they discussed when they met.

Dr Barnett, a long-standing resident of Fremantle, took an interest in all aspects of the physical and social landscape around him. He had grown up watching the harbour in Belfast being redeveloped and had visited harbours across the world in his days as a ship's surgeon. The developments at the river mouth in Fremantle would have intrigued him. But he could not have failed to compare the money being borrowed to fund the harbour works, and other engineering projects, with the begrudging amounts the government allowed for the asylum.

Chief Engineer O'Connor could not have been unaware of the situation at the asylum. The newspapers reported on the overcrowding regularly. His own Public Works Department was responsible for designing and contracting out any extensions that were built. His Minister, Harry Venn, had been on Dr Scott's select committee when it inspected the asylum in 1891.

As O'Connor liked to point out, his role as a public servant was to carry out the government's wishes, after proffering his advice. He could not initiate projects. If he ever quietly suggested to Minister Venn that the works department should take the advice of its own architect, George Temple Poole, and push for funding for a new asylum as soon as possible, it was off the record and went unheeded. Perhaps O'Connor and Dr Barnett restricted their conversations to more neutral topics—their memories of Ireland, sport, geography or the weather.

On one occasion, their relationship produced a negative, though unintended, consequence. Dr Barnett's presence at Aileen O'Connor's wedding in May 1895 would lead, indirectly, to a worsening of his relationship with the Premier's department.

Archdeacon Brown, the manager of the 'Swan Native and Half Caste Mission' in Guildford, wrote to Dr Barnett on Saturday 1 May, asking that a young Aboriginal girl be admitted to the asylum. The girl, aged just ten, was described as having fits of 'homicidal insanity' which made it difficult for the mission to keep her.

The evidence of her insanity included that, 'On several occasions knives have been found hidden about her person or amongst her bed clothes or the mattresses; also refusing to eat or take nourishment of any sort being certain that some girl had poisoned it.'[392] She had told the doctor who examined her that she wanted to kill two of the girls who she believed had led to her being ill-treated at the mission.

Although there were technical issues with the way she had been certified as a 'dangerous lunatic', her age itself was not a barrier to admission to the asylum.[393] But Dr Barnett, who was attending Aileen's wedding on the Saturday, did not receive the Archdeacon's letter in time. He replied by telegram and then by letter the following day, saying he would be glad to take the girl if he could, but it was impossible. Since the government had not yet met his repeated requests for the means to separate dangerous from quiet patients, he had no way of separating a dangerous patient from other patients. 'I cannot take in such a case to mingle with the quiet, harmless and elderly women,' he wrote.

His letter reached Archdeacon Brown too late. The girl had already been dispatched to Fremantle in the custody of the mission's matron. When they arrived at the asylum, the girl was refused admission and had to return to Guildford.

Archdeacon Brown, unsure what to do, wrote to the secretary of the Aboriginal Protection Board on 7 May for advice. The secretary, Charles D'Oyley Forbes, passed on the letter to the Premier's under-secretary, Octavius Burt. He in turn informed the Premier, in writing, of what had happened, adding 'I think Dr Barnett should admit her. There must be less danger both to herself and others inside the asylum where there is a staff to look after her, than outside where she is under minimal supervision.'

After receiving a note in reply from the Premier, 'I hope Dr Barnett will be able to assist in this matter, even if extra expense has to be incurred', the under-secretary sent the file to Dr Barnett, marked 'For your information.'

Henry Barnett responded to Burt with a barely polite letter. 'The preamble of the Lunacy Act states that it is expedient to provide for prevention of crimes by persons dangerously insane, and in this and other instances, [I have merely?] done my duty in pointing out that to mingle dangerous lunatics with harmless and quiet...is likely to cause, and has caused, murderous attacks.'

He went on; 'It is my duty to obey the directions of my official superiors, therefore having done my duty by entering my protest, I now...write to Archdeacon Brown requesting him to send the patient, and we must do the best we can.'[394] The child was admitted and remained at the asylum until she was discharged in December 1896.[395]

In general, Dr Barnett had a reputation for treating all his patients with compassion regardless of their race.[396] He also had some insight into the way incarceration away from their own family and land affected indigenous people, whether in the asylum or in prison. Back in 1878, he wrote of one female indigenous patient at the asylum:

'Her confinement in (the) Asylum makes her mental affliction worse and her presence irritates all the other female patients. Her husband and sister are anxious to take charge of her to the Murray. It will give her a better chance of recovery to be in the bush and the husband promises to bring her back if she gets worse.'[397]

In 1884, while he was the visiting medical officer to the Aboriginal prison on Rottnest, he had campaigned for a better diet for prisoners. He was also quoted as being in favour of Aboriginal prisoners from the North-West being kept closer to home. By the time they arrived at Rottnest, he said, they were 'depressed by confinement and sickness'.[398]

It may be that the antipathy of other patients towards non-white, non-British people was causing problems for Dr Barnett and his staff in running the overcrowded asylum. In his annual report for 1895, Dr Barnett regretted that 'the aliens - Chinese, Malays, Aboriginals &c now number thirty-four, and are increasing'.[399] It is understandable that he might have felt that those who arrived in the colony with mental illness should be returned to their home country for care. It would free up beds for other patients. It's not clear where he expected 'Aboriginals' to go if they became mentally unwell, or why he classified them with 'aliens'. They were legally entitled to the same treatment as anyone else under the *Lunacy Act* of 1871.[400]

But Dr Barnett's refusal to admit the child from the Swan River Mission seems to have been motivated neither by compassion nor by prejudice. He wanted to make a point. The asylum was too crowded and too understaffed to take on patients needing special attention.

* * *

If the advice of Dr Scott and the Select Committee into the asylum had been followed in 1891, a new asylum might well have been completed by 1895. As it was, in April 1895, four years after the committee's investigation, the *West Australian* reported that the government would be setting aside 20,000 pounds for a new asylum in that year's budget estimates. The paper gave no source for this information but added that the new asylum would be built on the forty-acre site in the Darling Ranges previously offered by Mr James Morrison.

Before the matter had even been discussed in parliament, the *West Australian* suggested ways to repurpose the current building. It could be used as an industrial school (for delinquent youths or girls) or be taken up by some other charitable institution. Or perhaps it could become a convalescent home for those 'seeking health and change from the goldfields in the pleasant and bracing summer climate of Fremantle.'[401]

The government had already intimated to the Fremantle Municipal Council in March that the Knowle, where elderly patients from the asylum were currently housed, would soon be handed over as a much-needed hospital for Fremantle.[402]

When the treasurer, John Forrest, gave his budget speech on 8 August, he made much of the fact that the revenue of Western Australia now exceeded that of Tasmania, with a credit balance that compared favourably with the much older colony's debts. The population of Western Australia had increased by nearly 45,000 in the previous five years, and in the last twelve months the increase had been over 1,000 per month. The healthy state of the colony's economy was attracting interest and investment from abroad. 'The future is bright and promising,' he told the members.[403]

In the same speech, he expressed impatience over how long the Fremantle harbour works were taking, while recognising that they couldn't proceed any faster. 'As everyone who has been to see the work must admit and acknowledge, it is a very great work indeed,' he said. 'It is also a very long and a very tedious work. It is on so great a scale that one is apt to be wearied with its apparently slow progress.'

Among the many items of planned expenditure, he briefly mentioned that £30,000 would be allocated for the new asylum, though he didn't name a site.[404] Most people welcomed this long-overdue news. The editor of the Coolgardie Miner, Frederick Vosper, took a different view.

Downplaying the government's planned expenditure on railways, public buildings and other facilities in the goldfields, he focused on the £30,000 specifically set aside by the treasurer for 'the development of our gold and mineral resources'.

The co-incidence between this amount and what was to be spent on the asylum provided Vosper with the ammunition he needed to accuse the government of having its priorities all wrong. He claimed it was ignoring the needs of the people of the goldfields, who created the wealth and paid heavy taxes. Sir John Forrest was buying himself voters in the centres of population around Perth, he said.

'Is it the act of a financier and a statesman to set apart £30,000 for the development of the goldfields of this colony and a similar amount for a lunatic asylum!' he wrote (punctuation original).[405]

Dissatisfaction with the government in the goldfields was widespread enough for this to find a receptive readership. By October, the theme had been picked up by those campaigning for increased representation in Parliament. At a public meeting in Kalgoorlie, the Chairman of the Chamber of Mines and Commerce for Coolgardie took it up.

'In his Budget speech, the Premier stated that £30,000 had been set apart for expenditure upon goldfields, and he also alluded to the fact that it was proposed to set aside £30,000 for a lunatic asylum in Perth. The Premier, therefore, considered that the Perth lunatics were entitled to consideration equal to that of the whole of the people upon the goldfields,' he is reported to have said.[406]

Meanwhile, work continued on the extensions to the southeast end of the Fremantle asylum that had been announced in February the previous year. Two wings of sixteen rooms each were built of the same limestone blocks as the existing buildings.[407] The contractor, John Milne, had found it difficult to obtain stone of the quality needed at the price he had quoted. After he entered bankruptcy in June, the contract was handed over to a Mr Ferguson.[408]

By November, the building work was completed, and all the female patients were transferred to the new wings. The thirty elderly patients from the Knowle were moved back, under police escort, to the rooms vacated in the main asylum building.[409] The additional space temporarily made conditions slightly less cramped for the patients and staff. The extensions included a large new dining room, which was used on 29 November for a concert given by the Fremantle Orchestral Society and the pupils of Miss Clare Robinson.[410]

But Dr Barnett still didn't have the facilities that he had long wished for, to separate the mild and curable cases from the rowdy and incurable and create a pleasant environment. More of the asylum grounds had been enclosed by a high wall, but the ground itself had not been levelled so that patients could use it for exercise.[411]

As well as the patients returning from the Knowle, thirty-six patients had been admitted during the year, offset by sixteen discharges and ten deaths. By December the asylum housed one hundred and sixty.

When John Forrest had announced, a year earlier, that Dr Barnett would be appointed full-time superintendent of the asylum, he mentioned that a residence for him would be built nearby.[412] Perhaps in the expectation of moving into quarters at the asylum, Henry Barnett had begun advertising some of his land in Fremantle for sale early in 1895.[413] In November he announced Park Bungalow itself for sale, describing it as a 'commodious, beautifully situated dwelling house'.[414] The two adjacent blocks had by then been subdivided into four, to be sold singly or together with the house.[415]

The obvious buyer for Park Bungalow would have been C. Y. O'Connor. He and his family had previously lived in the house for eighteen months and were aware of its benefits, in terms of size, location and amenities. But O'Connor never bought any land or property in Western Australia, possibly to avoid any hint of self-interest in the location of the projects he worked on. He continued to live in rented properties up until his death, and would, in fact, rent Park Bungalow again from 1897.

With no buyer forthcoming, in January 1896 Park Bungalow was advertised 'for sale or to let for a term of years'.[416] Dr Barnett also began advertising a 'newly-built ten-roomed House, in Quarry Street' to let.[417] This had been recently built on one of the empty blocks next door to Park Bungalow, facing Barnett Street. Eventually the Barnetts came to own two cottages on Barnett Street, 'Pendennis' and 'Logan'.[418] They moved into one of these.

The promised accommodation near the asylum never eventuated. Nor would Henry Barnett live long enough to see a new asylum built. The

Public Works Department could barely keep up with the numerous projects it was being asked to deliver. As Engineer-in-Chief and Acting General Manager of railways, C. Y. O'Connor had so much work to attend to that even reporting on its progress was sometimes delayed for years.

TWENTY-THREE: Railway blues – 1895 – 1896

In September 1895, the Commissioner for Railways, Harry Venn, tabled a hefty one-hundred-page report in the lower house of parliament. The long-awaited Railways Department report for the years 1892 to 1895 had been produced under the direction of C. Y. O'Connor and was largely written by him.

Venn did his best to be sanguine about the fact that this was the first report for four years. Every page, he said, showed the carefulness so characteristic of the Engineer-in-Chief, to whom he owed his warmest thanks. The report's comprehensiveness gave a far better picture of the state of the railways than his own brief annual reports to parliament had done. If the members compared the figures for one year with another, they would appreciate the progress that had been made.

He apologised that he had been unable to present a report earlier, 'owing to the great pressure of work in the department, and the necessity for attending closely to the business of the moment.' But he presented it now 'as a happy indication of what this House may expect in the future.'

The report showed that the railway system had grown extensively in the past five years, while the annual revenue had increased from 45,000 pounds to 296,000 pounds. The railways, which had once been a burden on the colony, were now paying their way, thanks largely to the untiring attention of C. Y. O'Connor.

'There is no doubt in my mind that we are at this moment constructing more railways for our money than was ever anticipated, and this is mainly due to the care and ability of the Engineer-in-Chief,' said Venn.[419]

But within the report was an item which Venn largely glossed over. The Chief Engineer had asked to be relieved of the responsibility of being Acting General Manager of railways.

'It is not that there is so very much actual work involved in it,' wrote O'Connor in his long report '—and, as regards the actual management of the traffic, I have never taken any active part in that at all—but the position necessarily involves a great deal of responsibility.

'It also necessitates a great deal of study of other than purely engineering questions, to keep in touch with modern ideas on the subject, and it also absorbs a great deal of time in interviewing persons who have new ideas to propound, or new commodities to dispose of and last but not least, there are numberless applicants for employment in the railway service who seem to all wish to see me personally on the subject.'[420]

Despite calmly offering advice on how the department might be reorganised, and even making an attempt at humour, the Chief Engineer was saying he'd had enough.

Just how desperately he needed to be relieved of some of his responsibilities became clear when he visited the eastern colonies in October to look at their railway workshops. The *West Australian* reported that he had been 'indisposed' recently and hoped the trip would be 'beneficial and recuperative' for him.[421] In November the paper was still reporting that he was suffering from ill-health brought on by overwork.

His solution was to leave the office and sail aboard the *Sultan* to Carnarvon for a short holiday. The three week 'holiday' would include inspecting the harbour there and advising the government on what improvements were needed.[422]

Less than two weeks after returning from Carnarvon, he travelled south with the Premier to Cape Leeuwin, for the laying of the foundation stone for a new lighthouse.[423] On 20 December, he received a deputation, on Mr Venn's behalf, of water carriers from the mining town of Coolgardie. The Woolgangie water tank, which supplied water on route to Coolgardie, was running dry.[424] Having listened, he dealt swiftly with the impending crisis. He spoke to the Premier and arranged for water to be sent by rail to replenish the tank.

The following day he again accompanied the Premier, this time on the long train journey to Albany, to welcome the new Governor, Sir Gerard Smith.[425]

If the first two years as Engineer-in-Chief in Western Australia had seemed to him 'the most trying and unremitting labour' that he had ever undertaken, nothing had happened to improve that situation since.[426] Apart from the workload itself, which would have been enough for two or three lesser men, he was under constant criticism from those who didn't like his way of doing things.

Local contractors and businessmen, in particular, were critical of the fact that he used government-employed labour on the harbour scheme rather than giving the work to contractors. When he did employ contractors, for instance in building the railway lines to Bunbury and Southern Cross, he took the lowest quote offered. These often came from companies outside Western Australia.

The year 1895 had been difficult personally as well as professionally. The death in January of John Irvine, whom he had known since his New Zealand days, was unsettling. In May, Frank Martin, who was employed as engineer in charge of existing railways in Western Australia, dropped dead at the age of forty.[427] He had been a pupil of O'Connor in New Zealand, and O'Connor esteemed him as 'an old and valued friend'.[428] In June, Fred Calver, the thirty-two-year-old traffic manager for the northern rail system, died of typhoid which he contracted in Southern Cross.[429] O'Connor had attended all their funerals.

Aileen's wedding in May was a cause for celebration, but perhaps even that had taken its toll. Aileen had been a part of his marriage to Susan literally from day one. For many years she had been a third adult in the family, someone who supported Susan practically and acted as her confidante during her father's many absences. She also sometimes served as her father's personal secretary.[430] Her moving out of home changed the family dynamic and everyone, including O'Connor, had to adjust.

The government and the newspapers acknowledged O'Connor's request to be relieved of the post of General Manager of the railways. But it would be another year before anyone was appointed to replace him.[431] In the meantime he would be dragged into an escalating conflict between the Premier, John Forrest, and his minister, Harry Venn. The management of the railways would be one of the conflict's precipitants.

The population of Western Australia had been steadily growing, as a result of the booming gold mining industry, with most of the influx coming from the eastern colonies. By early 1896, the stream of new arrivals had become a flood. The recession in the east was biting hard, while news that the West Australian government was working on plans to deliver a reliable water source to the goldfields encouraged those who might otherwise have hesitated to head west. Not every new arrival went to the goldfields. Many established themselves in Perth and Fremantle or in country towns.

One result of this influx was a shortage of rolling stock for the railways. Demand for both passenger trains and transport of goods had increased well beyond expectations. The opening of new lines to Bunbury, the Midlands and Southern Cross also necessitated more rolling stock. The locomotive works in Fremantle were busy building trucks as fast as they could unload the parts from the wharves.[432]

Increased demand for goods and building materials led to more ships arriving, while lack of transport meant the cargoes that arrived couldn't be moved away quickly. Early in January 1896, goods began piling up on the wharves at Fremantle. Shipping companies lost money as ships waited in port to be offloaded. A fire in Fremantle the previous October had destroyed some of the railway goods sheds, along with several trucks, which made things worse.[433]

It was suggested that some of the trucks being used on the harbour works should be diverted to ease the congestion, or even that the harbour works should be suspended for a while to allow all the trucks to be used for transporting goods. In February, O'Connor, the General Traffic Manager,

John Davies, and Harry Venn as the Commissioner for Railways, met to discuss this proposal. They decided that twenty-five trucks could be put to use between Fremantle and Perth during the weekends, after work on the harbour railway lines ceased at lunchtime on Saturdays.[434]

The lack of rolling stock was also affecting the delivery of water to the tank at Woolgangie, leading to claims that the government was reneging on its promise.[435] A reporter from *The Inquirer* interviewed O'Connor on 16 January and asked him about the allegations that some of the money allocated for buying new rolling stock had not been spent. O'Connor replied that all the money had been spent and the trucks purchased were already in the colony and being used. The problem was the enormous and unanticipated increase in demand, coupled with the fact that the amount allocated had never been adequate.[436]

He was questioned again about rolling stock when he came before the Civil Service Commission for the first time, in January 1896. The Commission had been in progress since 1894, and many, including members of parliament, felt it was time to wind it up. But others with an axe to grind insisted that it continue until it had reviewed the Public Works Department.

One of the commission members, George Simpson, MLA, had created an uproar in parliament a few months earlier, by revealing some of the commission's findings before they had been formally presented to the Governor. In particular, he quoted from evidence already given by John Davies, the General Traffic Manager for the railways, which was critical of both the Engineer-in-Chief and Mr Venn. Davies evidence, printed in the newspapers' reports on parliament, helped to inflame the idea that money allocated for rolling stock hadn't been spent, and that the Railways Department was poorly run.[437]

O'Connor's first of many meetings with the commissioners, most of whom were current or former members of parliament, took place on 9 January 1896.[438] They began with formal questions about his position. How long had he been employed as Engineer-in-Chief? What was his role?

He outlined how he had been employed. 'I asked, I may say, what the duties involved in the position were,' he said, 'whether they included railways or harbours or roads or what, and the answer by cable was "everything"'.[439]

The commissioners asked if he had previous experience in railway engineering. 'Oh yes, I was almost brought up on railways in England, and had an intimate knowledge of all branches there from when I was about seventeen years of age,' he answered.[440]

He was diplomatic in answering questions about his working relationship with John Davies, saying that although he, as Acting General Manager, was nominally in control of the traffic branch, he made it a distinct practice not to interfere with the actual running of trains.

But he became less guarded when asked about the shortage of rolling stock. He gave a detailed account of how the need for rolling stock was estimated and how it was purchased, adding, 'We have never yet had sufficient allocation to bring us up to date—not sufficient funds.'

Then, referring to evidence already given to the commission by Davies, he disputed the traffic manager's contention that he hadn't been properly consulted about requirements.

Tensions between Davies and O'Connor continued to simmer. On 23 January 1896, Davies attended a banquet in Fremantle, held to celebrate the arrival of a new steamship service. In his speech welcoming the service, Davies again implied that the Engineer-in-Chief and the Commissioner of Railways were to blame for the lack of rolling stock.

He did not like to speak of the motives of his superiors, he said, but in his four years as General Traffic Manager he had never had a free hand, and consequently he had never been able to make provision for the rapid increase in the traffic of Western Australia. His speech, and those of others critical of the government, were reported in the newspapers.[441]

On 24 January, a delegation of shipping agents from Fremantle attempted to meet with Minister Venn to discuss their concerns about lack of berths at the jetty. But due to some 'slight mistake' in the timing of their visit, Harry Venn was unavailable, and they met instead with the General Traffic Manager, John Davies. They then visited the Premier, who said he was reluctant to spend money on the jetty unless it was absolutely necessary but promised to recommend that the jetty be extended.[442]

By the end of February, dissatisfaction among businessmen and citizens in general had reached boiling point. Not only was the railway system failing to meet demand, but the postal and telegraphic services were also totally inadequate. Reports appeared regularly in the press of letters taking months to arrive at their destination.

A public meeting, held in the Perth Town Hall on 25 February 1896, drew a large and rowdy crowd. It was chaired by the newly elected mayor of Perth, Henry Saunders. (Alexander Forrest, the retiring mayor, had left earlier in the month on a trip to England.)

All the speakers were agreed that the Public Works and Railways Department and the Postal and Telegraphic Department weren't functioning as they should. Some blamed Sir John Forrest and his 'one-man government'. The Premier was accused, in his parsimony as treasurer, of having refused to supply the funding for rolling stock requested by the Minister for Railways. But most speakers laid responsibility for the chaos on Mr Venn and his 'autocratic' Engineer-in-Chief, who 'ruled him with a rod of iron'.

The meeting resolved that, 'to avert the ruin that will surely befall the community if the present Minister of Works and Railways be permitted to continue in office, and the present telegraphic muddle be permitted to any longer exist', they would present the Premier with what was essentially an ultimatum. Sort out the mess or face the consequences. Replace the Minister for Railways and put someone with some ability in charge of telegraph and postal services. If the Premier failed to respond, or worse, refused to meet with them, they would approach the Governor with their grievances.[443]

A similar public meeting occurred in Fremantle a few days later, at which those attending called for 'a reconstruction of the whole cabinet, as soon as possible'.[444]

Harry Venn was not happy with what he read in the papers. On 26 February, he wrote a long memo to the Premier, accusing him of not supporting him in his ministry.

> *'At the hands of the Press for some time past I have been personally assailed for want of foresight in providing rolling stock to meet the growing demands of the traffic, and, however unfair this criticism has been, I have stoutly defended the Government...'*

He reminded the Premier that in the discussion of the Loans Bill in 1894, the department had asked for 200,000 pounds worth of stock for open lines, and 130,000 pounds for lines proposed to be constructed.

> *'...this sum you said you were quite unable to grant, as you were not prepared to face Parliament with a larger loan than 1,500,000 pounds. You will remember the circumstances because, having cut the sum total down to 174,000 pounds, Mr. O'Connor saw you personally, and urged that the items should be increased, when he was distinctly told that the Government were not prepared to increase the amount of the loan, nor were they prepared to cut out any item in favour of rolling stock.*
>
> *I have no hesitation in saying that had the Government at the time seen their way clear to have met the wishes of the department, and had Parliament voted the money, our present difficulties would not have arisen'.*

Venn attached a report and a memo from the Chief Engineer to support his claims.

When he didn't get the response he wanted from John Forrest, he sent the memo to the *West Australian.* They published it on 29 February.[445] Other newspapers followed suit.

Most people, including Premier Forrest, expected Minister Venn to resign after this outburst. What followed instead was a war of words in the press. On 2 March, one of the key speakers from the public meeting in Perth, Frank Wilson, released a series of letters between himself and the Premier, in which John Forrest disputed Wilson's claim, based on Venn's information, that the lack of rolling stock was due to his government's refusal to accept the request for funds.[446]

Forrest had declined to meet with the delegation from the public meeting to discuss most of their resolutions, claiming that the motions agreed to were unconstitutional and unprecedented.[447] This aroused much ill feeling towards the usually popular Premier among the public.

Harry Venn, meanwhile, refused to resign, even when asked to do so by the Premier and cabinet. After only five years of self-government, the colony was facing a political crisis without precedent in the other colonies.

On Sunday, 8 March 1896, John Forrest visited the Governor.[448] The following day he telegraphed Venn, who had gone to his country home at Dardanup, informing him of his formal dismissal from office by His Excellency the Governor. The news reached Venn late at night, after he had gone to bed. He received it in his nightgown and delayed replying until the next morning.

His initial response to Forrest simply acknowledged receiving the news of his dismissal. But later he also wrote another, more bitter, letter to his former colleague. He would have expected, he wrote, that such an important announcement would have been conveyed to him directly from the Governor. He had every intention of resigning. In fact, his letter of resignation was already written and signed. He had planned to deliver it after being given the opportunity to put his case to the cabinet when it next met.

'I can only add I am unable to appreciate the indecent haste and hostility you have shown by your actions towards one with whom you have been so closely associated, for so many years shoulder to shoulder in the development of the political life of this colony.'

All these letters, and many more, appeared in the newspapers in the days that followed, including Harry Venn's unsent letter of resignation. Some were highly personal. The *West Australian*, though it published the letters and memos in full, expressed 'extreme surprise' that they should have been made public.[449]

Soon the Chief Engineer was pulled further into the fray. John Forrest, still wanting to vindicate himself, forwarded to the newspapers a copy of the report written by O'Connor to Venn in February 1896, which Venn had sent to Forrest with his original memo. Forrest also submitted to the papers letters from O'Connor to Venn and from Venn to himself as Premier. Forrest had annotated what he claimed were errors in O'Connor's figures and recollections of dates. Almost every item in the report carried a comment from the Premier. For instance, to item 4 of O'Connor's report:

> *'On 20th July 1894, I forwarded on this requisition for your consideration, at the same time stating that the number of trucks asked for would entail locomotives to work them ...'*

John Forrest added, 'This must be an error, as the requisition had been complied with on the 6th July...'

Item 13 of O'Connor's report:

> *'On 18th January, 1895, prior to making recommendation to the Minister, I asked Mr. Jull how the funds stood and got reply to effect that the balance of loan allocation (excluding the provision for Collie and Bridgetown railways, which was not voted) was only £27,000.'*

John Forrest's comment on this: 'Why was not this £27,000 used? It would have purchased 270 trucks, and why was indent not sent forward at once on the 8th November, 1894?'

After two items describing the process within the department, O'Connor's report came to item 16:

> *'On April 9th, 1895, I informed the General Traffic Manager of the condition of affairs in order that he might have an opportunity of still further urging the matter if he so chose.'*

John Forrest commented: 'From the 12th January, when Mr. Davies made the requisition, to the 9th April, when he was replied to [is] three months, rather a long time, I should say.'

Forrest repeated the claim that some of the money allocated for rolling stock hadn't been spent and denied that any representation had been made 'in a formal manner' to himself or the cabinet on the matter.

Such adverse comments, if made in a private meeting, would be considered frank but possibly fair. Published in a newspaper without O'Connor's knowledge or consent, they were disrespectful.[450]

O'Connor had been in Bunbury inspecting the harbour there while much of this was taking place. On his return, he was called to an extended interview with John Forrest to discuss the operations of the Public Works Department.[451] Until Forrest appointed Frederick Piesse in April to replace Harry Venn, he was not only Premier, treasurer and colonial secretary (following the resignation of Stephen Parker in December 1894) but also acting Commissioner for Railways and Minister for Public Works.[452]

No record exists of what was said at the meeting, but it must have been a very uncomfortable situation for O'Connor. Minister Venn had always been supportive of him and his work, both inside and outside parliament, while Forrest had only recently attacked his reputation publicly by calling into question the accuracy of his figures and his memory of events.

As he returned home to Fremantle later that day, it must have been soothing and satisfying to see the river mouth come into view before him, with the Indian Ocean as its backdrop. Under John McDonald's supervision, the harbour works were progressing well. Where once there had been turbulent water washing over the rocky bar, the river now flowed smoothly. The two dredges were still busy at work, while out on the pontoons, blasting continued to deepen and widen the channel. A flotilla of other craft assisted with the work, carrying supplies and a small army of workers.

Across the river, from Rous Head, tall-masted ships were already berthed alongside the completed north mole. Nearly fifteen hundred feet of the south mole had already been constructed from Arthur Head.

Along the river on the south side, an embankment ten feet high above the low water mark had been thrown up along the river's edge, all the way from the river mouth to the railway bridge. This embankment would soon become a retaining wall, holding back silt deposited by the pump dredge. Once the process was completed, this reclaimed land would be used to build the wharves on the south bank. The port town was becoming unrecognisable to anyone who had seen it just four years earlier.[453] Here in Fremantle, at least, O'Connor's vision was being vindicated.

TWENTY-FOUR: Running amok – 1896

The population boom that created so many problems for the railway and telegraph services was proving even more disastrous for the Fremantle Lunatic Asylum. And Dr Barnett's once polite relationship with the government was rapidly declining into animosity.

Among the thousands of men attracted to the colony by the lure of gold, many had a history of unstable mental health. Conditions on the goldfields were not conducive to mental stability. Relentless heat, thirst, overuse of alcohol, disease, disappointment and loneliness could affect even the strongest mind. With only one asylum in the colony, those afflicted found their way to Fremantle. The number of male admissions to the asylum had always outnumbered females, but now the disparity became far more marked.

During the previous year, 1895, Dr Barnett had admitted thirty-six new patients. In 1896 this rose to ninety, and only stopped at that number because there was simply no more room. That was despite fifteen deaths, and forty-nine patients discharged during the year. The discharges included seventeen Chinese patients transferred to Singapore.

Dr Barnett had foreseen what would happen. In his annual report for 1895, submitted in January 1896, he warned the government that:

> *'...the continual influx of patients will soon fill the present building and make it impossible to admit more; and even should the Government determine to build an asylum on some other site it would take years to do so, and as population augments we must look for a rapid increase in*

(the) number of lunatics.'[454]

The government and its officials seemed oblivious. Not long after this warning from Dr Barnett, a woman named Louise Scanlon arrived at the asylum with her son Victor, an ungainly looking boy of about twelve with a disfigured face. The woman told the attendant who opened the gate that she had come to have her son admitted, and produced a letter from the under-secretary, Octavius Burt, along with a medical certificate from a doctor.

'Madam,' the letter said, 'in reply to your letter, undated, I have the honor to inform you that if you can obtain the necessary certificate under the lunacy act from a medical man, your son can be admitted to the Lunatic Asylum at Fremantle.'

Mrs Scanlon explained that Victor was her second child, one of six. She had written to the Premier, John Forrest, asking for her son to be admitted to an asylum because 'the poor boy is a very serious loss and trouble to me by reason of his being demented and injuring himself and the other children, breaking the furniture and crockery in the house. He is more than one person's work to watch so as to keep him from injuring himself.'

Dr Barnett listened to her story then explained that he simply couldn't admit the boy until he had the staff to take care of him. Mrs Scanlon left, disappointed, with her son. The next morning, Dr Barnett took a sheet of the official letterhead paper used for internal communication with the government and wrote to the under-secretary.

> *'Under the circumstances I would at once have admitted him, had it been practicable, but the case is a special one, requiring constantly to be looked after, and I have no attendant suitable for this duty.'*

If he admitted the boy to the women's ward 'he would create an excitement which you cannot imagine'. The effect of leaving 'this weak-minded, epileptic boy' unattended even for a few moments among some of the male patients 'who have no more control of their passions than so many wild beasts' would be disastrous.

'The boy is quite helpless, frequently falls down, his face is now badly burned from falling into the fire,' he wrote. He requested authority to advertise for an additional male attendant. When he had this help, he would write informing Mrs Scanlon that her son could be admitted.

Octavius Burt sent back a terse note in point form. Though couched as questions, there were no question marks:

1. *Were the medical certificates forthcoming. If so, I think he should have been admitted. Surely your staff is already large enough.*
2. *How many male patients have you, and how many are decrepit, half-dead creatures*
3. *Do you really mean that this lad must have a special attendant*

Dr Barnett responded. Regarding point one, he had already explained why he couldn't admit the boy, despite the necessary medical certificate being produced. In answer to point two:

> *'There are 115 males, of whom more than twenty are totally helpless. These are the patients who are most bothersome, and on whom incessant care has to be bestowed. Most of them cannot retain their urine or their motions. Daily, and sometimes several times a day, the poor creatures have to be stripped, the filth washed from them, and dry clothing put upon them, while the filthy clothing has to be washed, work which the attendants must do, though they abhor it.*
>
> *As I understood your forgoing letter to be an order, I shall direct that the boy be admitted.'*

As to point 3,

> *'... epileptic imbeciles are not fit to mingle with other patients and cannot do so without being at risk of what (among some people) would be called criminal attack. I already have one poor imbecile boy named Francis*

> *who is totally unable to walk or stand, and who could be looked after by same attendant.'*

After signing his letter, Dr Barnett added a postscript: 'I have written to Mrs Scanlon that the boy will be admitted.'

Mrs Scanlon returned with Victor and left him at the asylum. Dr Barnett's reservations about admitting the boy would only be reinforced by events a few months later.

Dr Barnett's thoughts apparently ran in gloomy channels during these months. On 13 February, the West Australian published a letter from him, headed 'Disposal of town refuse and of the dead'.

'Sir,' it began,

> *'The offensive refuse of our cities should be disposed of in whichever way is least injurious to mankind, and the same statement applies to those bodies which during life we inhabit, and which after death should not be converted into a cause of disease and death.... In both cases there is but one effectual way—they should be consumed by fire.'*

Dr Barnett gave no reason for why he had been thinking about incineration, cremation and disposing of the dead. There had been no discussion of these topics in the newspapers. But the numerous examples he gave of cremation being used around the world, complete with statistics, suggested he had given it a lot of thought and done his research.

Perhaps he was motivated only by his long-standing interest in public health. Perhaps the proximity of the Skinner Street cemetery to the asylum had brought the question to mind.[455] It was Fremantle's main cemetery and funeral processions would regularly pass the asylum. Or perhaps he was mindful of his own mortality.

His letter concluded:

> *'West Australia possesses abundance of fuel, not merely in its forests but*

> *in its extensive coal deposits, and I hope that soon a properly planned crematorium may be erected, and that gradually we may cease to perpetuate the odious and dangerous system of interment.'*

There would be no crematorium in Fremantle for another fifty years. It must have seemed at times that the promised new asylum was just as far off. A committee, which included Dr Barnett, had been set up to examine potential sites, but it would be many months before they submitted their report. Meanwhile the present asylum was in crisis.

In April 1896, the government commissioned the architectural branch of the Public Works Department, under George Temple Poole, to draw up plans for a new female wing on the south side of the existing asylum buildings, so that the quarters currently occupied by the women could be taken over for male patients. But by August, the plans were still waiting for Poole's approval.[456] No tenders were called, and by the end of the year the extensions had not even been started.[457]

The ever-increasing workload placed an immense strain on all the staff. In February, one of the longest serving warders, James McKeown, was presented with a watch in appreciation of his thirty years' service to the colony. He had spent twelve years as a prison warder and eighteen as a warder at the asylum. The staff wished him 'a happy continuance of his long and usefully applied energies.'[458]

By 31 March he was dead, the result of a burst blood vessel.[459] Doctors Barnett, Wheeler and Lotz tried unsuccessfully to resuscitate him. He was fifty years old.

In July, admissions to the asylum for the year had already exceeded those of the previous year. Overcrowding inevitably led to more difficulties in managing violent patients. That same month, a temporary warder, Harrington, was assaulted and seriously injured by a patient. Another warder, Gallagher, who came to his help was also injured. His ankle was badly dislocated, and he required several months' recuperation. But because of the shortage of staff, he returned to work as soon as he could walk.[460]

Even in far-away Coolgardie, people were aware of the dire situation at the

Fremantle asylum. On 4 July, the *Coolgardie Miner* noted that the generally inept Public Works Department was wisely hurrying forward plans for the new building. In what would prove a strangely prophetic comment, the columnist remarked:

'...even when that useful building is erected, we suppose the usual game of contraries will be played and the harmless poet or political driveller will be confined in a strait waistcoat and a padded cell, while the demoniac afflicted with homicidal mania roams at large with a meat-axe down High-street.'[461]

Overcrowding wasn't the only problem Henry Barnett had to deal with. A letter published in the West Australian on 27 August created great consternation among the staff of the asylum. The anonymous letter writer, calling himself (or herself) 'One Behind the Scene', claimed that a boy of about ten or eleven years of age, named Victor Scanlon, was being kept in the men's wing of the asylum. The letter's author also claimed that the boy, who had fits but showed no evidence of insanity, was subject to assaults by the other patients which left scars on his face.[462]

The warders immediately wrote in protest to Dr Barnett, pointing out that the claim that Scanlon was uncared for and even maltreated was 'nothing short of a base and abominable falsehood,' intended to discredit them.

'We are not perfection, but our humanity has not yet descended to such a degenerate state as to tolerate a boy of tender years being ill-treated when placed in our charge. Victor Scanlon not only gets what is allowed him by the rules of this institution, but is actually made a pet of both by the employees and patients,' they wrote.

Dr Barnett included their letter of protest when he responded to 'One Behind the Scene' in a letter to the *West Australian,* published on 29 August. The claims made were utterly untrue, he said. He had recently examined the boy thoroughly and the only mark of violence found was a swollen lip, which the boy himself said was the result of a seizure.

'He tells me that no one ever hurt him, and I know that the warders, as a rule, are very kind and careful of the poor child. I am fortunate in having a staff who are forbearing and gentle to these unfortunate inmates, though they frequently have much provocation to bear with.'

An anonymous attack on his staff's integrity and competence was grossly unfair, he said. He requested that the letter writer's name be published, or at least that the original letter be forwarded to him.

Dr Barnett used the opportunity to remind everyone, especially the government, of how overcrowded the asylum had become. He also reminded readers that he had been saying for years that children with congenital disabilities, such as Victor Scanlan, should be cared for in their own institution, for their own sake and for the sake of other asylum patients. After quoting his own annual report from ten years earlier, he concluded,

'...circumstances compel me to once again repeat the words, for, though additions have been made to the buildings, the increase of lunacy is so rapid that the urgency now is worse than it was then.'[463]

'One Behind the Scenes' responded on 5 September. He had not intended to cast any slur on the staff of the asylum, he said. Nor did his letter allege that the boy was maltreated by them. However, he was certain that the boy had been assaulted by another patient, despite Dr Barnett's claim that his scar was due to a fit. The writer reiterated his main concern, that the child was not, in fact, insane and should therefore not be in the asylum at all.[464]

Nothing further appeared in the press. No inquiry was held. Victor Scanlon's death in May the following year went unnoticed by the press.[465]

On 4 July 1896, one of Fremantle's most popular residents died.[466] William E. (Bill) Marmion had been born in Fremantle and had been the town's representative in parliament since the 1870s. He was Minister for Mining and Commissioner for Lands in the Forrest government until he resigned in 1894, due to conflicts with his own mining and other business interests.

His scepticism about the harbour scheme and his support of those opposed to moving the railway workshops may not have won him any credit with C. Y. O'Connor. But he was an old friend of Henry Barnett, who attended his funeral at St Patrick's church. They had shared an interest in the Fremantle Rowing Club, the Literary Society and musical events. Dr Barnett joined a committee formed to raise a memorial to Marmion in Fremantle.[467]

Though Dr Barnett's involvement in the community was reduced now that he was no longer colonial surgeon, it still took up much of his spare time. He was elected as one of the vice-presidents of the Fremantle Literary Institute on 2 October, and vice-president of the Fremantle Musical Association three days later.[468]

On 11 November he attended the opening of the new North Fremantle Town Hall. Sir John Forrest, in opening the building, spoke of the many achievements of his government, including the new harbour, and the healthy state of the economy. He also provided an insight into his government's thinking.

'In a few words, the policy of the Government was summed up as "better facilities of transit, with the object of making the colony more productive."'[469]

The colony was certainly making great progress in improving its transport facilities under O'Connor's direction. But such a policy offered little to those who might be deemed unproductive and immobilised due to incarceration in the asylum. A few days after the speech, Henry Barnett visited the Premier, to personally impress on him the urgent need for more accommodation for the asylum patients. He reported that he came away 'comforted with the assurance that it would be attended to at once.'[470]

When nothing had happened by the beginning of December, Dr Barnett took matters into his own hands. He had a notice published in the *Government Gazette*, announcing that the asylum was full, and magistrates should not forward any more cases until they were sure that they could be accepted.

He also wrote to Dr Lovegrove, the colony's Principal Medical Officer, reminding him once again of the urgent need for more accommodation at the asylum, and informing him about the notice.

> *'The building of a new asylum will occupy years to build (sic) and the present asylum is full,' he wrote, underlining the words for emphasis. The Premier had given him assurances, but nothing had yet been done, 'nor will be until matters are placed in the hands of a contractor.'*

Dr Lovegrove, annoyed by Dr Barnett's action, wrote to under-secretary Burt:

> *'That additional temporary accommodation is required at the asylum there is no doubt. The Works Department however seems unable (or unwilling) to understand the kind of building required and appears determined to erect structures of a permanent kind and expensive [?] design or worse. All that is required is two large plain wards, a few good sized cells...which should be put up in a few weeks.*
>
> *'I do not think Dr Barnett should have notified in the gazette his inability to receive more patients. I see no reason why a few extra beds should not be placed in the larger wards and the corridors utilised for quiet patients.'*

This was not the response Dr Barnett had hoped for. But the under-secretary did at least contact the Works Department and asked that an officer discuss with Dr Lovegrove what could be done.

The discussion never took place. By the end of December, under-secretary Burt was advising Dr Lovegrove to see the Director of Public Works, Mr Piesse, himself.[471] By this time, George Temple Poole had resigned from the Public Works Department after he had been severely criticised in parliament for the slow pace at which public buildings were approved and constructed.[472] At a farewell function in his honour on 22 December, C. Y. O'Connor spoke warmly in defence of his 'great friend' George Poole, and his comments were reported in the newspapers.[473]

About this same time, newspaper reports arriving from London described the role of Henry Barnett's relative by marriage, Francis Hart, in an 'unseemly' disruption of a lecture given by David Draper, a geologist from South Africa. Francis had been the ringleader of a flag-waving group which objected noisily to Dr Draper's alleged pro-Boer, anti-British stance.[474]

Francis had left Perth for London in April, planning to set up a 'bureau of information' to promote Western Australia, particularly its mining industry.

He effectively abandoned his wife, Lilian, and their nine-year-old daughter, Geraldine, for the next two years.[475]

But George Poole's resignation and Francis Hart's outrageous behaviour looked insignificant beside other events in Fremantle that December. The *Coolgardie Miner*'s remark earlier in the year about homicidal maniacs roaming free, while the harmless were confined to the asylum, seemed horribly fulfilled.

On 3 December 1896, just after midday, Dr Wheeler was driving down High Street when he saw a crowd of people outside Church and Co.'s hardware shop. They were gathered around something on the ground.

As he came nearer, he realised it was the body of a man lying in the gutter in a pool of blood. He rushed over to help. The unconscious man, a wharf labourer named Griffiths, had a dreadful gash to his forehead, penetrating his skull to the cheekbone. The agitated onlookers were desperately but ineffectively trying to staunch the flow of blood with handkerchiefs.

Everyone was talking at once, but Dr Wheeler was able to gather that an Afghan man had rushed at Griffiths from behind, as he was leaning against one of the verandah posts outside the hardware store. Wielding an axe picked up from a pile outside the store, the Afghan had struck Griffiths in the head. He struck him again in the hip, before running off down High Street, shouting something unintelligible.

Dr Wheeler could see another crowd gathered further up the street, outside the Commercial Hotel, with policemen in attendance. People were running from all directions. Cries of 'Lynch him! Lynch him!' came as the police, with difficulty, bundled the handcuffed culprit away. His name was Jumna Khan.

The doctor arranged for Griffiths to be transported to the hospital, but the badly injured man died within minutes of arriving. Dr Wheeler assisted Dr Hope to perform a post-mortem.

Khan appeared in the Fremantle magistrates court the following morning. He had come to Western Australia from India and had been working as a camel driver between Morowa and Cue, north of Perth. Two days earlier he had arrived in Fremantle and had wandered aimlessly about the streets.

His intention was apparently to return to India but his attempts to buy tickets from several shipping companies were unsuccessful. He tried to find somewhere to stay but also failed at that. Several times he was moved on by the police.

On the morning of the attack, after retrieving his belongings from a coffee shop where he had left them the previous night, he went to buy a revolver at the Union Stores. He left without the gun when the shop assistant refused to load it for him.

Khan met with the same response when he tried to buy a gun at another shop. Asked why he wanted it, he said he wanted to shoot 'two men out in the bush who are drunk'. For the next three hours he wandered up and down the streets, a blanket over his shoulders, complaining to passers-by that he had been robbed. Then he grabbed the axe from the doorway of the ironmongers.[476]

After fatally striking Griffiths, he pursued, and would have killed, an elderly man, Thomas Henderson, if a bystander hadn't tried to deflect the axe blow. As it was, Henderson received a nasty gash to his shoulder. A young policeman, Constable Normoyle, managed to bring Khan down.

On the day of the hearing, the courtroom and the footpath outside overflowed with curious and angry onlookers. The local newspapers had described Khan as an 'insane Afghan' who killed in a 'fit of madness' or insanity.[477] Many in the crowd feared that Khan would indeed be found insane and escape the death penalty that they were determined should be applied.

Khan's appearance in court was brief. The charge was translated for him by an interpreter employed by the police, who reported that the prisoner understood what was said. The police magistrate, Mr Fairbairn, remanded Khan for eight days.[478]

When Khan reappeared in court on 11 December, his solicitor announced that his client would not be answering any questions or making any statements. Evidence was taken from witnesses, including Constable Normoyle and Dr Wheeler. Dr Hope reported the autopsy findings. He also gave evidence that he had visited Jumna Khan at the prison several times. He said Khan didn't speak good English, but he gave rational answers to the questions that he did understand.[479]

Khan was committed for trial at the Supreme Court in Perth. When he appeared in a packed courtroom on 19 December, before Mr Justice Stone, his lawyer asked that the case be adjourned, as he had not had time to gather his evidence. That Khan was guilty of killing Griffiths would not be denied, but he wished to show that Khan had shown signs of insanity on other occasions. Mr Stone and the Crown Solicitor agreed to the adjournment.[480] Khan returned to prison until the following March.

Dr Barnett's thoughts about Jumna Khan were not recorded. He seems never to have been consulted about the case. One thing was certain—there was no room for Khan at the asylum.

TWENTY-FIVE: Standing in tights on Mount Burgess – 1897

The Jumna Khan episode was disturbing to everyone living in Fremantle, including, no doubt, the O'Connor family. Such events might happen elsewhere, to be read about in the newspapers. But a murder in the main street of Fremantle, in broad daylight, created more than just a sense of wonder at the strange ways of humankind.

C. Y. O'Connor would have read about the case and heard it being discussed among his colleagues. Perhaps his family talked about it at home. But by the time Khan appeared in the Supreme Court to be tried for murder, O'Connor was far away in London. He was there to discuss plans to build a pipeline that would become one of the world's greatest engineering marvels.

The question of how to provide water to the Coolgardie goldfields had continued to trouble the government. As the population living on the goldfields rapidly increased, the problem grew in intensity. Not just residents, but also the mining industry, needed water. In September 1895, with another summer approaching, and the threat of a worsening typhoid outbreak looming, the mayor of Coolgardie wrote to Sir John Forrest imploring the government to act immediately 'to stem the tide of dissatisfaction verging on despair that is setting in here.'[481] John Forrest and his government were increasingly unpopular amongst goldfields residents.

Water conservation, tank building and carting water by road or rail could only stave off the crisis for so long. Drilling had shown that there was no great underground artesian basin in Western Australia, as in Queensland.

The solution was one which an imaginative child could have come up with—build a pipeline to carry water from the coast to the goldfields. The real question was how to build it. The pipeline would be over 350 miles long. There would have to be pumping stations at regular intervals. But the terrain it would have to cross would not pose any great difficulty from an engineering point of view.

C. Y. O'Connor made no claim to have originated the idea of building a pipeline to Kalgoorlie. He was not a hydraulic engineer, as his detractors would soon delight to point out. But his gifts and vision as an engineer, his ability to gather and inspire a team, and his reputation for producing what he promised, would enable him to bring it into being.

A letter from J. S. Talbot, a prospector, had appeared in the papers in early 1894, discussing the pipeline possibility.[482] In September 1894, John Maher, a New Zealand contractor, proposed to build a pipeline from the Swan River to the goldfields, but failed to get government approval for what would have been a privately owned and operated water supply.[483] The idea of a privately built scheme had the support of Alexander Forrest.[484] John Forrest was against such an important resource being in the hands of a private company. But once he saw that a pipeline might be possible, he liked the concept.

Forrest asked O'Connor to examine the feasibility of building a pipeline, fed by a dam in the Darling Ranges. Despite being in poor health at the time, O'Connor began working on the project in the last months of 1895, gathering information and measurements and consulting with hydraulic engineers. He continued working on it while attending more interrogations on the running of the railways by the Civil Service Commission.

In February 1896, when the crisis over lack of rolling stock for the railways was at its peak, newspapers began reporting details of the proposed pipeline scheme. The Premier promoted it boldly in Coolgardie when he opened the new railway line in March 1896. He promised the cheering locals that his government would not only provide them with better railways and increased representation in parliament, but also with a water supply scheme that would bring water from the coast to the top of Mount Burgess (a local landmark to the northeast of Coolgardie).[485]

By 17 July 1896, the Engineer-in-Chief had presented his report to the new Minister for Public Works, Fred Piesse, and the government began pushing the *Goldfields Water Supply Scheme Loan Bill* through parliament.[486]

Inevitably, the project had its opponents. Harry Venn, the former Minister for Works, was incensed by John Forrest's adoption of the scheme as if it was his own idea. Speaking in the Legislative Assembly on 6 August, for the first time since his dismissal, he said he had asked the Chief Engineer to look at the figures for such a scheme when he was minister, chiefly with the intention of showing that it would be prohibitively expensive.

'It was some time after this,' he continued, 'that the Premier, standing, as it were, in tights on Mount Burges (sic), balanced himself on one leg on top of a balloon, and talked about living waters converting the wilderness into smiling farms and enchanting flower gardens. When this thing took on with the honourable gentleman, as usual with him, everything was swept out of his way like a tornado.'[487]

The scheme's estimated cost of two and a half million pounds was certainly enough to make many parliamentarians wince. Some doubted that it was necessary and disputed the rainfall figures O'Connor quoted in his report. They wanted alternatives, such as drilling, to be further investigated.

Others were concerned that the gold mining boom might be short-lived, leaving the colony unable to pay the debt for a pipeline that was no longer needed.[488]

Then there were those who misunderstood how the scheme would work and doubted that water could be pumped up a gradient of 2,500 feet over several hundred miles. (Coolgardie is only 1,400 feet above sea level, but O'Connor took into account the effect of friction in calculating the height the water had to be lifted.)[489]

In his report, O'Connor responded to all these objections and strongly defended himself against the accusation that he was pushing the scheme onto the government.

'...I never urged, nor do I now propose to urge, upon the Government or

the country, the undertaking of this work. [B]ut while it would evidently be quite improper for me to do that, it is equally evident that if I am called upon by the Government to give an opinion as to the best way of attaining a certain object, it is clearly my duty to give such opinion to the best of my ability.'

The cost of pumping 5 million gallons of water daily to Coolgardie would be offset by selling the water in Coolgardie and along the way, he explained. It was already clear that other sources of water, such as artesian bores, were neither viable nor cost-effective. As to the objection that it was impractical to pump water to the height required, it was based on the false assumption that the water would have to be pumped to that height from its origin in the Darling range. The scheme involved a series of eight to ten pumping stations along the route, each of which had to raise the water only 300 feet or so.[490]

O'Connor concluded his report by recommending that the government arrange to consult with specialists in England about various aspects of the scheme.

With John Forrest's keen support, the bill passed through the Legislative Assembly in August and the Council in September 1896. O'Connor had forwarded plans to Sir John Carruthers, an old friend and consulting engineer in London, to pass on to a commission of engineers for their review.[491] In order to persuade bankers to lend the huge sum required to build the pipeline, it would be important to have the backing and advice of reputable engineers experienced in such major undertakings.

Encouraged by the government, O'Connor made plans to go to London himself to discuss the project in person.[492] John McDonald, currently in charge of harbour works, would be appointed acting engineer-in-chief in his absence.

Due to a number of delays, O'Connor didn't leave Albany for England until 23 January 1897. The staff of the Public Works Department gave him a hastily organised but warm-hearted farewell at the Criterion Hotel in Perth on the morning of 19 January. Everyone, from the minister down, wished him *bon voyage.* Martin Jull, the under-secretary of the Works Department, spoke of the good feeling which existed between the Engineer-in-Chief and the staff generally. He said Mr. O'Connor possessed their high esteem, both personally and professionally.[493]

O'Connor was leaving the department in good order. During the previous year, the unwieldy department had been reorganised into three divisions, each under its own engineer-in-charge, and each with its own office space. This was something O'Connor had been urging the government to do ever since his arrival in the colony and it had lifted the burden of dealing with every minor matter from his own shoulders.[494]

On 23 December 1896, the government had also finally relieved him of the post of General Manager of railways, appointing John Davies in his place.[495] Whatever O'Connor's thoughts about this appointment, he left the colony for London with the knowledge that there were competent engineers in charge of the work he left behind.

He travelled without his family. The two youngest children, Bridget and Murtagh, were still at school. Taking Susan and the family would have been expensive and there was little point in uprooting them for what was meant to be a short business trip.

Almost as soon as he arrived in London, the newspapers in Western Australia announced that the Commission of Engineers had 'virtually adopted' the goldfields pipeline plans.[496] But the commissioners—John Carruthers, George F. Deacon and Professor William Unwin—needed to go through the scheme in detail with O'Connor. He wanted their advice on the best type of pipe to use, where to locate the pumping stations and other details. While in London, O'Connor also planned to consult with manufacturers and engineers on matters related to the railways and Fremantle Harbour.

As a base, he rented an office in Victoria Street, above the Agent General's Department. This was convenient for meeting with the Agent himself, who acted as a representative in England for the West Australian government. Once the project had the go-ahead, the Agent General would be the one to call for tenders to supply materials. But it was also an opportunity to catch up with his old friend and mentor, Sir Malcolm Fraser, who still held the position.[497]

Just after his arrival in London, O'Connor was interviewed by a reporter on behalf of the *Coolgardie Miner.* The report was published on 3 May, the day before the harbour at Fremantle would be unofficially opened.

O'Connor first explained to the interviewer why he was in England, the role of the expert commissioners, and when he expected to receive their report.

'By the way,' he added rather testily, 'I do not wish this scheme to be misunderstood. I court the fullest criticism, but before people commence to write about it, they should certainly make themselves acquainted with all the facts. The allegations which appeared in the 'Saturday Review' of January 30 last to the effect that the water scheme is impracticable is simply ridiculous.'

He was referring to an article by 'A Coolgardie correspondent' that appeared in the London newspaper, *Saturday Review.* Sceptical about the whole scheme, the writer had in effect warned the London money market not to invest in it.[498]

'...It is not a compliment either to the Parliament or to the Government of Western Australia,' O'Connor continued, 'to suppose that they would have passed a scheme that was impracticable, and still less to suppose that they would have approved of the altogether ridiculous scheme which the writer in the "Saturday Review" seems to have evolved out of his inner consciousness, and which bears no resemblance whatever to the scheme actually proposed by the Government engineers.

'...As I explained to a friend of mine the other day, what I proposed to do was to pump the water up eight or ten separate steps—not to jump the whole flight of stairs in one leap, as the writer in the "Saturday Review" led people to suppose.'

'But it has been stated here, Mr O'Connor,' the interviewer said, 'that the scheme is not wanted, and that in the near future the goldfields will have more water than they know what to do with?'

'So it has been stated in the colony, but that fallacy I think by this time has been exploded,' O'Connor replied. He produced details to support his argument.

After several more questions, the interviewer asked, 'And how are the Fremantle harbour works progressing?'

'By next December, I think,' O'Connor replied, 'we shall be able to let in ships drawing 20ft., but it will be two years later before we can let in ocean steamers drawing 30ft. As a matter of fact, however, there is really no reason why they should not go to Fremantle now, for along the southern slope of the North Mole we are erecting a water berth wharf 1,000ft. in length with a depth of 27ft. at the ocean end...I have to-day received a cable gram stating that 300ft. of this wharf has been completed, and will be ready for shipping in a fortnight.'[499]

It would indeed be nearly three years before ocean steamers such as the mail ships were able to enter the new harbour. But O'Connor had overestimated how long it would be before other ships would berth, not just outside along the mole, but inside the inner harbour itself.

TWENTY-SIX: The Sultan arrives – 1897

Under John McDonald's able supervision, the harbour works had progressed more rapidly than anyone, including O'Connor, could have imagined. With work going on around the clock, except for blasting, the first 1000 feet of the wharf along the river's southern edge was completed by 27 February 1897.[500] There was still much work to be done, but by April 1897 the harbour was ready to accept steam ships, though not yet the larger mail ships.

O'Connor had originally intended to return to Western Australia by April. When interviewed in London, he said he would be returning in June. But when the Queen's Jubilee Honours list was announced on 22 June, it included Charles Yelverton O'Connor's name among those appointed Companions of St Michael and St George (C.M.G.). The honour came in recognition of his services to the colony.[501] Sir John Forrest, who would arrive in London with Lady Forrest on 7 June, was to be appointed a member of the Queen's Privy Council. There was no question of O'Connor leaving London until after the investiture ceremony at St James Palace on 21 July.

Consequently, when the owners of the steamship *Sultan* asked, and were granted, permission in April to berth at the new wharf at Fremantle on her next voyage from Singapore, O'Connor was still at work in London.[502] As things turned out, he would not arrive back in Fremantle until September. The ceremony to welcome the *Sultan* would have to proceed without him.

The *Sultan* would be the first ocean-going vessel to enter the inner harbour and the occasion, on 4 May 1897, would become the unofficial but much-celebrated opening of the new port.

Preparations for the event were marred by tragedy. On the evening of 1 May, a boat manoeuvring the anchor of the dredge *Parmelia* capsized when the anchor's weight shifted unexpectedly. All the crew were sucked down into the water by the sinking boat. Five men struggled to the surface and were rescued by other boats. Two—Richard Ingram and Edward Phillips—disappeared.

Despite a desperate search in the dark, rescuers could not find them. The search continued the following day, using the dredges from the harbour works and a diver. The sunken boat and the anchor chain were recovered, but the two men's bodies remained missing.

The water police informed John McDonald, and George H. Royce, the resident engineer in charge of the harbour works. Both were to be aboard the *Sultan* when it entered the harbour a few days later. Perhaps, the searchers speculated, the drowned men had been washed out to sea by the current. But there remained the awful possibility that their swollen bodies might re-appear in front of the *Sultan* and her cargo of dignitaries.[503]

Just after 11 o'clock, on the morning of Tuesday, 4 May, the *SS Sultan* left its temporary moorings at the long jetty in Gage Roads, under the command of Captain Frank Pitts.[504] The ship, with its distinctive blue funnel, slowly rounded the recently completed south mole. In the clear but chilly air of early winter, the multicoloured flags festooning the *Sultan's* rigging fluttered like carnival bunting. Many smaller boats, similarly decorated, accompanied the steam ship on this short but historic voyage. Captain McDonald from the dredge 'Fremantle' was aboard as pilot.

As the ship approached the mouth of the Swan River, Captain McDonald handed the wheel to Lady Margaret Forrest. She would have the honour of steering the first ocean-going steam ship into the newly constructed harbour.

If Lady Forrest was nervous about taking a 2,000-ton ship with a draft of nineteen feet into a channel that had, until recently, been impassable to anything bigger than a sailing boat, she didn't show it. Sir John Forrest's broad chest swelled with pride at his wife's poise and grace, but even more at the success of his government's greatest project so far.

Some aboard the flag-bedecked ship watched nervously as the *Sultan* began turning to dock alongside the wharf on the south quay. Sceptics had long claimed that the channel was too narrow for an ocean-going steam ship to rotate. But when the *Sultan* arrived at the south quay, just on noon, she proved the sceptics wrong as she effortlessly swung around in the channel and moored alongside the wharf.

This was not an official opening ceremony. The wharf was still a construction site, littered with piles of timber, railway trucks and building materials. The dredges, moored for now, would soon be back at work on the unfinished channel. Flags of all the shipping companies trading with Fremantle flew from their temporary site on the tower of the harbour works office.

But the crowds lining the quay—men and boys in suits, women in dark winter dresses, some holding young children aloft, some with umbrellas unfurled against the sun—cheered and applauded as the *Sultan* arrived. At last Fremantle had a harbour capable of receiving ocean-going vessels.

The wharf on which they were standing had been a sandbank where children swam and played just five years earlier.[505]

On board the *Sultan*, the invited dignitaries moved from their seats on the forward decks, down the mid-ship staircase into the saloon. They included members of both houses of parliament, the mayor of Fremantle, officials from the Public Works Department, the Railways Department and of course, the Fremantle Harbour works. Many of the guests were accompanied by their wives.

Consular representatives from the United States and Sweden also joined them, along with Captain Thomas, who had been sailing in and out of Fremantle as a trading mariner for sixty-seven years.

The ship's crew moved about quietly serving lunch to the gathered guests seated in the brown velvet-cord upholstery of the saloon. The *Sultan*, along with its sister ship the *Saladin*, had been built three years earlier, specifically for trading between Australia and Asia.[506] Her crew were all recruited from

Asia, a fact that didn't go unnoticed.

'The boat which occupied the post of honour, was a Chinese trader, manned by a crew of heathens,' said a letter to the *West Australian* newspaper a few days later. Couldn't a British-crewed ship have been found for such an important occasion, the indignant writer asked.[507]

When all had eaten and drunk sufficient, Charles Bethell, the London-based owner of the *Sultan*, proposed a toast to the health of Sir John and Lady Forrest. The advancement of the colony under Sir John had been marvellous, he said. People in London had heard of the railways and public works spreading in all directions in Western Australia, and news had reached them of the grand scheme to build a water pipeline to Coolgardie. Last but not least, they had heard that the grand harbour scheme at Fremantle was a *fait-accompli*. No-one in London could have imagined that such undertakings could have made such progress in so short a time, he said. He might have added 'in what was once such a small and backward colony' but refrained.

Wherever he travelled along the West Australian coastline, he continued, pastoralists, storekeepers, mining men and pearlers all told him that they believed Sir John was doing his utmost to further their interests.

After an enthusiastic toast was raised and drunk, Sir John Forrest stood and responded. 'It is a proud day for the people of Fremantle, the people of the colony and for myself and other members of the government,' he said, 'in having the privilege of coming into the Fremantle harbour in an ocean-going steamer.'

The chief credit of the scheme, he went on, was due to the Engineer-in-Chief, Mr. C. Y. O'Connor.

'I cannot speak too highly of the conduct of this gentleman with regard to this work. Mr O'Connor took upon himself a great responsibility and risked his reputation as an engineer by putting forward proposals that did not accord with those of engineers of world-wide reputation,' said Forrest, alluding to Sir John Coode.

His audience applauded politely, though a little uncertainly. Perhaps they recalled Sir John Forrest's own initial objections to Mr O'Connor's harbour scheme.

'In this colony we have had the civilisation and wealth of the old world passing by us for a half-century, and it was passing by us today. We did not realise it,' said Sir John.

'The works have progressed at a rate beyond all anticipation, and this is due to the admirable work done by the engineering staff under the direction of the executive engineer, who is at present the acting engineer-in-chief, Mr. J. A. McDonald.

'Twelve months ago, that gentleman had to complete a dredged channel of sufficient width to admit ocean-going steamers drawing 20 feet of water, together with the construction of 1,000 feet of wharf on the south side of the river. Not only has he been able to carry out those works, but actually had them finished three months sooner than the time stipulated.'

After more applause, Sir John listed the progress made by the colony since being granted responsible government in 1890, along with the work still to be done. 'We have covered the country with railways and telegraphs. But if we had never done anything else than form the harbor at Fremantle, we would have done enough to immortalise the establishment of self-government in Western Australia,' he said, to a cheer from the crowd. 'Looking back on all that has been accomplished, I think that we have great cause for congratulating ourselves.'

'I am going to the old country in a few days,' Sir John continued. 'It will assist me considerably at home in promoting future plans, to be able to tell the people in England that a large ocean-going steamer has already berthed alongside the river wharf.'

'Above all,' he concluded, 'I am pleased that my wife should have had the honour of steering the first steamer into the river and to a safe mooring in the port of Fremantle.'

It was a long speech. But the applause was loud as he proposed a toast to the health of the *Sultan's* owners, Mr and Mrs Bethell.

Sir James Lee Steere, Speaker in the Legislative Assembly and a former midshipman in the merchant navy, proposed a toast to the engineering staffs of the Harbour Works. It proved to be a back-handed toast.

They had come into the harbour on the *Sultan* on an exceptionally fine day, with favourable weather, he said. Consider what might happen in the event of a nor-west gale. The place would be most unsafe for large vessels such as the mail steamers, which were double the length of the *Sultan*.

'Engineers have two faults', he went on. 'First, they will not take advice from anyone.'

The audience laughed, unsure where this was heading.

'If they had taken advice from people versed in nautical matters,' Sir James continued, 'more could have been done to make Fremantle harbour suitable for mail steamers.

'Second, engineers don't know the value of the money expended in carrying out the work entrusted to them. However, if I blame anyone, I blame the government.'

An awkward silence followed. John McDonald stepped in.

'I would be very pleased,' he responded, 'to enter the harbour under the conditions suggested by Sir James Lee Steere, with dead low water, a norwesterly gale and a larger vessel.

'And I would be more than pleased if Captain Pitts were in command,' he added, with a nod to the Captain of the *Sultan*.

'Hear, hear,' cried the audience, laughing.

'As a matter of fact, the works have been carried out at a cost of forty per cent less than the scheduled price approved by Parliament,' chipped in George Royce, the acting Executive Engineer.

'And part of the works at fifty-five percent less,' added McDonald.

Royce had the last word.

'It was engineering skill that effected this saving, and as the staffs were working night and day to bring the works to a speedy conclusion, it must be conceded that the undertaking had progressed satisfactorily.'

As the applause died away, Fred Piesse, Director of Public Works, proposed a toast to the *Sultan's* Captain Pitts, and thanked the two engineers for their tireless work. Bonhomie was restored and Sir John Forrest brought the luncheon to a close.[508]

Charles Yelverton O'Connor's genius in designing and building the harbour had been acknowledged in his absence. But the day belonged very much to Sir John Forrest. It was also an auspicious day for Frederick Vosper, the editor of the Coolgardie Miner, who was elected to the Legislative Assembly as a member for North-East Coolgardie the same day.[509]

Two days after the Sultan's triumphant entry to the harbour, the disfigured body of a man came to the surface of the harbour near the south mole. It belonged to one of the harbour workers missing after the boating accident on 1 May. The body of the other man was found on the same day, not far from where their boat had sunk.

The jury at the inquest found that the two men, Richard Ingram and Edward Phillips, were accidentally drowned while performing their duty. Six hundred people, including all the officers and men employed on the harbour works, attended their funeral.[510]

Their deaths brought to at least eight those killed while working on the harbour, with many others seriously injured. 'While performing their duty', men like Phillips and Ingram had helped transform not just Fremantle harbour but the whole landscape of Fremantle.

Six months later, another man would die 'while performing his duty', not at the harbour this time but at the asylum.

TWENTY-SEVEN: A valued government official – 1897

On 22 January 1897, the newly renovated and extended 'Knowle' was officially opened as Fremantle Government Hospital. 'The wards are splendidly airy and bright rooms, opening by means of French windows towards the sea. Around the whole front a 10ft. balcony runs, forming one of the best features of the building, and providing a promenade and lounge for convalescents where they may reap the full benefit of the invigorating sea breezes,' the *West Australian* reported enthusiastically.[511] Fremantle residents were delighted.

A few days prior to the opening, the government announced that a 1,000-acre site had been selected, and land purchased, for the new asylum.[512] It would be built at Whitby Falls, a rural area thirty miles south of Perth. The location had its attractions. The surrounding countryside was picturesque, and the property already had several buildings which might be adapted for use while the new asylum was built. It also had an established orchard and gardens. The nearest railway siding, at Serpentine, was only a mile away.

But Dr Barnett was not happy. He had visited potential sites with the other members of the Asylum committee, headed by the Principal Medical Officer, Dr Thomas Lovegrove. In Dr Barnett's opinion, the Whitby Falls site would be difficult for patients and visitors to access and would condemn the staff to an isolated existence, far from the city or any large town.[513] His objections went unheeded. By June, a group of twelve inmates from the asylum had been sent to Whitby Falls under the care of attendant Gallagher, to clear land and cultivate the gardens.[514]

On 10 February, Henry Barnett celebrated his sixty-fifth birthday. He had spent the last twenty-five years as superintendent of the asylum. The staff marked the occasion by presenting him with a specially commissioned photo collection, mounted in a frame. Portraits of all the nurses and warders surrounded one of Dr Barnett himself, while an artist's impression of the asylum building formed the background. After the presentation, the staff and invited guests drank his health and that of Mrs Barnett 'with enthusiasm'.[515]

The photo of Henry shows him looking unwell. His unsmiling face is thin, his cheeks hollow, and his eyes gaze into the distance in a melancholy way. Two weeks after celebrating his birthday, he wrote a frank letter to Dr Lovegrove, the Principal Medical Officer:

> *'For some time I have felt this continuous strain telling on me bodily and mentally and as my weakness increases I am at last forced to claim a rest, as otherwise I shall utterly break down.*
>
> *In a letter you sent me some time ago you said Government would give me three weeks holiday each year and pay for a* locum tenens.'

He suggested Dr Wheeler to act as locum, then went on:

> *'I think I might be able to go to Mandurah or some other place by March 5th and would try to keep up the work till then.'*[516]

The leave was granted, and Dr Wheeler appointed. Dr Barnett's next appearance in public was at a cricket tournament in Fremantle on 13 April. He was absent from Fremantle during the trial of Jumna Khan in the Supreme Court.

Louis Wheeler appeared as a witness at the trial on 4 March, and testified about the autopsy findings on William Griffiths.

Khan's defence lawyer, Mr Edmunds, argued that his client was insane. In evidence, he produced two of Jumna Khan's associates, who said he had been acting strangely in Coolgardie before he went to Fremantle, and that he claimed someone was trying to kill him. He had been desperate to return to his home country.

Further evidence of Khan's insanity was provided by Dr Paget, medical partner to Dr Hope, who testified that he had examined Jumna Khan at Fremantle Prison and in his opinion, the prisoner was suffering from delusional insanity.[517]

Justice Stone carefully explained to the jury the legal technicalities of a plea of insanity. Eight minutes after leaving the court, the jury members returned with their verdict: guilty.[518] Jumna Khan was executed by hanging on 30 March.

If Henry Barnett had still been colonial surgeon for Fremantle, he would likely have been invited to dine on board the *Sultan* when she sailed into Fremantle Harbour, in May, for the unofficial opening ceremony. As superintendent of the asylum, however, there was no reason for him to receive such an invitation. He may have joined the crowd that gathered on the wharves to welcome the ship into port, but he was not listed among the guests on board the vessel.

Lady Forrest did include him and Emily Barnett among the five hundred guests invited to an 'at home' the following day. She and Sir John were about to leave for London to join the celebrations for the Queen's Golden jubilee.

Susan O'Connor and her daughters were also invited.[519] They knew by now that Charles O'Connor would not be returning in June, as he had intended. During his absence, the O'Connor family moved back into Park Bungalow.[520] They would remain there until 1902, when they returned to Cantonment Road.

Apart from his absence in March, Dr Barnett remained fully involved in the community during 1897. He was present at the planting of a tree to commemorate the Queen's jubilee in June. Despite wet and squally weather, he attended the Fremantle Rowing Club's annual regatta. He and Emily both took part in the Rowing Club ball in August, with Henry proposing the toasts as patron of the club.[521] The Fremantle Orchestral Society re-elected him as president that same month. He also continued to appear on the bench as a justice of the peace in the Fremantle police courts and was part of a committee set up to organise a farewell dinner for the magistrate, Mr Fairbairn, on 11 August.

But his health was deteriorating. While mentally still alert, his physical strength was waning, and he lost the ability to walk. He ordered a three-wheeled 'Velociman' tricycle which could be propelled using only the arms. It would take several months to arrive, and he would never get to use it.[522]

By September, Henry Barnett had taken to self-medicating his dreadful insomnia with sulphonal, a sedative and sleep-inducing agent. He continued to do this despite the protests of his wife, Emily, and Dr Wheeler. Sulphonal was widely known to be dangerous because of its unpredictable effects and ease of overdosing.[523]

On 2 October, Dr Barnett sat on the police court bench, with the acting magistrate, to hear the case of a drunken seaman charged with using obscene language in High Street. The rest of the morning was taken up with other cases of disorderly conduct, and that of a father charged with neglecting his children.[524] The strain on his dwindling reserves of strength was telling. It would be the last time the newspapers mentioned Henry's appearance in public.

On 13 October he wrote a will, appointing the West Australian Trustee and Agency Company and the Reverend Thomas Bird (one of Emily's relatives) as executors. He left the two cottages in Barnett Street, 'Pendennis' and 'Logan', with all the household contents, outright to Emily, along with a sum of one hundred pounds.

His eldest daughter, Florence Bullock, was to receive one hundred and thirty pounds, while his three other children by his first marriage, Alexander, Harry and Olive, would each receive fifty pounds. The trustees were directed to manage the rest of his properties, as they saw fit, with the proceeds to be divided equally, on a regular basis, between Emily and the four children. Park Bungalow wasn't mentioned specifically, but it seems it was to be either sold or let by the trustees.[525]

As Henry Barnett's personal physician, Dr Wheeler was aware of the precarious state of his colleague's health. One way or another, there would soon be a vacancy at the asylum. He had frequently worked alongside, or in place of, Dr Barnett, and felt that this experience should count for something. After trying unsuccessfully to see John Forrest in his offices, he wrote to the Premier on 11 October:

> *'Some time back you gave me reason to believe I would have your support in the appointment of Superintendent of the Asylum if Dr Barnett retired and I trust I may rely on your good offices in the matter. Knowing you are exceptionally busy just now I will not take the liberty of again trying to see you personally, but hope these few lines will serve as a reminder when the matter comes under your consideration.'*

The letter went to John Forrest and returned to the under-secretary with a pencilled note from someone, 'I think it would be better to get a specially trained man from Eng(land). I certainly could not support Dr Wheeler's appointment.' In ink, Forrest instructed Burt on what to write.

On 15 October, the under-secretary replied to Dr Wheeler:

> *'I am directed by Sir John Forrest to inform you... that when the position is vacant it will be necessary for the government to obtain the services of a tried man of large experience in lunatic asylums.'* [526]

Dr Wheeler's hopes were once more disappointed.

Although Dr Barnett was still keeping up his duties at the asylum, his health continued to deteriorate, both physically and mentally. On 15 October, he scrawled a letter to the principal medical officer, Dr Lovegrove:

> *'My sad mental condition remains unimproved. I am worn out and am*

totally without sleep. I beg to apply for six months leave on full pay and shall try what a little travel will do for my overworked brain.'

In a footnote, he added, 'You did not send me the medicines you spoke of.' Whether he was referring to medicines for himself or for the asylum is unknown.

Dr Lovegrove replied five days later, in a letter devoid of sympathy or compassion, or even recognition of Dr Barnett's condition.

'The Superintendent
Lunatic Asylum

Regarding your application for leave of absence...I am directed to inform you that the leave asked for will be granted but that only three of it can be on full pay, the remaining term must, in accordance with the regulations, be on "half pay".

I am further instructed to ask when you desire your leave shall commence and what arrangements you propose for the discharge of your duties while away and whether you intend to resign at the end of your six months leave?

T. H. Lovegrove, PMO'

Dr Barnett asked Dr Wheeler if he would be willing to act in his place and waited another two days for Dr Wheeler's response in writing. He then wrote to the under-secretary a letter that betrayed not just how unwell he was, but how wounded he felt by the way he had been treated.

'Dear Sir,

I am so exhausted from illness brought on by continuous overwork, and want of sleep that I scarcely know what I write.

I am anxious to have an opportunity of explaining matters personally to Sir John Forrest.

In reply to your enquiry I do not know of anyone capable of doing asylum duty for the present except Dr Wheeler whose letter I enclose.

I accept the offer of 3 months on full pay, commencing November 1st and 3 more on ½ pay—though I do not know how I am to make ends meet on the latter income.

Should my health improve I may in 6 months be able to resume duty on full pay but if not—I trust that Government will in consideration of my long and exhausting service, continue to me—during what little life may be left to me, continue me on full pay for I have tried faithfully to perform my duty until I broke down.

Yours truly

H C Barnett.[527]

The leave he requested was granted, though Dr Hope, not Dr Wheeler, was appointed to relieve him.[528] But the announcement came too late for Henry Barnett.

On Tuesday evening, 2 November, utterly weary but unable to sleep, Henry took a large dose of sulphonal. The following morning, Emily couldn't rouse him. Alarmed, she called for Louis Wheeler, who called in Dr Paget and together they did what they could to resuscitate him. They called in a third doctor to assist. But their efforts were all futile. At seven in the evening, Henry Barnett died without ever having regained consciousness.[529]

Dr Wheeler wrote a death certificate, giving the cause of death as 'insomnia and narcotic poisoning.'[530] No inquest was held, though it was usual to hold an inquest when death was thought to be the result of an overdose.[531] If anyone pondered how, or why, a doctor as experienced as Henry Barnett would have accidentally overdosed himself, they kept their thoughts to themselves.

Henry's funeral was held on 5 November and his body laid to rest, without cremation, in the Anglican section of the cemetery in Skinner Street, next door to the asylum. The service was conducted by his old friend, Archdeacon Watkins.

C. Y. O'Connor, who had returned from London in September, was one of the eight pall bearers. His presence in this role, along with seven other men of high status—doctors, magistrates and politicians—was a measure of the respect in which Dr Barnett was held. But perhaps O'Connor's presence was also an indication of the understanding that existed between the two fellow Irish men.

Grieving representatives of the asylum staff and members of the Rowing Club accompanied numerous civic dignitaries to the graveside. Some had missed the popular Perth High School annual sports day, held the same afternoon, to attend.

Sir John and Lady Forrest sent flowers but decided to keep their commitment to attend the sports day.[532] Mr Fairbairn represented the Premier at the funeral. When the *Morning Herald* had asked Sir John for his response to Dr Barnett's death a few days earlier, he was reported to have said 'he was very sorry to hear of the death of Dr. Barnett, who had been an old and valued Government official.' He referred to the great interest which the late Dr. Barnett had always taken in the affairs of the colony, especially in literary matters, but made no mention of the asylum.[533]

Henry's last report on the asylum, for the year 1896, was tabled in parliament a few days after his death. It made pitiful reading. The *West Australian*, after noting the huge increase in admissions and the overcrowding, commented on the sad lack of progress in tackling the problem.

'Early in 1895 the superintendent had to report that there would shortly be no available accommodation, and at his urgent request Mr. Poole, Colonial Architect, submitted to Government plans of a new wing for females and female staff…Had this course been adopted and the proposed buildings been placed in the hands of a contractor, it would by this time have been fit for occupation, and the present disastrous state of things would have been averted. But the repeated and urgent representations of the superintendent were totally neglected; no tenders were called for, and, saving that an occasional party of prisoners were sometimes sent to level a site, nothing was done.'

Dr Barnett had requested in his report that a permanent assistant superintendent be appointed to help him with the asylum work, so that he might have 'occasional mental and bodily rest'. He had proposed Dr Wheeler for the position. But this hadn't happened either.[534]

In the Legislative Assembly on 6 December, during a discussion of who would replace Henry Barnett as superintendent, the question of paying a gratuity to Henry's widow was raised. Sir John Forrest, as treasurer, said he would like to see more information about whether Dr Barnett's widow needed relief by the government. Each case should be decided on its merit, and unless she was in want, there was no justification for the House moving in the matter.[535]

The question was raised again on 17 December, during the estimates debate. This time it came with a recommendation from the Governor himself that Mrs Barnett be paid a gratuity of five hundred pounds. Sir John still asserted that each case should be considered on its merits, but now he was full of praise for Dr Barnett and his many years of service to the colony.

'When an officer has served his country for so long—over 30 years—and has occupied an important, responsible, and irksome position, which I think controlling a lunatic asylum is, when he dies and leaves a widow ill-provided for, I think a case is made out for the consideration of honourable members. I should be very glad if honourable members approved of this small grant of money to the widow of this old officer', Sir John said.

In his speech, he noted that the letter granting six months leave had reached Dr Barnett's home the day after he died. He revealed that the letter had given the doctor permission to retire on an annual pension of four hundred pounds on his return from leave. Henry Barnett died unaware of this.[536]

After Henry Barnett's death, the position of acting superintendent of the asylum was temporarily filled by Dr Hope, who took on the role in addition to all his other duties. In September 1900, following the death of a female patient at the hands of another patient, Vosper's *West Australian Sunday Times* ran a series of articles with sensational headings, such as: 'THE LIFE OF A LUNATIC! How Patients are Treated. DONE TO DEATH By a Violent Maniac. The Facts Suppressed. The Coroner Deceived.'[537]

At the instigation of Vosper, who was still member for North East Coolgardie, the Legislative Assembly set up a select committee in October 1900, to inquire into the conditions of the Fremantle and Whitby Falls asylums.[538] Vosper headed the committee.

It reported back to parliament in November, having found that the Fremantle Asylum 'is utterly unfit for the purposes for which it is used [and] its continued occupancy as an asylum is calculated to retard, if not altogether prevent, the cure of patients.'[539] Whitby Falls was found to be adequate, but inconveniently located. All Dr Barnett's complaints were vindicated.

Dr Sydney Montgomery, a native of Belfast like Dr Barnett, arrived in June 1901, to take up the position of full-time superintendent of the asylum.[540] He quickly rejected Whitby Falls as totally unsuitable as a site for the asylum and a new building was begun in the Perth suburb of Claremont.[541] It was opened two years later, in August 1903. After all the patients had been transferred, the old asylum building in Fremantle was converted into a home for older women.

TWENTY-EIGHT: The Final Chapter

C. Y. O'Connor arrived back in Western Australia aboard the Royal Mail Ship *Oceana* in September 1897, two months before Dr Barnett's death. He disembarked in Albany, just as he had when he arrived in the colony six years earlier. During his time in London, he and Sir John Forrest had met with the managing directors of the Orient Shipping Company. The directors showed great interest in the improvements made to the Fremantle harbour, but it would be some time before any of the shipping companies could be persuaded to have their mail ships call at Fremantle.

O'Connor was met in Albany by a reporter from the *West Australian*, who had apparently interviewed the Chief Engineer before. He found him noticeably more energetic than when he left and brimming with information on every topic raised. The reporter enquired about his trip.

The change of scene, climate, and employment during his eight-month absence had done him good physically, said O'Connor. The relief from the overwhelming amount of routine work which he had on his hands before he left Perth had been of great benefit to him.

Not that he had been relaxing on the job. Apart from spending time in London, he had also visited Glasgow, Newcastle-on-Tyne, Middlesborough, Sheffield, Leeds, Birmingham, Liverpool and Essex in England, Cardiff in Wales, Belfast and Dublin in Ireland.

He had also travelled to Germany and Belgium and to Brindisi in Italy, gathering information, examining pipes and engines and pumps, and looking at harbours and railway lines. He was particularly intrigued by the huge Krupps manufacturing company in Germany. Large towns had grown up around the factories, where the old and infirm were provided with pensions, and young men instructed and entertained. The concept appealed to him.

Although he didn't mention it in the interview, he had also taken the opportunity to visit his sister Frances, and other family and friends, in England and Ireland.[542] But he was pleased to be home.

'After all my travels' he said, 'I am glad to get back again, because however interesting it was to see so many new places, it was hardly a restful time. I would like to take this opportunity of saying that I feel exceedingly grateful to the Government, and also to the many influential persons in the colony whom I believe were instrumental in giving me this change of work and a trip to Europe.

'Prior to leaving for England my health was far from perfect, and I was beginning to feel very severely the effects of over-work and over-anxiety which belonged not to the time immediately preceding my departure, but to some years before. This trip, therefore, has been an enormous boon to me.'[543]

For Charles Yelverton O'Connor, 1897 had been a very good year, probably the best he'd had since arriving in Western Australia.

On his return to Fremantle, O'Connor declared himself well pleased with the way the harbour works had advanced during his absence. Under the management of acting engineer-in-chief, John McDonald, progress had been 'beyond his most hopeful anticipation.'[544]

As O'Connor had confidently predicted, evidence of sand travel had been minimal in the five years since the work began. The rocky bar had been almost totally removed and dredging continued day and night to deepen and lengthen the navigable channel. Land reclamation and wharf building was progressing rapidly.

It would be almost three years before the first Royal Mail ship, the *Ormuz*, called at Fremantle, on 13 August 1900, to great celebration. O'Connor was present on this occasion and received the recognition due to him. The harbour wasn't formally completed and opened until 1903. But from 1897, with the inner harbour opened to steamships and John McDonald in charge of the harbour work, O'Connor was able to turn most of his attention to the Coolgardie Water Pipeline scheme.

He had returned from England refreshed, with his medal and title from the Queen providing tangible evidence of his success as an engineer. But he soon found himself facing the same pressure of work and even greater opposition and criticism than before he left.

The pipeline project did not proceed as smoothly as O'Connor had hoped. In 1899, during the building of the dam wall in the Helena valley at Mundaring, a fault line was found in the underlying rock that caused delays while it was repaired. In July that year, the *Carlisle Castle* went down off Garden Island in a storm, taking with it a shipment of locking bars needed for constructing the pipeline.[545]

By January 1902, substantial progress had been made, but the project, and O'Connor, were still under attack from disgruntled businessmen, from members of parliament and from the press.

Sir John Forrest, who had generally supported O'Connor in parliament, even as he leaned on him for his own ends, left Western Australia in 1901, to take up a post in the new Federal Parliament in Canberra. He had been replaced as Premier by George Leake, who had never been in favour of the pipeline scheme, and now only half-heartedly defended it and the colony's Chief Engineer.

O'Connor's old nemesis, Alexander Forrest, died from complications of kidney disease on 20 June 1901 at the age of fifty-one.[546] O'Connor was among the hundreds who attended his funeral. Forrest's last few years had been filled with tragedy, with the death of his wife in 1897, and his seventeen-year-old son, Anthony, on the battlefields of South Africa in May 1901.

O'Connor might have hoped for some relief from being criticized and denigrated in parliament. But Forrest's role was soon taken up by others. Robert Hastie, member for Kanowna, for instance, was reported in February 1902 as saying that 'as far as he knew, not one of the public works under the control of the Engineer-in-Chief had ever been finished by the time stated.'[547]

The *West Australian Sunday Times*, edited by Frederick Vosper, ran several derogatory editorials, questioning O'Connor's competence and integrity.[548] After Vosper's early death in 1901 from acute appendicitis, the new editor, Thomas Walker, continued and intensified the attacks.

In 1902, O'Connor made a decision that gave the *WA Sunday Times* deadly ammunition. In January that year, he agreed to let out the contract for completing the laying of pipes to a Victorian company, Couston, Finlayson and Porritt. A caulking machine invented by Couston had already been introduced to replace the hand-caulking method used up until then to join the pipes. It took time for the workers to learn how to use it.

Couston suggested that progress would be quicker if he could employ his own men. He was supported by engineer Thomas Hodgson, who was second only to O'Connor in charge of the project. Although O'Connor preferred to employ labourers directly through the Public Works Department on all his projects, he was convinced to accept the contract.

He did this without calling for tenders, reasoning that it would serve little purpose and cause further delay. Couston knew his own machine, and a lower tenderer might not have the same expertise.[549] O'Connor left the state on 23 January 1902, with the Premier's permission, to consult on the outer harbour in Adelaide. It was a fateful decision.

The *West Australian Sunday Times* of 26 January described the Couston contract as a scheme 'which smacks of nauseous suspicion, if not of putrid corruption, from start to finish.' It accused O'Connor of fleeing the state to avoid responsibility.[550]

On 9 February 1902, the *Sunday Times* published a particularly malicious article headed 'Corruption by Contract'. It read in part:

> *'It is open rumour everywhere that this shire engineer from New Zealand has absolutely flourished on "palm grease" since the first day when the harbor works and the Coolgardie water scheme were agreed upon. If he is not now immensely rich there is a mystery somewhere. And apart from any distinct charge of corruption, this man has exhibited*

> *such gross blundering, or something worse, in his management of great public works that it is no exaggeration to say he has robbed the taxpayers of this State out of millions of money.'*[551]

When O'Connor discovered the article on his return from Adelaide, he was so incensed that he circled the most offensive parts in blue pencil and kept the newspaper. He showed it, with shaking hands, to engineering contractor Charles Hoskins on 6 March.[552]

O'Connor was particularly stung that false accusations and inaccurate reports had been made in parliament while he was away in South Australia. He couldn't refute the accusations and believed no-one had come to his defence.[553]

During O'Connor's absence, the West Australian parliament had set up a select committee, to examine 'the conduct and completion of the Coolgardie Water Scheme'. The committee, which clearly wanted to find O'Connor at fault, recommended the establishment of a Royal Commission.

O'Connor, who seems to have used alcohol for many years to numb his emotional pain and anxiety, along with sleeping tablets to deal with his lack of sleep, faced months of grilling, misunderstanding and claims and counterclaims by all involved.[554]

Those close to him became concerned about his state of mind. He had difficulty concentrating, to the point that he couldn't multiply simple numbers. He would speak in an agitated way to colleagues then sit in morose silence at home.[555] But there was no-one close enough, with enough authority, to help him. His family doctor, Dr Birmingham, was on holiday. One of his closest colleagues, under-secretary for Works, Martin Jull, was also away. If Dr Barnett had ever been a confidante, he was long gone.

Early on the morning of Monday, 10 March, O'Connor rode his horse to the ocean at South Beach. He usually went riding with his daughter Bridget, but she felt unwell that morning and didn't ride with him. After dismounting, he waded into the calm water and stood with his back to the waves. Then, with a revolver taken from the drawer of his son's desk, he shot himself through the mouth.[556]

Historians continue to debate whether the note found among his papers by his twenty-year-old son Roderick, the day after his death, was a suicide note or simply the outpouring of a mind racked by anxiety but still focused on completing the job of building the pipeline. It read:

> *10/3/02*
>
> *The position has become impossible.*
>
> *Anxious important work to do and three commissions of inquiry to attend to.*
>
> ~~*If we have not neglected our business in the past we*~~
>
> *We may not have done as well as possible in the past but we will necessarily be too hampered to do well in the imminent future.*
>
> *I fear that my brain is suffering and I am in great fear of what effect all this worry will have upon me — I have lost control of my thoughts.*
>
> *The Coolgardie scheme is all right and I could finish it if I got a chance and protection from misrepresentation but there's no hope for that now and it's better that it should be given to some entirely new man to do who will be untrammelled by prior responsibility. PS Put the wing walls to Helena Weir at once.*[557]

An inquest was opened in Fremantle on the afternoon of O'Connor's death, before the district coroner, Dr Black, and a three-man jury. After viewing the body, the coroner adjourned the inquest until the following Thursday, 13 March. The note became evidence.

Dr Anderson, who carried out the autopsy, found O'Connor's death was due to injuries to the brain caused by a bullet. He also described vascular changes consistent with O'Connor's age (fifty-nine), and shrinkage and 'slight cirrhosis' of both the liver and the kidneys.

Although liver cirrhosis has several possible causes, the most common is heavy, prolonged alcohol intake. The kidneys are not usually affected until the liver is quite severely damaged. Significantly, the symptoms of progressing cirrhosis include 'confusion, difficulties thinking, memory loss, personality changes, and sleep disorders'.[558] While O'Connor used alcohol to self-medicate his anxiety, insomnia and distress, it ultimately worsened his mental state.

Those who had been with O'Connor in the days before his death, including his son Roderick, gave evidence about his state of mind. The jury at the inquest reached a verdict of 'death by his own hand…while in a state of mental derangement caused through worry and overwork.'

Archdeacon Watkins once again found himself officiating at the funeral of a friend. At least a thousand men joined the funeral procession, and thousands more members of the public lined the streets of Fremantle on Tuesday, 11 March, as the cortege wound its way to the new Fremantle cemetery some two and a half miles from the O'Connor's home in Beach Street. O'Connor's sons and sons-in-law were among the public mourners, but Susan and his daughters remained at home.[559]

The Minister for Public Works at the time, C. H. Rason, had never given O'Connor the level of support that he'd received from his predecessors, Harry Venn and Fred Piesse. But in a letter of condolence to Mrs O'Connor, published in the *West Australian* on the day of the funeral, Rason wrote:

> *'Had Mr. O'Connor never carried out any other undertaking than the Fremantle Harbour Works, he would have done enough, in my opinion, to justify his reputation as an engineer of the first rank.*
>
> *It is to be deeply deplored that he was not spared to see the crowning success of that other great work, so ably initiated by him, and in which he took so deep and active an interest (the Coolgardie water scheme).'*

O'Connor's confidence in the scheme was ultimately vindicated. On 22 January 1903, the pumping machinery at Mundaring weir was officially and ceremonially turned on by Lady Forrest, who had returned with Sir John Forrest for the occasion.[560] In reality, water had been flowing in the pipes for some time.

Two days later, the pipeline was opened at Coolgardie by Sir John. He spoke 'at great length', before turning on a silver tap to release a fountain of water. After many more speeches and ceremonies, the party went on to Kalgoorlie, where Sir John opened a valve that allowed water to flow into the Mount Charlotte reservoir.[561]

Epilogue

Far from lining his pockets with corruptly obtained funds, O'Connor died with no property other than his two horses, his household goods and personal effects. He never bought or invested in land in Western Australia. After his liabilities were subtracted, his total assets when he died amounted to less than two hundred pounds plus a small insurance policy.

In September 1902, after a debate in which O'Connor was eulogised for his character, his achievements and his dedication, the West Australian parliament voted to provide his widow with an annuity of 250 pounds. In opening the debate, the Minister for Public Works, C.H. Rason, noted that C. Y. O'Connor had taken only seventeen days leave of absence in eleven years, and was owed more than twenty months leave of absence on full pay and fifty-four months on half pay, amounting in total to 2,906 pounds. Had he retired, he would also have been entitled to a pension of 525 pounds per annum. [562]

Susan O'Connor lived on in Western Australia, surrounded by her family, to the age of ninety-three.[563]

Two years after Henry Barnett's death, his widow, Emily, married John Palmer Scott Main, an English mechanical engineer employed as Locomotive Superintendent by the West Australian government railways.[564] They moved to England not long afterwards. Park Bungalow and the two cottages in Barnett Street were eventually sold. Park Bungalow was demolished in the 1960s.

Lilian Hart, Emily Barnett's niece, left Western Australia with her daughter

Geraldine in mid-1898 to join Francis Hart in London. But the relationship between Lilian and Francis was untenable. In 1904 she successfully filed for divorce, on the grounds of desertion and adultery.[565] Francis seems to have drifted into anonymity. The *Sunday Times* in Perth mentioned him as 'the late "Cocky" Hart in January 1930, but there was nothing in the papers to mark his death.[566]

Dr Louis Wheeler, no doubt bitterly disappointed that he had once again been overlooked in the appointment of the asylum superintendent, remained in Western Australia until July 1898. After applying for six months' leave from his post as Health Officer for the North Fremantle council, he went to London.[567] While there, he resigned from the Fremantle post.[568]

On 3 January 1906, he and Lilian Hart were married at the Marylebone Presbyterian church.[569] Louis obtained a Diploma in Tropical Medicine and Health in 1916 and spent many years working in Malaysia, a move his old mentor and friend in Fremantle would surely have approved.[570]

Afterword

Often, I struggle to find a title for something I've written. In this case, though, I had a title for the piece before I'd finished the first draft. As I was writing about Western Australia in the 1890s, I sensed a streak of madness running through the whole society. It was a product of the insularity of West Australian society, and was fuelled by the gold rushes. Yet there was also much to marvel at. And many surprises came to light along the way.

Although I began with the intention of focusing on O'Connor and Barnett, John Forrest proved to be an important link between them, and he elbowed his way into the story more often than I had expected. Both men included him in their social circle. Both needed his support for their work, though only O'Connor received it much of the time. Yet I was frequently surprised at how flimsy Forrest's support for O'Connor proved to be. I'd read many times that one of the reasons for O'Connor's downfall and suicide was the loss of the protection he had received previously from John Forrest, after Forrest left for Canberra in 1901. O'Connor supposedly became more exposed to his critics from then on.

It seemed, in reality, that Forrest used O'Connor for his own ends. He might praise the Chief Engineer's character and expertise, but he also hid behind this expert opinion when his own decisions were being questioned. His treatment of O'Connor during his own very public dispute with Harry Venn (who really did support O'Connor) could hardly be considered gallant. Forrest played a vital role in exploring and mapping Western Australia and in developing the West Australian economy. But in the context of O'Connor's story, his role often appeared somewhat less than noble.

I came to see C. Y. O'Connor as an example of the tragic hero—a man of virtuous character but with a fatal flaw that leads to his downfall at the hands of the gods he has offended.[571]

O'Connor was well-born, gifted at his chosen career and dedicated to it, a natural leader, generous and well-liked by most people. His great virtue, which became his fatal flaw, was his integrity. To be accused of incompetence was galling to him but could be refuted by facts. To be accused of dishonesty or corruption was intolerable to him. This, when coupled with his pride and a strong sense of honour, drove him into conflict with the local 'gods' of West Australian society and ultimately led to his death.

What sets O'Connor apart from the classical tragic hero is his apparent failure to develop any insight into how his own actions contributed to his downfall. The idea that he might sometimes forgive, or at least overlook, an insult, rather than demanding an apology, seemed foreign to him. Nothing in his last few conversations or his suicide note suggest introspection into how he might have made so many enemies or whether he could have handled things differently.

In another place, or in a later age, O'Connor might not have faced the same barrage of personal criticism, innuendo and insults he experienced from the politicians, businessmen and newspaper editors of 1890s Western Australia. His cosmopolitan outlook on life, his willingness to try innovative ways of doing things, his apparent disdain for 'the way we've always done it' and his failure to tread carefully around the established social hierarchy marked him out almost from the day he arrived in Perth.

The attacks made on him were often quite personal, perhaps because he threatened some people's personal sense of entitlement. Today, the deterioration in his mental health might have been diagnosed and treated rather than being passed off as 'overwork'. All of which adds to the tragedy of his death.

The epitaph written by railway engineer Daniel Gooch for one of O'Connor's engineering heroes, Isambard Kingdom Brunel, could, with a change of country, be apt for O'Connor himself:

> *'By his death the greatest of England's engineers was lost, the man with the greatest originality of thought and power of execution, bold in his plans but right. The commercial world thought him extravagant; but although he was so, things are not done by those who sit down to count the cost of every thought and act.'*[572]

Henry Barnett appears less the tragic hero, more the prophet crying in the wilderness. Not that he was overtly spiritual, but like many of the biblical prophets, he was a complicated character, a dreamer of dreams with an unconventional life story, a man called by providence to a position that would not have been his first choice of career.

For years he faithfully delivered his message and warned of forthcoming disaster, even when no-one seemed to be listening. He wasn't opposed to progress or prosperity—he bought property and owned shares in a goldmine—but like the prophets, he reminded the powerful that the poor and needy were being overlooked.

While his life story doesn't have the same acclaim, the same depths of nobility and tragedy as O'Connor's, I felt a sadness in watching the life of such an adventurous, creative and sensitive man being slowly constricted by circumstances. Who could not be moved by a man who wanted to share his love of flowers with his patients? By restricting this story mainly to events of the 1890s, I have barely touched on his life and there is much more that could be written about him.

The rest of the quote from Don Quixote in *Man of La Mancha* which began this book seems a fitting end to this story:

> *'When life itself seems lunatic, who knows where madness lies? Perhaps to be too practical is madness. To surrender dreams, this may be madness. To seek treasure where there is only trash... too much sanity may be madness! And maddest of all... to see life as it is and not as it should be!'*[573]

Acknowledgements

I'm grateful to the many people who have contributed in some way to the writing of this book.

In the research stage, the staff of the State Library of Western Australia and the State Records Office were invariably helpful. I especially thank the archivist who searched out records that were hard to find. Thanks also to the staff of the History Centre at Fremantle Library, the Robert Muir bookshop and Mainly Books bookshop.

Much of the information I used came from the newspaper pages on Trove, the online portal for the National Library of Australia. The wonderful people ('voluntroves') who correct the OCR-generated text to make it more accessible and searchable do a magnificent job.

Numerous people offered me suggestions and advice when I needed it, including the members of the Historical Writers Forum on Facebook. Historian and fellow writer, Irene Saurman, gave me particularly helpful feedback during the editing process. And I couldn't have done without the editorial skills, insights and encouragement of my daughter Amy Budrikis.

So many friends have kept me going along the way simply by asking 'How's it going?' At last I can say, 'I've finished!' I hope you have found the wait worthwhile.

As always, I'm grateful to my husband Gary for providing me with the space and means for researching and writing, and for his suggestions, comments and encouragement to keep going. It's not easy living with someone whose thoughts are constantly wandering into another era.

Bibliography

Archival sources:

State Records Office of Western Australia:

Chief Secretary's Department, and Colonial Secretary's Office. 'Appointment of Superintending Medical Officer - Fremantle Asylum.' Item, 7 January 1908. AU WA S675- cons527 1897/3176.

———. 'Asking That His Official Medical Duties May for the Time Be Confined to Superintendence of and Attendance on All Lunatics in Asylums - Colonial Surgeon at Fremantle'. Item, 10 March 1894. AU WA S675- cons527 1894/0325.

———. 'Colonial Surgeon at Fremantle. For Post of, - Louis Wheeler'. Item, 4 October 1894. AU WA S675- cons527 1894/1671.

———. 'Extension of Leave of Absence to End of the Year. Telephone to House of Medical Superintendent Lunatic Asylum - Colonial Surgeon at Fremantle'. Item, 24 November 1892. AU WA S675- cons527 1892/1836.

———. 'Insane Half Cast Girl "Emily Jones" Belonging to the Swan N and H.C [Native and Half Cast] Mission Refused Enter to the Fremantle Lunatic Asylum'. Item, 29 May 1895. AU WA S675- cons527 1895/1175.

———. 'L. Wheeler - Superintending Medical Officer Lunatic Asylum When Vacant - for Post Of.' Item, 15 October 1897. AU WA S675- cons527 1897/3127.

———. 'Official Letter of Recommendation to Colonial Government, Asks for. - H. C. Barnett, Surgeon Superintendent Lunatic Asylum.' Item, 7

April 1891. AU WA S675- cons527 1891/0653.

———. 'Superintendent Lunatic Asylum - Attack on a Warder - Reporting.' Item, 3 July 1896. AU WA S675- cons527 1896/2039.

———. 'Superintendent Lunatic Asylum - Fremantle - Absence of Leave Doctor H.C. Barnet - Asking for - from March 5th for Three Weeks - Doctor Wheeler as Acting Superintendent during His Absence.' Item, 4 March 1897. AU WA S675- cons527 1897/0537.

———. 'Surgeon Superintendent Lunatic Asylum - Additional Accommodation Urgently Required.' Item, 12 January 1897. AU WA S675- cons527 1896/3977.

Crown Law Department, and Judicial Department. 'Re: Death of C. Y. O'Connor'. Item, 14 March 1902. AU WA S2664- cons997 1902/0976.

Supreme Court of Western Australia, and Civil Court of Western Australia. 'Henry Calvert Barnett'. Item. AU WA S34- cons3403 1897/150.

Colonial Secretary's office, minute paper 94, 13 March 1894, Cons 1003 1900-0301 (not yet indexed)

Parliament of Western Australia

'Report of the Civil Service Commission (Appointed 13th April 1894) 1896.' *www.parliament.wa.gov.au/intranet/libpages.nsf/WebFiles/Royal+Commission+Civil+Service+Commission+1896/$FILE/6669.pdf*

Parliament of Western Australia, Hansard archive 1870-2000 *parliament.wa.gov.au/hansard/hansard1870to1995.nsf/Screen1870s*

Parliament of Western Australia, 'The Constitution Act Amendment Act 1893 (57 Vict. No. 14)' *classic.austlii.edu.au/au/legis/wa/num_act/tcaaa189357vn14396/*

Parliament of Victoria

'An Act to amend the Factories and Shops Act 1890 and for other purposes', 1896. *www.austlii.edu.au/au/legis/vic/hist_act/fasa1896196.pdf*

Public Records Office Victoria

Inward Overseas Passenger Lists, VPRS 947/P0000, Oct - Dec 1894

State Library of Western Australia

Members of the Legislative Assembly 1896. 1896. Photograph.

Working on the Bar at Fremantle Harbour. 1900. Photograph.

'Police Gazette, Western Australia', No 44, 3 November 1897, *slwa.wa.gov.au/pdf/battye/police_gazettes/PG189711.pdf*

State Library of Western Australia. 'Post Office Directories 1893–1899'. *slwa.wa.gov.au/collections/collections/post-office-directories*

Royal Australasian College of Physicians History of Medicine Library

(Items located by searching for 'Fremantle Asylum' on the search page)

'Report Upon the Lunatic Asylum at Fremantle for the Year 1891 by the Acting Surgeon Superintendent. No. 16', 1893.

'Report Upon the Lunatic Asylum at Fremantle for the Year 1892 by the Acting Surgeon Superintendent' No. 10, 1893.

'Report Upon the Lunatic Asylum at Fremantle for the Year 1893 by the Surgeon Superintendent.' No. 13, 1894.

'Report Upon the Lunatic Asylum at Fremantle for the Year 1894 by the Superintending Medical Officer.' No. 6', 1895.

'Report Upon the Lunatic Asylum at Fremantle for the Year 1895 by the Superintending Medical Officer.' No. 6, 1896.

'Report Upon the Lunatic Asylum at Fremantle for the Year 1896 by the Superintending Medical Officer.' No. 25, 1897.

'Report of the Select Committee of the Legislative Assembly appointed to consider and report as to what is necessary to place the Asylum for the Insane on a satisfactory basis, as to accommodation and maintenance.' A5 1891

Government of Western Australia Department of Justice

Registry of Births, Deaths and Marriages, death certificate for Henry Calvert Barnett, 1897.

Newspapers

Argus (Melbourne, Vic)

Australian Advertiser (Albany, WA)
Belfast Newsletter (Belfast, Ireland)
Brisbane Courier (Brisbane, QLD)
Bunbury Herald (Bunbury, WA)
Clare's Weekly (Perth, WA)
Coolgardie Miner (Coolgardie, WA)
Daily News (Perth, WA)
Daily Telegraph (Hawkes Bay, New Zealand)
Eastern Districts Chronicle (York, WA)
Evening Journal (Adelaide, SA)
Evening Star (Dunedin, New Zealand)
Express (Fremantle, WA)
Freemans Journal (Dublin, Ireland)
Geraldton Advertiser (Geraldton, WA)
Geraldton Murchison Telegraph (Geraldton, WA)
Grey River Argus (Greymouth, New Zealand)
Hannan's Herald (Kalgoorlie, WA)
Herald (Fremantle, WA)
Hobart Town Courier and Van Diemen's Land Gazette (Hobart, TAS)
Inquirer and Commercial News (Perth, WA)
Kalgoorlie Miner (Kalgoorlie, WA)
Meath Herald (County Meath, Ireland)
Northam Advertiser (Northam, WA)
People (Perth, WA)
Perth Gazette and Independent Journal of Politics and News (Perth, WA)
Pilot (Dublin, Ireland)
South Australian Register (Adelaide, SA)
Southern Cross Herald (Southern Cross, WA)
Southern Times (Bunbury, WA)
Sunday Times (Perth, WA)
Sydney Morning Herald (Sydney, NSW)
Timaru Herald (Timaru, New Zealand)
Umpire (Fremantle, WA)

Victorian Express (Geraldton, WA)
W. A. Bulletin (Fremantle, WA)
W. A. Record (Perth, WA)
West Australian (Perth, WA)
West Australian Sunday Times (Perth, WA)
West Coast Times (Hokitika, New Zealand)
West Australian Goldfields Courier (Coolgardie, WA)
West Australian Times (Perth, WA)
Western Mail (Perth, WA)

Books (including books online)

Belfast, Queen's University of. *The Belfast Queen's College Calendar*. Simms and M'Intyre, 1852.

Bolton, G. C. 'Forrest, Alexander (1849–1901)'. In *Australian Dictionary of Biography*. Canberra: National Centre of Biography, Australian National University. *adb.anu.edu.au/biography/forrest-alexander-6208.*

Calendar of the Royal College of Surgeons of England. 1888. Taylor & Francis

Churches, Steven. 'Put Not Your Faith in Princes (or Courts) – Agreements Made from Asymmetrical Power Bases: The Story of a Promise Made to Western Australia's Aboriginal People'. In *What Good Condition? Reflections on an Australian Aboriginal Treaty 1986–2006*, edited by Peter Read, Gary Meyers, and Bob Reece, 1st ed. ANU Press, 2006. *doi.org/10.22459/WGC.12.2006.01.*

Cowan, Peter. *A Unique Position: A Biography of Edith Dircksey Cowan, 1861-1932.*' University of Western Australia Press,1978.

Crawford, D. R. 'Coode, Sir John (1816–1892)'. In *Australian Dictionary of Biography*. Canberra: National Centre of Biography, Australian National University. *adb.anu.edu.au/biography/coode-sir-john-3250.*

Crowley, F. K. 'Forrest, Sir John (1847–1918)'. In *Australian Dictionary of Biography*. Canberra: National Centre of Biography, Australian National University. *adb.anu.edu.au/biography/forrest-sir-john-6211*

Curtin, Amanda. *Kathleen O'Connor of Paris*. Fremantle Press, 2018.

Evans, A. G. *C. Y. O'Connor: His Life and Legacy*. Crawley, W. A: University of Western Australia Press, 2001.

Hasluck, Alexandra. *C. Y. O'Connor*. Oxford University Press, 1965.

Hitchcock, J. K., and J. W. B. Stevens. *The History of Fremantle: The Front Gate of Australia, 1829-1929*. Fremantle: Fremantle City Council, 1929.

Jaggard, E. 'Vosper, Frederick Charles Burleigh (1869–1901)'. In *Australian Dictionary of Biography*. Canberra: National Centre of Biography, Australian National University. *adb.anu.edu.au/biography/vosper-frederick-charles-burleigh-8933.*

Kimberly, W. B., ed. *History of West Australia: A Narrative of Her Past Together with Biographies of Her Leading Men*. Carlisle, Western Australia: Hesperian Press, 2015. *nla.gov.au/nla.obj-30010617*

McPherson, Margaret. *History of Fremantle Arts Centre 1864 - 1946: Part 3: Dr. Henry Calvert Barnett Medical Superintendent - 25 Years*, 2012. Fremantle City Library Local History Collection

Phillips, Harry C. J. (Harry Charles John), and (issuing body) Western Australia. Parliament. 'Parliamentary Committees in the Western Australian Parliament: An Overview of Their Evolution, Functions and Features. Volume 1, 1870-2000'. Perth, [Western Australia]: Parliament of Western Australia, 2017.

Royal Geographical Society. *Proceedings of the Royal Geographical Society*. Stanford,1866 *www.google.com.au/books/edition/Proceedings_of_the_Royal_Geographical_So/HU9DAAAAcAAJ*

International Congress of Hygiene and Demography. *Seventh International Congress of Hygiene and Demography: London, August 10 - 17, 1891: Official Directory. London. wellcomecollection.org/works/m32ckb3r/items.*

Senate, United States Congress. *Senate Documents, Otherwise Publ. as Public Documents and Executive Documents: 14th Congress, 1st Session-48th Congress, 2nd Session and Special Session*, 1859. (Viewed at Google Books)

Shorter, Edward. *A History of Psychiatry: From the Era of the Asylum to the Age of Prozac*. Wiley, 1997.

Stevens, Abel, and James Floy (ed) *The National Magazine: Devoted to Literature, Art, and Religion*. Carlton & Phillips, 1858. (viewed at Google Books)

Tauman, Merab. *The Chief: C. Y. O'Connor*. Nedlands: University of Western Australia Press, 1978.

The Lancet London: A Journal of British and Foreign Medicine, Surgery, Obstetrics, Physiology, Chemistry, Pharmacology, Public Health and News. Elsevier, 1860.

The Saturday Review of Politics, Literature, Science and Art 1897-01-30: Vol 83 Issue 2153. Out-of-copyright, 1897. *archive.org/details/sim_saturday-review_1897-01-30_83_2153.*

Articles and papers

'Curthoys, Ann, "Settler Self-Government versus Aboriginal Rights, 1883 – 2001: The Shocking History of Section 70 of the Western Australian Constitution." *https://branchcollective.org (search 'Curthoys')*

Fox, Charlie. 'Jumna Khan'. *Studies in Western Australian History*, no. 16 (1 January 1995): 53–68.

'Front Matter'. *The Journal of the Royal Geographical Society of London* 41 (1871): i–cxxxiv. https://www.jstor.org/stable/3698048.

Johnston, Peter W —- "The Repeals of Section 70 of the Western Australian Constitution Act 1889: Aborigines and Governmental Breach of Trust" [1989] UWALawRw 16; (1989) 19(2) University of Western Australia Law Review 318'. *http://classic.austlii.edu.au/au/journals/UWALawRw/1989/16.html.*

Kabir, Nahid Afrose. 'The Culture of Mobile Lifestyle: Reflection on the Past - the Afghan Camel Drivers, 1860-1930'. *Continuum* 23 (2009): 791–802. *https://www.academia.edu/16650974*

Martyr, Philippa. '"Behaving Wildly": Diagnoses of Lunacy among Indigenous Persons in Western Australia, 1870-1914'. *Social History of Medicine* 24, no. 2 (1 August 2011): 316–33. *https://doi.org/10.1093/shm/hkq046.*

———. 'Equal under the Law? Indigenous People and the Lunacy Acts in Western Australia to 1920', n.d.

———. 'Unlikely Reformer: Dr Henry Calvert Barnett (1832–1897)'. *Australasian Psychiatry* 25, no. 5 (1 October 2017): 497–500. *https://doi*

.org/10.1177/1039856217715992.

Papers in Labour History No. 9, June 1992, Ed Lenore Taylor, Charlie Fox. papers-in-labour-history-no-9_wa.pdf (*labourhistory.org.au*).

Piddock, Susan. 'A Place for Convicts: The Fremantle Lunatic Asylum, Western Australia and John Conolly's "Ideal" Asylum'. *International Journal of Historical Archaeology* 20, no. 3 (2016): 562–73. *https://www.academia.edu/83799529*

'POISONING BY SULPHONAL.' *Journal of the American Medical Association* XVII, no. 11 (12 Sept 1891). *https://doi.org/10.1001/jama.1891.02410890039014*

Pugh, Don. 'Constructing Australia: Pipeline Dreams', n.d.

Tull, M. T. 'The Development of the Port of Fremantle, Australia's Western Gateway'. *The Great Circle* 7, no. 2 (1985): 116–38. www.jstor.org/stable/41562520.

Virtue, Roger. 'Lunacy and Social Reform in Western Australia, 1886-1903'. *Studies in Western Australian History*, no. 1: 29–65. *https://doi.org/10.3316/ielapa.780601581.*

Wallis, Alexandra. 'Hysterical Women: Moral Treatment of Female Patients in the Fremantle Lunatic Asylum, 1858 – 1908'. Ph D thesis, Notre Dame Australia, 2020. *https://researchonline.nd.edu.au/theses/260.*

Wallis, Alexandra. 'Driven to Insanity: Marital Cruelty and the Female Patients at the Fremantle Lunatic Asylum, 1858-1908'. *Limina* 24 (2019).

Websites

Lennon Wylie, 1843 Belfast/Ulster Street Directory, *www.lennonwylie.co.uk/BSD1843StreetsNames.htm*

'APA Dictionary of Psychology', *https://dictionary.apa.org*

City of Fremantle, *www.fremantle.wa.gov.au*

'Fremantle Stuff", *https://freotopia.org.*

'Google Books', *https://books.google.com/*

'MP Biographical Register', *www.parliament.wa.gov.au/parliament/library/MPHistoricalData.nsf*

National Museum of Australia, *www.nma.gov.au/defining-moments/resources/harveste*

judgement.

Anthropology from the Shed. 'Pre-Contact Indigenous Fremantle', *https://anthropologyfromtheshed.com/project/map-pre-contact-indigenous-fremantle/.*

History of Ireland, *www.historyireland.com/pandemic-cholera-in-belfast-1832/*

'Sheet 37 - History of Parliament House.Pdf'. *https://www.parliament.wa.gov.au/WebCMS/webcms.nsf/resources/file-37-history-of-parliament-house/$file/Sheet%2037%20-%20History%20of%20Parliament%20House.pdf*

Public Records Office of Ireland (PRONI), Freeholders, *https://apps.proni.gov.uk/freeholders*

'SROWA Perth Metro Maps'. *https://mapping.sro.wa.gov.au.*

National Institute of Diabetes and Digestive and Kidney Diseases. 'Symptoms & Causes of Cirrhosis | NIDDK'. *https://www.niddk.nih.gov/health-information/liver-disease/cirrhosis/symptoms-causes.*

'The Suicide Disease: Trigeminal Neuralgia - 1327 Words | Bartleby'. *https://www.bartleby.com/essay/The-Suicide-Disease-Trigeminal-Neuralgia-P3B27W3FT8X.*

'Victor Scanlan (1884-1897) - Find a Grave…' *https://www.findagrave.com/memorial/206948272/victor-scanlan.*

Videos

Constructing Australia (2007) Pipe Dreams, 2013. *https://www.youtube.com/watch?v=p8C8zr9QPZQ.*

CY O'CONNOR: LOVED AND ABANDONED? 2012. *https://www.youtube.com/watch?v=a0qiy9QO0Mw.*

About notes

Abbreviations used:

ADBO Australian Dictionary of Biography (online)

Ancestry Ancestry.com

DOJWA Department of Justice Western Australia

Hansard Western Australia, *Parliamentary debates* (parliament.wa.gov.au)

NLA National Library of Australia

RACPHML Royal Australasian College of Physicians, History of Medicine Library

(online at https://racp.intersearch.com.au)

SROWA State Records Office of Western Australia

Notes

PREFACE

1 'The Perth to Coolgardie Water Scheme | National Film and Sound Archive of Australia', https://www.nfsa.gov.au/latest/perth-coolgardie-water-scheme

2 Alexandra Hasluck, C. Y. O'Connor. Oxford University Press, 1965.

3 Merab Tauman, The Chief: C. Y. O'Connor (Nedlands: University of Western Australia Press, 1978).

4 A. G. Evans, C. Y. O'Connor: His Life and Legacy (Crawley, W. A: University of Western Australia Press, 2001).

5 Philippa Martyr, 'Unlikely Reformer: Dr Henry Calvert Barnett (1832–1897)', Australasian Psychiatry 25, no. 5 (1 October 2017): 497–500.

ONE: THE BOY FROM BELFAST

6 See Belfast Newsletter, June 03, 1828; Page: 4

7 History Ireland, Pandemic cholera in Belfast, 1832, https://www.historyireland.com/pandemic-cholera-in-belfast-1832

8 Died, *Belfast Newsletter*, 4 September 1832, 2

9 'A Card', *Belfast Newsletter*, 8 April 1825, p 2

10 Freeholders, Volume 77, Page 2, Line 40, apps.proni.gov.uk/freeholders

11 Lennon Wylie, 1843 Belfast/Ulster Street Directory, 1843 BSD Street Names (lennonwylie.co.uk)

12 *Belfast Newsletter*, April 13, 1841, p3

13 *Freemans journal*, 26 May, 1847.

14 *Belfast Newsletter*, 7 Jan 1848, p 1

15 Queen's University of Belfast, The Belfast Queen's College Calendar (Simms and M'Intyre, 1852), 84. (Viewed at Google Books, https://books.google.com)

16 Calendar of the Royal College of Surgeons of England. 1888 (Taylor & Francis, 1888), 100. Viewed at Google Books

17 'CELESTIAL RECOLLECTIONS.', *Victorian Express*, 18 June 1887, http://nla.gov.au/nla.news-article212630303; 'History of West Australia: A Narrative of Her Past Together

with Biographies of Her Leading Men', 89 (image 500) Trove, https://nla.gov.au/nla.obj-30010617.

18 Senate, United States Congress. Senate Documents, Otherwise Publ. as Public Documents and Executive Documents: 14th Congress, 1st Session-48th Congress, 2nd Session and Special Session, 1859. P 873-874. (viewed at Google Books)

19 Stevens, Abel, and James Floy (ed) *The National Magazine: Devoted to Literature, Art, and Religion.* Carlton & Phillips, 1858. 255 (Viewed at Google Books)

20 *Belfast Newsletter*, Friday, February 10, 1860; Page: 3

21 'A visit to Yosemite Valley, Falls and the Mammoth Trees of Calaveras, California', *Belfast News-Letter,* 27 July 1859, 4.

22 The Lancet London: Vol 1, May 1860. List of Licentiates of the Royal College of Physicians of Edinburgh. (Viewed at Google Books)

23 'List of Fellows of the Royal Geographical Society, The Journal of the Royal Geographical Society of London 41 (1871): xx, www.jstor.org/stable/3698048.

24 "Court for Divorce and Matrimonial Cause." *The Western Australian Times,* 11 September 1877: 2. http://nla.gov.au/nla.news-article2978070.

25 The National Archives; Kew, Surrey, England; Court for Divorce and Matrimonial Causes, later Supreme Court of Judicature: Divorce and Matrimonial Causes Files, J 77; Reference Number: J 77/34/L102. Viewed at Ancestry.com.au.

26 Medical Trials', *British Medical Journal,* 30 Nov. 1867, 509, viewed at https://books.googl e.com.

TWO: STORMY TIMES

27 "YORK." *The Inquirer and Commercial News,* 8 July 1868: 3. http://nla.gov.au/nla.news-ar ticle69387064

28 'Mr. Henry Calvert Barnett, J. P.', *W.A. Bulletin,* 25 February 1888, http://nla.gov.au/nla. news-article227588509; 'DEATH OF DR. BARNETT.', *Daily News,* 4 November 1897, http://nla.gov.au/nla.news-article82744520.

29 "LOCAL" *The Express,* 2 May 1872: 3. http://nla.gov.au/nla.news-article256610331

30 "Literary Institute." *Herald,* 5 February 1876: 3. http://nla.gov.au/nla.news-article10990 2566

31 "Correspondence." *The Perth Gazette and West Australian Times,* 27 May 1870: 2. http://nl a.gov.au/nla.news-article3749696

32 "The Week." *Herald,* 26 October 1872: 2. http://nla.gov.au/nla.news-article114441731

33 "Topics of the Week." *Herald,* 5 October 1872: 3. http://nla.gov.au/nla.news-article11444 1105

34 No title. *The Western Australian Times,* 27 April 1875: 4. http://nla.gov.au/nla.news-articl e2974067

35 'POLICE COURT, FREMANTLE.', *The Express*, 3 May 1870: 3. http://nla.gov.au/nla.news-article256621510

36 'FREMANTLE POLICE COURT.', *Western Australian Times*, 12 January 1877, http://nla.gov.au/nla.news-article2976962.

37 'SUPREME COURT.', *Herald*, 8 September 1877, http://nla.gov.au/nla.news-article106305344.

38 'SUPREME COURT.', *Herald*, 8 September 1877, http://nla.gov.au/nla.news-article106305343.

39 'LAW INTELLIGENCE.', *Inquirer and Commercial News*, 12 September 1877, http://nla.gov.au/nla.news-article66302110.

40 'LAW INTELLIGENCE.', *Inquirer and Commercial News*, 12 September 1877, http://nla.gov.au/nla.news-article66302113.

41 Annie-Lee Frost Matthews COPPLESTONE, family tree online at Ancestry

42 'OLD TIME MEMORIES.' *Western Mail*, 30 March 1917: 44. http://nla.gov.au/nla.news-article37987968

43 'Advertising', *Herald*, 25 October 1884, http://nla.gov.au/nla.news-article109665138

44 'ARCHITECTS AND THEIR EMPLOYERS.', *Western Mail*, 1 June 1889. http://nla.gov.au/nla.news-article32728201.

45 'General News.', *Inquirer and Commercial News*, 29 September 1886, http://nla.gov.au/nla.news-article66038339. 'FREMANTLE MUNICIPAL COUNCIL.', *Western Mail*, 9 October 1886, http://nla.gov.au/nla.news-article32698048.

46 Park Bungalow, 'Art Collection Catalogue', https://www.parliament.wa.gov.au/parliament/artcollect.nsf/WebPP/190FCB12726A086E48256D260022DE49?opendocument.

THREE: CHARLES YELVERTON O'CONNOR

47 Tauman, The Chief, 3

48 The Pilot, 29 March 1848

49 *Waterford News*, 19 October 1849

50 Tauman, The Chief, 10

51 Evans, C. Y. O'Connor, 96-97

52 Evans, C. Y. O'Connor, 67-69

53 C Y O'Connor and wife, 1865 - C. Y. O'Connor - Wikimedia Commons

54 *Grey River Argus*, Volume XXIII, Issue 3614, 25 March 1880, Page 2, https://paperspast.natlib.govt.nz/newspapers/GRA18800325.2.6.5

55 'Interprovincial.', *Evening Star*, 23 March 1880, https://paperspast.natlib.govt.nz/newspapers/ESD18800323.2.12.3; 'The Grey River Argus. Published Daily. Tuesday, March 23,

1880.', *Grey River Argus*, 23 March 1880, https://paperspast.natlib.govt.nz/newspapers/GRA18800323.2.4.

56 'Interprovincial.', *Evening Star*, 23 March 1880, https://paperspast.natlib.govt.nz/newspapers/ESD18800323.2.12.3.

57 'West Coast Times. Monday, March 22, 1880.', *West Coast Times*, 22 March 1880, https://paperspast.natlib.govt.nz/newspapers/WCT18800322.2.6.

58 Evans, C. Y. O'Connor, 85

59 'New Under – Secretary for Public Works.', *Daily Telegraph*, (New Zealand) 17 November 1883, https://paperspast.natlib.govt.nz/newspapers/DTN18831117.2.16.4

FOUR: DR BARNETT AND HIS GUESTS – 1891

60 'LADIES' COLUMN. LOCAL GOSSIP.', *Western Mail*, 24 January 1891, http://nla.gov.au/nla.news-article33063762.

61 'GENERAL NEWS.', *Daily News*, 18 December 1890, http://nla.gov.au/nla.news-article77425733.

62 'GOVERNMENT GAZETTE', *Herald*, 15 May 1880, http://nla.gov.au/nla.news-article110470833.

63 'A VISIT TO THE FREMANTLE LUNATIC ASYLUM.', *Daily News*, 27 February 1891, http://nla.gov.au/nla.news-article77425510.

64 Martyr, 'Unlikely Reformer', 498

65 Martyr, Philippa. 'Unlikely Reformer', 498

66 'Vigilans et Audax', *West Australian*, 24 January 1890, http://nla.gov.au/nla.news-article3131563.

67 'GOVERNMENT GAZETTE.', *Daily News*, 4 July 1890, http://nla.gov.au/nla.news-article76931252.

68 'Report upon the Lunatic Asylum at Fremantle, for the year 1890, by the Surgeon Superintendent.' Government Printer, Western Australia, 1891. Viewed at RACPHML

69 'THE FREMANTLE LUNATIC ASYLUM. (No. II.)', *Inquirer and Commercial News*, 9 April 1890, http://nla.gov.au/nla.news-article66928746.

FIVE: AN INQUIRY INTO THE ASYLUM – 1891

70 'Report upon the Lunatic Asylum at Fremantle, for the year 1889, by the Surgeon Superintendent.' Government Printer, Western Australia, 1890. Viewed at RACPHML

71 Hansard, Legislative Assembly, 2 Feb 1891, 103-109 (parliament.wa.gov.au); 'PARLIAMENT.', West Australian, 3 February 1891, http://nla.gov.au/nla.news-article3140328

72 'THE REVENUE RETURNS.' *Western Mail*, 24 January 1891, http://nla.gov.au/nla.news-article33063764.

73 'POINTS.', *Inquirer and Commercial News,* 30 January 1891, http://nla.gov.au/nla.news-article67197273.

74 'METEOROLOGICAL REPORT. WEDNESDAY, FEBRUARY 11.', *South Australian Register,* 12 February 1891, http://nla.gov.au/nla.news-article48089405.

75 Roger Virtue, 'Lunacy and Social Reform in Western Australia, 1886-1903', *Studies in Western Australian History,* no. 1: 36.

76 'REPORT OF THE SELECT COMMITTEE of the Legislative Assembly appointed to consider and report as to what is necessary to place the Asylum for the Insane on a satisfactory basis, as to accommodation and maintenance.' Viewed at RACPHML

77 'THURSDAY, FEBRUARY 19.', *Western Mail,* 21 February 1891, http://nla.gov.au/nla.news-article33064209.

78 Hansard, Legislative Assembly, 19 Feb 1891, 330

79 'PARLIAMENT.', *West Australian,* 20 February 1891, http://nla.gov.au/nla.news-article3140719. The subsequent discussion in the Council suggests that the wording and intent of the message from the Council to the Assembly had been misunderstood. The Council's real concern was to have the proposed loan of £150,000 earmarked for the Fremantle Harbour works listed separately, given the hotly debated nature of the proposed harbour developments.

80 'THE LEGISLATIVE CHAMBER.', *Inquirer and Commercial News,* 30 November 1870, http://nla.gov.au/nla.news-article66032093.

81 'Members of the Legislative Assembly 1896 [Picture] 000999d.Jpg', SLWA, accessed 9 January 2023, https://slwa.wa.gov.au/images/cof/000999d.jpg.

82 'LADIES SOCIAL GOSSIP.', *Western Mail,* 21 February 1891, http://nla.gov.au/nla.news-article33064254.

83 Hansard, Legislative Assembly, 11 Feb 1891, 238

84 Hansard, Legislative Assembly, 13 Feb 1891, 271

SIX: DR BARNETT TAKES LEAVE – 1891

85 'GENERAL NEWS.', *Daily News,* 17 March 1891, http://nla.gov.au/nla.news-article77422558.

86 Chief Secretary's Department and Colonial Secretary's Office, 'Official Letter of Recommendation to Colonial Government, Asks for. - H. C. Barnett, Surgeon Superintendent Lunatic Asylum.' (Item, 7 April 1891), AU WA S675- cons527 1891/0653, SROWA

87 The West Australian described him as a "Manillaman" i.e., Filipino

88 'SUICIDE AT THE LUNATIC ASYLUM.', *West Australian,* 30 March 1891, http://nla.gov.au/nla.news-article3141600.

89 'NEWS AND NOTES.', *West Australian,* 23 April 1891, http://nla.gov.au/nla.news-article3019201.

90 'Advertising', *Daily News*, 31 March 1891, http://nla.gov.au/nla.news-article77424769.

91 'Classified Advertising', *West Australian*, 28 April 1891, http://nla.gov.au/nla.news-article 3019349.

92 'Advertising', *Daily News*, 18 May 1891, http://nla.gov.au/nla.news-article76463341.

93 'Advertising', *Inquirer and Commercial News*, 27 May 1891, http://nla.gov.au/nla.news-art icle66229736.

94 'GENERAL NEWS.', *Daily News*, 6 June 1891, http://nla.gov.au/nla.news-article7646201 4.

95 'NEWS AND NOTES.', *West Australian*, 9 June 1891, http://nla.gov.au/nla.news-article30 20878.

96 'Report upon the Lunatic Asylum at Fremantle, for the year 1894, by the Superintending Medical Officer.' Government Printer, Western Australia, 1895. Viewed at RACPHML

97 Chief Secretary's Department and Colonial Secretary's Office, 'Extension of Leave of Absence to End of the Year. Telephone to House of Medical Superintendent Lunatic Asylum - Colonial Surgeon at Fremantle' (Item, 24 November 1892), AU WA S675-cons527 1892/1836, https://archive.sro.wa.gov.au/index.php/extension-of-leave-of-abs ence-to-end-of-the-year-telephone-to-house-of-medical-superintendent-lunatic-asylu m-colonial-surgeon-at-fremantle-1892-1836.

SEVEN: C. Y. O'CONNOR ARRIVES IN FREMANTLE – 1891

98 *Timaru Herald*, 14 May 1891, Page 2, https://paperspast.natlib.govt.nz/newspapers/THD 18910514.2.9

99 'A TRIP TO WESTERN AUSTRALIA AND YILGARN GOLDFIELDS.', *Evening Journal*, 28 March 1891, http://nla.gov.au/nla.news-article198405113.

100 'MR JOHN A. WRIGHT.', *Daily Telegraph*, 2 March 1891, http://nla.gov.au/nla.news-arti cle235882093.

101 Evans, *C. Y. O'Connor*, 108

102 'HEAVY RAIN AT ALBANY.', *West Australian*, 2 June 1891, http://nla.gov.au/nla.news-ar ticle3020644.

103 'NEWS AND NOTES.', *West Australian*, 1 June 1891, http://nla.gov.au/nla.news-article30 20601; 'ALBANY.', *Australian Advertiser*, 1 May 1891, http://nla.gov.au/nla.news-article2 60749803.

104 'THE LATE REV. W. LOWE.', *Eastern Districts Chronicle*, 6 June 1891, http://nla.gov.au/nl a.news-article148137840.

105 'NEWS AND NOTES.', *West Australian*, 2 June 1891, http://nla.gov.au/nla.news-article30 20636.

106 Evans, C. Y. O'Connor.

107 'GOVERNMENT GAZETTE.', *Western Mail*, 23 May 1891, http://nla.gov.au/nla.news-article33065823.

108 'NEWS AND NOTES.', *West Australian*, 3 June 1891, http://nla.gov.au/nla.news-article3020677.

109 J. K. Hitchcock and J. W. B. Stevens, *The History of Fremantle: The Front Gate of Australia, 1829-1929* (Fremantle: Fremantle City Council, 1929), 10 See https://freotopia.org/hitchcock.html.

110 'THE PERTH CROSSINGS QUESTION.', *Inquirer and Commercial News*, 17 June 1891, http://nla.gov.au/nla.news-article66233129.

111 'NEWS AND NOTES.', *Southern Times*, 22 June 1891, http://nla.gov.au/nla.news-article164855550.

112 'NEWS OF THE WEEK.', *Western Mail*, 11 July 1891, http://nla.gov.au/nla.news-article33066746.

113 'Government Notices.', *West Australian*, 15 September 1891, http://nla.gov.au/nla.news-article3024746.

114 'WESTERN AUSTRALIA.', *West Australian*, 27 August 1891, http://nla.gov.au/nla.news-article3023998.

115 'GENERAL NEWS.', *Inquirer and Commercial News*, 20 October 1891, http://nla.gov.au/nla.news-article69706011.

116 'The Daily News. TUESDAY, OCTOBER 20, 1891.', *Daily News*, 20 October 1891, http://nla.gov.au/nla.news-article77392590.

117 'THE MAYOR'S BALL.', *Daily News*, 10 July 1891, http://nla.gov.au/nla.news-article76465313.

118 'THE MAYOR'S BALL.', *West Australian*, 11 July 1891, http://nla.gov.au/nla.news-article3022037.

119 'GENERAL NEWS.', *Daily News*, 14 September 1891, http://nla.gov.au/nla.news-article76464160.

120 'THE CELEBRATION OF PROCLAMATION BAT.', *Daily News*, 10 October 1891, http://nla.gov.au/nla.news-article77388870.

121 'POINTS.', *Daily News*, 13 October 1891, http://nla.gov.au/nla.news-article77392367.

EIGHT: DR BARNETT'S TRAVELS - 1891-1892

122 'GOVERNMENT GAZETTE.', *W.A. Record*, 11 June 1891, http://nla.gov.au/nla.news-article211680737.

123 'FATALITY AT THE LUNATIC ASYLUM.', *West Australian*, 16 June 1891, http://nla.gov.au/nla.news-article3021145.

124 'SHIPPING.', *West Australian*, 29 June 1891, http://nla.gov.au/nla.news-article3021566.

125 The four were the Britannia, Arcadia, Victoria and Oceana

126 'THE P. AND O. COMPANY'S JUBILEE YEAR.', *Sydney Morning Herald*, 17 March 1887, http://nla.gov.au/nla.news-article13629578.

127 'GENERAL NEWS.', *Inquirer and Commercial News*, 1 May 1891, http://nla.gov.au/nla.news-article66229459.

128 'OLD TIME MEMORIES.', *Western Mail*, 30 March 1917, http://nla.gov.au/nla.news-article37987968.

129 'WESTERN AUSTRALIA.', *Daily News*, 20 October 1925, http://nla.gov.au/nla.news-article84181608.

130 'SHIPPING.', *Inquirer and Commercial News*, 7 August 1891, http://nla.gov.au/nla.news-article66231538.

131 'Seventh International Congress of Hygiene and Demography: London, August 10 -17, 1891: Official Directory.', Wellcome Collection, https://wellcomecollection.org/works/m32ckb3r/items. Henry Barnett's name isn't listed in the published handbook, nor is there any mention of a delegate from Western Australia. It's possible that Dr Barnett enrolled in the Congress too late for his name to be included.

132 In 1876, alarmed at the way household sewage in Fremantle was collected in cesspits which then drained into the drinking water sources, he published a pamphlet on how sanitation could be improved in Western Australia. It was still being cited years later.

133 'Singular Irish Probate Suit', *Freemans Journal*, 10 Dec 1897,5

134 The *Daily News* reported in July that Dr Barnett was making a close inspection of 'British, American and Continental Asylums', but there is no other suggestion that Dr Barnett travelled outside the British Isles. 'The Daily News. SATURDAY, JULY 29,1892.', *Daily News*, 23 July 1892, http://nla.gov.au/nla.news-article76456375.

135 Chief Secretary's Department and Colonial Secretary's Office, 'Extension of Leave of Absence to End of the Year. Telephone to House of Medical Superintendent Lunatic Asylum - Colonial Surgeon at Fremantle' (Item, 24 November 1892), AU WA S675-cons527 1892/1836, SROWA.

136 'Report upon the Lunatic Asylum at Fremantle, for the year 1894, by the Superintending Medical Officer.' Government Printer, Western Australia, 1895. Viewed at RACPHML

137 'APA Dictionary of Psychology', https://dictionary.apa.org/.

138 The Australian author Henry Handel Richardson described this process of mental, physical and social deterioration, in her three-part novel *The Fortunes of Richard Mahoney*. She based the work on her own experience of her father's illness.

139 Edward Shorter, A History of Psychiatry: From the Era of the Asylum to the Age of Prozac (Wiley, 1997) 49-61

140 'MEN AND THINGS.', *Daily News*, 22 January 1892, http://nla.gov.au/nla.news-article77392693.

NINE: O'CONNOR PLANS A HARBOUR – 1892

141 'FREMANTLE HARBOUR.', *West Australian*, 15 October 1912, http://nla.gov.au/nla.news-article26523758.

142 'LOCAL AND GENERAL.', *Western Australian Times*, 1 February 1878, http://nla.gov.au/nla.news-article2978689.

143 'LOCAL AND GENERAL.', *Western Australian Times*, 26 March 1878, http://nla.gov.au/nla.news-article2978940.

144 'SIR JOHN COODE'S REPORT ON FREMANTLE HARBOUR.', *Western Australian Times*, 4 June 1878, http://nla.gov.au/nla.news-article2979337.

145 'SIR JOHN COODE'S REPORT.', *West Australian*, 21 May 1887, http://nla.gov.au/nla.news-article3764893.

146 'Western Australia. Report on the Blue Book, 1887', *Inquirer and Commercial News*, 2 November 1888, http://nla.gov.au/nla.news-article66084725.

147 'HARBOR WORKS FOR FREMANTLE.', *Daily News*, 21 May 1887, http://nla.gov.au/nla.news-article76067694.

148 'The Daily News. FRIDAY, MAY 27,1887.', *Daily News*, 27 May 1887, http://nla.gov.au/nla.news-article76068227.

149 'THE ORIENT STEAMERS.', *West Australian*, 6 June 1891, http://nla.gov.au/nla.news-article3020805.

150 'THE OWEN ANCHORAGE HARBOUR SCHEME.', *West Australian*, 29 December 1891, http://nla.gov.au/nla.news-article3029480.

151 'HARBOR WORKS FOR FREMANTLE.', *Daily News*, 21 May 1887, http://nla.gov.au/nla.news-article76067694.

152 'FREMANTLE HARBOR WORKS.', *Australian Advertiser*, 25 September 1891, http://nla.gov.au/nla.news-article260753285.

153 No Title, *Australian Advertiser*, 28 September 1891, http://nla.gov.au/nla.news-article260753323.

154 'Vigilans et Audax.', *West Australian*, 25 September 1891, http://nla.gov.au/nla.news-article3025225; 'The Daily News. MONDAY, SEPTEMBER 28, 1891.', *Daily News*, 28 September 1891, http://nla.gov.au/nla.news-article76462186.

155 'THE OWEN ANCHORAGE HARBOUR SCHEME.', *West Australian*, 29 December 1891, http://nla.gov.au/nla.news-article3029480.

156 'PARLIAMENT.', *Daily News*, 8 December 1891, http://nla.gov.au/nla.news-article77389580; 'PURCHASE OF A HOPPER DREDGER.', *Australian Advertiser*, 13 November 1891, http://nla.gov.au/nla.news-article260754268.

157 'Vigilans et Audax.', *West Australian*, 29 December 1891, http://nla.gov.au/nla.news-article3029460.

158 'HARBOUR WORKS AT FREMANTLE.', *Daily News*, 7 January 1892, http://nla.gov.au/nla.news-article77392917.

159 Tauman, *The Chief*,68

160 Hansard, Legislative Assembly, 6 Jan 1892, 186-192

161 'The Daily News. FRIDAY, JANUARY 8, 1892.', *Daily News*, 8 January 1892, http://nla.go v.au/nla.news-article77388292.

162 'Vigilans et Audax', *West Australian*, 7 January 1892, http://nla.gov.au/nla.news-article30 29996.

163 'NEWS AND NOTES.', *West Australian*, 9 January 1892, http://nla.gov.au/nla.news-articl e3030126.

164 'THE FREMANTLE HARBOUR WORKS.', *Inquirer and Commercial News*, 13 January 1892, http://nla.gov.au/nla.news-article69704181.

165 Harry C.J. Phillips, 'Parliamentary Committees in the Western Australian Parliament: an overview of their evolution, functions and features - Volume 1: 1879-2000.' Parliament of Western Australia, 2017 73

166 Hansard, Legislative Assembly, 19 January 1892, 324

167 'The Courier.', *Hobart Town Courier and Van Diemen's Land Gazette*, 24 July 1840, http://nl a.gov.au/nla.news-article8748486.

168 'THE CHINESE QUESTION IN WESTERN AUSTRALIA.', *Western Mail*, 14 November 1891, http://nla.gov.au/nla.news-article33068749.

169 'THE CHINESE QUESTION.', West Australian, 18 January 1892, http://nla.gov.au/nla.n ews-article3030481.

170 'THE CHINESE QUESTION', People, 6 February 1892, http://nla.gov.au/nla.news-artic le257693207.

171 'PARLIAMENT.', West Australian, 3 March 1892, http://nla.gov.au/nla.news-article3032 623.

172 'PARLIAMENT.', Daily News, 11 March 1892, http://nla.gov.au/nla.news-article773915 53.

173 Hansard, Legislative Assembly, 19 January 1892, 315ff

TEN: O'CONNOR GRILLED – 1892

174 'The Daily News. TUESDAY, FEBRUARY 23, 1892.', *Daily News*, 23 February 1892, http://nla.gov.au/nla.news-article77389162.

175 'PARLIAMENT.', *Daily News*, 22 January 1892, http://nla.gov.au/nla.news-article773926 98.

176 Phillips, 'Parliamentary Committees in the Western Australian Parliament', 76 https://w ww.parliament.wa.gov.au/WebCMS/webcms.nsf/resources/file-parliamentary-committ ees-dr-harry/$file/Parliamentary_Committees-Dr_Harry_Phillips.pdf.

177 'PARLIAMENT.', *West Australian*, 22 January 1892, http://nla.gov.au/nla.news-article303 0704.

178 Phillips, 'Parliamentary Committees in the Western Australian Parliament', 77. 'Harbour Works at Fremantle.', *Inquirer and Commercial News*, 20 February 1892, http://nla.gov.au/nla.news-article69706103.

179 'THE FREMANTLE HARBOUR QUESTION.', *West Australian*, 19 February 1892, http://nla.gov.au/nla.news-article3032019.

180 'THE FREMANTLE HARBOUR QUESTION.', *West Australian*, 19 February 1892, http://nla.gov.au/nla.news-article3032019.

181 'The Daily News. TUESDAY, FEBRUARY 23, 1892.', *Daily News*, 23 February 1892, http://nla.gov.au/nla.news-article77389162.

182 'Report of the Joint Select Committee of the Legislative Council and the Legislative Assembly on the Question of Harbor Works at Fremantle, together with the Proceedings of the Committee Minutes of Evidence, and Appendix, Votes and Proceedings, 15 February 1892, 6. Quoted in Phillips, 'Parliamentary Committees in the Western Australian Parliament', 78

ELEVEN: PROGRESS – 1892

183 D. R. Crawford, 'Coode, Sir John (1816–1892)', in *ADB*, https://adb.anu.edu.au/biography/coode-sir-john-3250.

184 'FREMANTLE HARBOUR WORKS.', *West Australian*, 8 April 1892, http://nla.gov.au/nla.news-article3034184.

185 'Local and General', *W.A. Record*, 19 May 1892, http://nla.gov.au/nla.news-article211973878.

186 'The West Australian.', *West Australian*, 3 June 1892, http://nla.gov.au/nla.news-article3036274.

187 'EMPLOYMENT ON THE FREMANTLE HARBOUR WORKS.', *West Australian*, 2 August 1892, http://nla.gov.au/nla.news-article3038446.

188 'GENERAL NEWS.', *Daily News*, 1 August 1892, http://nla.gov.au/nla.news-article76456473.

189 'NEWS AND NOTES.', *West Australian*, 14 September 1892, http://nla.gov.au/nla.news-article3039991.

190 'FREMANTLE HARBOR WORKS.', *Inquirer and Commercial News*, 15 April 1898, http://nla.gov.au/nla.news-article66703439.

191 In fact, the Forrest government was intent on removing the one section of the constitution (Section 70) that acknowledged the rights and needs of indigenous people in Western Australia. See 'Johnston, Peter W. "*The Repeals of Section 70 of the Western Australian Constitution Act 1889: Aborigines and Governmental Breach of Trust*" [1989].

192 'WOMEN'S CHRISTIAN TEMPERANCE UNION.', *Western Mail*, 20 August 1892, http://nla.gov.au/nla.news-article33072596.

193 Report says sandstone but elsewhere it is referred to as limestone

194 'FREMANTLE HARBOUR WORKS.', *Daily News*, 29 August 1892, http://nla.gov.au/nla.news-article76456586.

195 'People', https://freotopia.org/people/irvinejohn.html.

196 Evans, *C. Y. O'Connor*, 132; Tauman, *The Chief*, 243-244

TWELVE: THE CROSS AND THE INDIGNANT – 1892

197 http://nla.gov.au/nla.news-article3039603

198 Evans, *C. Y. O'Connor*, 139; Tauman, *The Chief*, p 115

199 Papers in Labour History No. 9, June 1992, Ed Lenore Taylor, Charlie Fox, 40-45 papers-in-labour-history-no-9_wa.pdf (labourhistory.org.au)

200 Evans, *C. Y. O'Connor*, 139

201 'Departure of Mr C. Y. O'Connor, District Engineer,', *Grey River Argus*, 25 March 1880, https://paperspast.natlib.govt.nz/newspapers/GRA18800325.2.6.5.

202 'THE SOUTHERN CROSS STRIKE.', *Daily News*, 16 September 1892, http://nla.gov.au/nla.news-article77386057.

203 'SOUTHERN CROSS NEWS.', *West Australian*, 26 September 1892, http://nla.gov.au/nla.news-article3040405; 'THE ENGINEER-IN-CHIEF AT SOUTHERN CROSS.', *Daily News*, 20 September 1892, http://nla.gov.au/nla.news-article77387835.

204 'NEWS OF THE WEEK.', *Western Mail*, 9 July 1892, http://nla.gov.au/nla.news-article33073568; 'PROSPECTS OF WESTERN AUSTRALIA', *Australian Advertiser*, 22 August 1892, http://nla.gov.au/nla.news-article260609366.

205 'THE LOCOMOTIVE WORKSHOPS.', *West Australian*, 21 September 1892, http://nla.gov.au/nla.news-article3040228.

206 'THE REMOVAL OF THE GOVERNMENT LOCO. SHOPS FROM FREMANTLE.', *Daily News*, 29 September 1892, http://nla.gov.au/nla.news-article77384028.

207 'SOUTHERN CROSS NEWS.', *West Australian*, 26 September 1892, http://nla.gov.au/nla.news-article3040405.

THIRTEEN: HEARTACHES AND HOSPITALITY – 1892

208 'SPORTING INTELLIGENCE.', *West Australian*, 8 September 1892, http://nla.gov.au/nla.news-article3039811.

209 'MUSICAL "AT HOME" AT GOVERNMENT HOUSE.', *West Australian*, 27 August 1892, http://nla.gov.au/nla.news-article3039344.

210 'NEWS AND NOTES.', *West Australian*, 1 August 1892, http://nla.gov.au/nla.news-article3038393.

211 The boy's name was not recorded in the newspaper accounts, but it seems more likely that Frank would be riding alone than 11-year-old Roderick or 4-year-old Murtagh.

212 'NEWS AND NOTES.', *West Australian*, 11 October 1892, http://nla.gov.au/nla.news-article3040926; 'SERIOUS ACCIDENT ON THE FREMANTLE ROAD.', *Inquirer and Commercial News*, 12 October 1892, http://nla.gov.au/nla.news-article66309965.

213 'FREMANTLE HARBOUR WORKS', *Daily News*, 17 November 1892, http://nla.gov.au/nla.news-article77385755; 'FREMANTLE HARBOUR WORKS.', *West Australian*, 17 November 1892, http://nla.gov.au/nla.news-article3042168.

214 'Classified Advertising', *West Australian*, 15 November 1892, http://nla.gov.au/nla.news-article3042100. ('Situations vacant')

215 'FREMANTLE HARBOUR WORKS.', *West Australian*, 17 November 1892, http://nla.gov.au/nla.news-article3042168; 'FREMANTLE HARBOUR WORKS', *Daily News*, 17 November 1892, http://nla.gov.au/nla.news-article77385755

216 'GARDEN PARTY AT GOVERNMENT HOUSE.', *West Australian*, 16 November 1892, http://nla.gov.au/nla.news-article3042126.

FOURTEEN: DR BARNETT'S RETURN – 1892-1893

217 'NEWS AND NOTES.', *West Australian*, 5 November 1892, http://nla.gov.au/nla.news-article3041764.

218 Chief Secretary's Department and Colonial Secretary's Office, 'Extension of Leave of Absence to End of the Year. Telephone to House of Medical Superintendent Lunatic Asylum - Colonial Surgeon at Fremantle' (Item, 24 November 1892), AU WA S675-cons527 1892/1836. SROWA

219 'NEWS AND NOTES.', *West Australian*, 18 January 1893, http://nla.gov.au/nla.news-article3044284.

220 'CORRESPONDENCE.', *West Australian*, 6 December 1892, http://nla.gov.au/nla.news-article3042845.

221 Report upon the Lunatic Asylum at Fremantle, for the year 1892, by the Acting Surgeon Superintendent, Government Printer, Western Australia, 1893. RACPHML

222 . 'NEWS AND NOTES.', *West Australian*, 30 January 1892, http://nla.gov.au/nla.news-article3031104.

223 'GENERAL NEWS.', *Daily News*, 13 May 1892, http://nla.gov.au/nla.news-article76460354.

224 'THE LUNATIC ASYLUM.', *Inquirer and Commercial News*, 15 June 1892, http://nla.gov.au/nla.news-article66311271.

225 'THE LUNATIC ASYLUM.', *Daily News*, 20 June 1892, http://nla.gov.au/nla.news-article76457896.

226 'LEGISLATIVE ASSEMBLY', *West Australian*, 24 February 1892, http://nla.gov.au/nla.news-article3032231.

227 'FREMANTLE MUNICIPAL COUNCIL.', *Inquirer and Commercial News*, 6 July 1892, http://nla.gov.au/nla.news-article66308797.

228 Report upon the Lunatic Asylum at Fremantle, for the year 1892, by the Acting Surgeon Superintendent, Government Printer, Western Australia, 1893. RACPHML

229 'HOSPITAL ACCOMMODATION FOE FREMANTLE.', *Inquirer and Commercial News*, 14 September 1892, http://nla.gov.au/nla.news-article66305275.

230 'FREMANTLE MUNICIPAL COUNCILS', *West Australian*, 7 July 1892, http://nla.gov.au /nla.news-article3037483.

231 'A HOSPITAL FOR FREMANTLE.', *Inquirer and Commercial News*, 17 March 1893, http://nla.gov.au/nla.news-article66244208.

232 'TO THE EDITOR.', *West Australian*, 12 June 1893, http://nla.gov.au/nla.news-article304 9292.

233 'GENERAL NEWS.', *Daily News*, 15 March 1893, http://nla.gov.au/nla.news-article7692 2563; 'The Daily News. PERTH, TUESDAY, MARCH 28, 1893.', *Daily News*, 28 March 1893, http://nla.gov.au/nla.news-article76922488; 'A CASE OF SMALLPOX IN PERTH.', *Australian Advertiser*, 29 March 1893, http://nla.gov.au/nla.news-article260602398.

234 'NEWS AND NOTES.', *West Australian*, 10 October 1893, http://nla.gov.au/nla.news-arti cle3053463.

235 'REPORTED SMALLPOX IN PERTH', *West Australian*, 28 March 1893, http://nla.gov.au /nla.news-article3046669.

236 'SMALL POX IN PERTH.', *Daily News*, 4 April 1893, http://nla.gov.au/nla.news-article7 6924823.

237 'PROTEST FROM FREMANTLE.', *Daily News*, 8 April 1893, http://nla.gov.au/nla.news-article76923045.

238 'LATER FROM FREMANTLE.', *Daily News*, 14 April 1893, http://nla.gov.au/nla.news-ar ticle76924221.

239 'NEWS AND NOTES.', *West Australian*, 24 April 1893, http://nla.gov.au/nla.news-article 3047521.

240 'THE SMALL-POX EPIDEMIC.', *West Australian*, 26 April 1893, http://nla.gov.au/nla.ne ws-article3047621.

241 . 'LOCAL BOARD OF HEALTH.', *West Australian*, 6 June 1893, http://nla.gov.au/nla.new s-article3049045.

242 'FREMANTLE LOCAL BOARD OF HEALTH.', Inquirer and Commercial News, 2 June 1893, http://nla.gov.au/nla.news-article66242177. The population of Fremantle in 1893 was about 8,000, see The Statesman's Year-Book - Google Books

243 'THE SMALL-POX SCARE.', *West Australian*, 8 April 1893, http://nla.gov.au/nla.news-ar ticle3047009.

244 'COLORED CHEAP LABOUR', *Daily News*, 13 June 1893, http://nla.gov.au/nla.news-ar ticle76927182.

245 Dr Scott had resigned as Mayor in 1891 (in fact he left for London on the same ship as Dr Barnett). He had been succeeded briefly by Edward Keene and Stephen Henry Parker.

246 'THE MAYORALTY.', *West Australian*, 2 December 1892, http://nla.gov.au/nla.news-article3042707.

247 'THE GOVERNOR'S BALL.', *West Australian*, 22 June 1893, http://nla.gov.au/nla.news-article3049630.

248 'NEWS AND NOTES.', *West Australian*, 10 July 1893, http://nla.gov.au/nla.news-article3050260.

249 'SUPREME COURT—CIVIL SITTINGS.', *Daily News*, 17 July 1893, http://nla.gov.au/nla.news-article77379151.

250 'FREMANTLE ROWING CLUB BALL.' *West Australian*, 5 August 1893, https://trove.nla.gov.au/newspaper/article/3051241.

251 'NEWS AND NOTES.', *West Australian*, 25 October 1893, http://nla.gov.au/nla.news-article3053966.

252 'A PEEP AT CEYLON.', *West Australian*, 28 October 1893, http://nla.gov.au/nla.news-article3054129.

FIFTEEN: THE OMNIPOTENT CHIEF ENGINEER – 1893

253 'FREMANTLE HARBOUR WORKS', *West Australian*, 1 March 1893, http://nla.gov.au/nla.news-article3045772.

254 'OPENING OF PARLIAMENT.', *Daily News*, 5 July 1893, http://nla.gov.au/nla.news-article76924286.

255 Hansard, Legislative Assembly, 19 July 1893, 117 ff; 'NEWS AND NOTES.', *West Australian*, 15 May 1893, http://nla.gov.au/nla.news-article3048279.

256 'MINING.', *Geraldton Murchison Telegraph*, 10 January 1893, http://nla.gov.au/nla.news-article260026894.

257 'SOUTHERN CROSS NEWS.', *Western Mail*, 21 January 1893, http://nla.gov.au/nla.news-article33076048.

258 'THE WATER SUPPLY QUESTION.', *West Australian*, 22 March 1893, http://nla.gov.au/nla.news-article3046474.

259 'NEWS AND NOTES.', *West Australian*, 21 March 1893, http://nla.gov.au/nla.news-article3046433.

260 'PROVINCIAL TELEGRAMS.', *Inquirer and Commercial News*, 7 July 1893, http://nla.gov.au/nla.news-article71893459.

261 'NEWS AND NOTES.', *West Australian*, 22 November 1893, http://nla.gov.au/nla.news-article3055018.

262 'PARLIAMENT.', *West Australian*, 29 August 1893, http://nla.gov.au/nla.news-article3052005.

263 'OUR OPEN COLUMN.', *Daily News*, 12 August 1893, http://nla.gov.au/nla.news-article 77376907.

264 'OUR OPEN COLUMN', *Daily News*, 20 June 1893, http://nla.gov.au/nla.news-article76 925127; 'THE WORKS AND RAILWAY DEPARTMENT.', *Inquirer and Commercial News*, 4 August 1893, http://nla.gov.au/nla.news-article71892319.

265 'THE PAY OF CIVIL SERVANTS.', *West Australian*, 6 September 1893, http://nla.gov.au/ nla.news-article3052288.

266 If 'Honor' was O'Connor, it would be tempting to guess that 'Jarrah' might have been the pseudonym of Alexander Forrest. However, letters to the paper under the name 'Jarrah' continued to appear after Forrest's death in 1901.

267 Hansard, Legislative Assembly, 5 July 1893; 'THE AUDITOR-GENERAL'S REPORT.', *West Australian*, 7 July 1893, http://nla.gov.au/nla.news-article3050185.

268 'THE WORKS DEPARTMENT AND THE AUDITOR-GENERAL.', *West Australian*, 7 September 1893, http://nla.gov.au/nla.news-article3052343.

269 'Vigilans et Audax', *West Australian*, 8 September 1893, http://nla.gov.au/nla.news-article 3052373.

SIXTEEN: MISHAPS, MEETINGS AND MEMORANDUMS – 1893

270 'GENERAL NEWS.', *Daily News*, 21 January 1893, http://nla.gov.au/nla.news-article773 85848; 'Local and General.', *W.A. Record*, 15 June 1893, http://nla.gov.au/nla.news-article 211986578

271 'THE ROCKY BAY QUARRY ACCIDENT.', *West Australian*, 4 October 1893, http://nla.g ov.au/nla.news-article3053282.

272 'NEWS AND NOTES.', *West Australian*, 23 October 1893, http://nla.gov.au/nla.news-arti cle3053935.

273 'NEWS AND NOTES.', *West Australian*, 26 October 1893, http://nla.gov.au/nla.news-arti cle3054002.

274 'BLASTING ACCIDENT AT ROCKY BAY.', *West Australian*, 4 November 1893, http://nl a.gov.au/nla.news-article3054369.

275 'THE LOCOMOTIVE WORKSHOPS QUESTION', *West Australian*, 6 November 1893, http://nla.gov.au/nla.news-article3054401.

276 Parliament of Western Australia, 'The Constitution Act Amendment Act 1893 (57 Vict. No. 14)' The Constitution Act Amendment Act 1893 (57 Vict. No. 14) (austlii.edu.au).

277 Hansard, Legislative Assembly, 24 July 1893, 135ff.

278 'PARLIAMENT.', *Australian Advertiser*, 28 July 1893, http://nla.gov.au/nla.news-article26 0607880.

279 In September 1893, women in New Zealand became the first in a self-governing country to win the right to vote.

280 'THE DRINK TRAFFIC AND THE WOMENS FRANCHISE.', *West Australian*, 21 November 1893, http://nla.gov.au/nla.news-article3055006.

281 The WCTU, the Karrakatta club and other supporters continued their campaign for women's right to vote. By 1899, John Forrest had come round to the view that, since most women lived in the metropolitan areas of Perth and Fremantle, and married women would likely vote the same way as their husbands, their votes would be a useful counterbalance to the labor-voting men of the goldfields. He supported the passage of the Constitution Acts Amendment Act, which passed through the Assembly with a majority of eleven votes in August 1899 and was proclaimed in May 1900. Women in Western Australia (other than indigenous women) went on to vote for the first time in the referendum on Federation held in July 1900.

282 'THE ENGINEER-IN-CHIEF AND THE AUDITOR-GENERAL.', *West Australian*, 16 February 1894, http://nla.gov.au/nla.news-article3058181.

283 'NEWS AND NOTES.', *West Australian*, 11 January 1894, http://nla.gov.au/nla.news-article3056834.

284 'THE WESTERN AUSTRALIAN GOLD-FIELDS.', *Argus*, 6 January 1894, http://nla.gov.au/nla.news-article8722447.

SEVENTEEN: A PHYSICAL DRAWBACK - 1894

285 'HOSPITAL REQUIREMENTS AT FREMANTLE.', West Australian, 8 January 1894, http://nla.gov.au/nla.news-article3056725; 'FREMANTLE MUNICIPAL COUNCIL.', West Australian, 26 January 1894, http://nla.gov.au/nla.news-article3057426.

286 'CORRESPONDENCE.', *West Australian*, 30 January 1894, http://nla.gov.au/nla.news-article3057543.

287 'THE FREMANTLE HOSPITAL QUESTION AND DR. BARNETT.', *West Australian*, 31 January 1894, http://nla.gov.au/nla.news-article3057593.

288 'DEATH AT THE FREMANTLE LUNATIC ASYLUM.', *Western Mail*, 13 January 1894, http://nla.gov.au/nla.news-article33099947.

289 'THE WESTERN AUSTRALIAN BANK.', *Western Mail*, 28 January 1893, http://nla.gov.au/nla.news-article33075994.

290 'NEWS AND NOTES', *West Australian*, 2 February 1894, http://nla.gov.au/nla.news-article3057669.

291 'THE REMOVAL OF THE ASYLUM', *Daily News*, 17 February 1894, http://nla.gov.au/nla.news-article76485599.

292 Chief Secretary's Department and Colonial Secretary's Office, 'Asking That His Official Medical Duties May for the Time Be Confined to Superintendence of and Attendance on All Lunatics in Asylums - Colonial Surgeon at Fremantle' (Item, 10 March 1894), AU WA S675- cons527 1894/0325, SROWA.

293 'SPORTING NEWS.', *Inquirer and Commercial News*, 25 May 1894, http://nla.gov.au/nla.news-article66245457.

294 Colonial Secretary's office, minute paper 94, 13 March 1894, Cons 1003 1900-0301 (not yet indexed) SROWA.

295 'The Suicide Disease: Trigeminal Neuralgia - 1327 Words | Bartleby', https://www.bartleby.com/essay/The-Suicide-Disease-Trigeminal-Neuralgia-P3B27W3FT8X.

296 . 'NEWS AND NOTES.', *West Australian*, 11 August 1894, http://nla.gov.au/nla.news-article3065314.

297 'SOCIAL NOTES.', *West Australian*, 15 August 1894, http://nla.gov.au/nla.news-article3065462.

298 'THE KARRAKATTA CLUB.', *West Australian*, 23 November 1894, http://nla.gov.au/nla.news-article3069369.

299 Western Australia Parliament, 'Report Upon the Lunatic Asylum at Fremantle for the Year 1893 by the Superintending Medical Officer. No. 13', 1894. RACPHML

300 'GENERAL NEWS.', *Daily News*, 30 July 1894, http://nla.gov.au/nla.news-article77282795.

301 'NEWS AND NOTES.', *West Australian*, 26 September 1894, http://nla.gov.au/nla.news-article3067069.

302 'POLICE COURT REPORTS.', *Inquirer and Commercial News*, 19 October 1894, http://nla.gov.au/nla.news-article66252692.

303 'PARLIAMENT.', *Daily News*, 2 October 1894, http://nla.gov.au/nla.news-article76467527; 'PARLIAMENT.', *West Australian*, 2 October 1894, http://nla.gov.au/nla.news-article3067261; Hansard, Legislative Assembly, 1 October 1894, 834.

304 Hansard, Legislative Assembly, 3 October 1894, 884.

305 Chief Secretary's Department and Colonial Secretary's Office, 'Colonial Surgeon at Fremantle. For Post of, - Louis Wheeler' (Item, 4 October 1894), AU WA S675- cons527 1894/1671.

306 'OPERETTA AT GOVERNMENT HOUSE.', *Inquirer and Commercial News*, 19 January 1894, http://nla.gov.au/nla.news-article66314749; '"PREDATOROS" IN MELBOURNE.', *West Australian*, 20 November 1894, http://nla.gov.au/nla.news-article3069238.

307 'Public Record Office Victoria Collection | PROV', https://prov.vic.gov.au/archive/428BE78B-F96C-11E9-AE98-8F34A61BA797?image=179. image 179; 'Public Record Office Victoria Collection | PROV', https://prov.vic.gov.au/archive/26A1A425-F7F0-11E9-AE98-EDAAD0290EC2?image=309. image 309; 'SHIPPING INTELLIGENCE.' *The Argus* 2 November 1894 http://nla.gov.au/nla.news-article8718448; 'SHIPPING INTELLIGENCE', Australian Advertiser, 3 December 1894, http://nla.gov.au/nla.news-article260682482.

308 'ORIGINAL POETRY.', *Daily News*, 13 October 1894, http://nla.gov.au/nla.news-article76470341.

309 'THE COUNCIL OF THE SWANS.', *Inquirer and Commercial News*, 15 June 1870, http://nla.gov.au/nla.news-article66031619.

310 'POETRY.', *West Australian*, 3 November 1894, http://nla.gov.au/nla.news-article3068516.

EIGHTEEN: THIS GENTLEMAN FROM NEW ZEALAND – 1894

311 'TABLEAUX AND CONCERT AT FREMANTLE.', *West Australian*, 3 April 1894, http://nla.gov.au/nla.news-article3060013; 'THE ALL NATIONS FAIR AT FREMANTLE.', *West Australian*, 13 September 1894, http://nla.gov.au/nla.news-article3066547.

312 'THE FREMANTLE MUSICAL FESTIVAL.', *Inquirer and Commercial News*, 12 October 1894, http://nla.gov.au/nla.news-article66251919.

313 Amanda Curtin, *Kathleen O'Connor of Paris* (Fremantle Press, 2018).

314 'FREMANTLE CHESS CLUB.', *Daily News*, 16 April 1894, http://nla.gov.au/nla.news-article76484032.

315 'SPORTING INTELLIGENCE.', *West Australian*, 23 April 1894, http://nla.gov.au/nla.news-article3060793.

316 'INSPECTION OF THE NEW RAILWAY STATION.', *Southern Times*, 26 May 1894, http://nla.gov.au/nla.news-article157521640; 'THE NEW RAILWAY STATION.', *Geraldton Murchison Telegraph*, 25 May 1894, http://nla.gov.au/nla.news-article260149218.

317 'THE IMPROVEMENTS ON THE EASTERN RAILWAY.', *West Australian*, 21 February 1894, http://nla.gov.au/nla.news-article3058367.

318 'NEWS AND NOTES.', *West Australian*, 24 January 1894, http://nla.gov.au/nla.news-article3057361.

319 'Vigilans et Audax', *West Australian*, 12 April 1894, http://nla.gov.au/nla.news-article3060338.

320 'NEWS AND NOTES.', *West Australian*, 9 May 1894, http://nla.gov.au/nla.news-article3061425.

321 'THE GOVERNMENT POLICY', *Daily News*, 26 May 1894, http://nla.gov.au/nla.news-article77279108; Hansard, Legislative Assembly, 24 Sept 1894, 718.

322 'THE POPULATION OF WESTERN AUSTRALIA.', *Brisbane Courier*, 12 April 1894, http://nla.gov.au/nla.news-article3577818.

323 'THE PREMIER'S SPEECH AT BUNBURY.', *Daily News*, 26 May 1894, http://nla.gov.au/nla.news-article77279138.

324 'A MINISTERIAL MINUTE.', *West Australian*, 20 June 1894, http://nla.gov.au/nla.news-article3063124.

325 'VIGILANS ET AUDAX', *West Australian*, 30 July 1894, http://nla.gov.au/nla.news-article3064760; 'THE AUDITOR-GENERAL AND THE RAILWAY DEPARTMENT', *Daily*

News, 31 July 1894, http://nla.gov.au/nla.news-article77282193; 'SATURDAY, AUGUST 11TH.', *Southern Times*, 11 August 1894, http://nla.gov.au/nla.news-article157523234.

326 'PARLIAMENT.', *Southern Times*, 2 October 1894, http://nla.gov.au/nla.news-article157524286; 'PARLIAMENT.', *West Australian*, 2 October 1894, http://nla.gov.au/nla.news-article3067261; Hansard, Legislative Assembly, 1 Oct 1894, 829.

327 'NEWS AND NOTES.', *West Australian*, 10 July 1894, http://nla.gov.au/nla.news-article3063939.

328 'NEWS AND NOTES.', *West Australian*, 12 July 1894, http://nla.gov.au/nla.news-article3063992.

329 'Pre-Contact Indigenous Fremantle', Anthropology from the Shed, https://anthropologyfromtheshed.com/project/map-pre-contact-indigenous-fremantle/.

330 'THE FREMANTLE HARBOUR WORKS.', *West Australian*, 30 August 1894, http://nla.gov.au/nla.news-article3066024.

331 'The Bar', *Perth Gazette and Independent Journal of Politics and News*, 12 February 1848, http://nla.gov.au/nla.news-article3169680.

332 'The Legislative Council.', *Perth Gazette and Independent Journal of Politics and News*, 21 April 1849, http://nla.gov.au/nla.news-article3170613.

333 'Topics of the Week.', *Bunbury Herald*, 15 August 1894, http://nla.gov.au/nla.news-article87104568.

334 'NEWS AND NOTES.', *Inquirer and Commercial News*, 31 August 1894, http://nla.gov.au/nla.news-article66249931.

335 'THE FORTUNE OF WAR MINE.', *Daily News*, 23 August 1894, http://nla.gov.au/nla.news-article77283534.

336 'PARLIAMENT.', *West Australian*, 24 August 1894, http://nla.gov.au/nla.news-article3065796.

337 'NEWS AND NOTES.', *West Australian*, 16 October 1894, http://nla.gov.au/nla.news-article3067764.

338 'SHIPPING INTELLIGENCE. SHIPPING NOTES.', *Western Mail*, 27 October 1894, http://nla.gov.au/nla.news-article33110109.

339 'THE NEW STEAM DREDGE FREMANTLE.', *West Australian*, 10 December 1894, http://nla.gov.au/nla.news-article3070095.

340 'NEWS AND NOTES.', *West Australian*, 28 November 1894, http://nla.gov.au/nla.news-article3069596.

341 Hansard, Legislative Assembly, 12 Nov, 1894, 1362-1378.

342 'THE RAILWAY WORKSHOPS IN FREMANTLE.', *Inquirer and Commercial News*, 16 November 1894, http://nla.gov.au/nla.news-article66253380.

343 Hansard, Legislative Assembly, 19 Nov, 1894, 1489-1494.

344 'THE COLONIAL SECRETARY'S RESIGNATION.', *Daily News*, 6 December 1894, http://nla.gov.au/nla.news-article76468227; 'THE RECONSTRUCTION OF THE CABINET.', *Daily News*, 4 December 1894, http://nla.gov.au/nla.news-article76469317.

345 'VIGILANS ET AUDAX', *West Australian*, 11 December 1894, http://nla.gov.au/nla.news-article3070124.

NINETEEN: FREMANTLE RATTLED – 1895

346 'THE SHOCK FELT IN PERTH.', *Daily News*, 2 January 1895, http://nla.gov.au/nla.news-article78356063.

347 'DYNAMITE EXPLOSION AT FREMANTLE.', *West Australian*, 3 January 1895, http://nla.gov.au/nla.news-article3071111; 'FURTHER PARTICULARS.', *Daily News*, 2 January 1895, http://nla.gov.au/nla.news-article78356061.

348 'DYNAMITE EXPLOSION AT FREMANTLE.', *Daily News*, 2 January 1895, http://nla.gov.au/nla.news-article78356029.

349 'The Dynamite Explosion at Fremantle.', *Western Mail*, 5 January 1895, http://nla.gov.au/nla.news-article33111772.

350 'THE EXPLOSION AT FREMANTLE.', *West Australian*, 5 January 1895, http://nla.gov.au/nla.news-article3071240; 'THE DYNAMITE EXPLOSION FREMANTLE.', *Inquirer and Commercial News*, 11 January 1895, http://nla.gov.au/nla.news-article66264672.

351 'NEWS AND NOTES.', *West Australian*, 8 January 1895, http://nla.gov.au/nla.news-article3071325.

352 'THE HARBOUR WORKS AT FREMANTLE.', *West Australian*, 12 January 1895, http://nla.gov.au/nla.news-article3071549.

353 'THE POSTAL CONFERENCE', *Daily News*, 2 February 1895, http://nla.gov.au/nla.news-article78359550.

354 'THE PORT OF FREMANTLE.', *Daily News*, 6 February 1895, http://nla.gov.au/nla.news-article78362062.

355 'FREMANTLE AS A PORT OF CALL FOR OCEAN STEAMERS.', *West Australian*, 11 February 1895, http://nla.gov.au/nla.news-article4541180.

356 'THE PORT OF FREMANTLE.', *Daily News*, 7 February 1895, http://nla.gov.au/nla.news-article78355342.

357 'VIGILANS ET AUDAX.', *West Australian*, 7 February 1895, http://nla.gov.au/nla.news-article4549351.

TWENTY: FALLEN IN A NOBLE STRUGGLE – 1895

358 'Advertising: DISSOLUTION OF PARTNERSHIP', *Daily News*, 4 January 1895, http://nla.gov.au/nla.news-article78358784.

359 'EXPLOSION AT ROCKY BAY.', *West Australian*, 8 February 1895, http://nla.gov.au/nla.

news-article4542762; 'THE ROCKY BAY EXPLOSION.', *West Australian*, 16 February 1895, http://nla.gov.au/nla.news-article4547163.

360 'THE ROCKY BAY EXPLOSION.', *West Australian*, 16 February 1895, http://nla.gov.au/nla.news-article4547163.

361 People/John & Minnie Irvine', https://freotopia.org/people/irvinejohn.html; 'THE ROCKY BAY EXPLOSION.', *West Australian*, 11 February 1895, http://nla.gov.au/nla.news-article4541195.

362 'NEWS AND NOTES.', *West Australian*, 22 February 1895, http://nla.gov.au/nla.news-article4543576.

363 'TO-NIGHT.', *Daily News*, 3 April 1895, http://nla.gov.au/nla.news-article78356090; 'FREEMANTLE V. IMPERIALS.', *Western Mail*, 8 June 1895, http://nla.gov.au/nla.news-article33115469; 'CORRESPONDENCE.', *Inquirer and Commercial News*, 31 May 1895, http://nla.gov.au/nla.news-article66263231.

364 'THE TAIPO EXPLOSION AT FREMANTLE.', *Inquirer and Commercial News*, 22 November 1895, http://nla.gov.au/nla.news-article72374058.

365 'THE ESTIMATES, 1898-9.', *West Australian*, 20 August 1898, http://nla.gov.au/nla.news-article3201126.

366 "The West Australian." *The West Australian*, 11 February 1895: 4. Web. 25 Oct 2023, http://nla.gov.au/nla.news-article4541194

367 State Library of WA, '009730PD: Working on the Bar at Fremantle Harbour, Western Australia, 1900: Slwa_b2543284_1', State Library of WA, https://purl.slwa.wa.gov.au/slwa_b2543284_1.

368 'THE FREMANTLE HARBOUR WORKS.', *West Australian*, 11 February 1895, http://nla.gov.au/nla.news-article4541209; 'THE FREMANTLE HARBOR WORKS.', *Inquirer and Commercial News*, 22 February 1895, http://nla.gov.au/nla.news-article66267369; 'THE FREMANTLE HARBOUR WORKS.', *Daily News*, 12 March 1895, http://nla.gov.au/nla.news-article78357622.

369 'NEWS AND NOTES.', *West Australian*, 23 April 1895, http://nla.gov.au/nla.news-article4538431; 'Local and General.', *W.A. Record*, 4 May 1895, http://nla.gov.au/nla.news-article212346596.

370 'ACCIDENT AT ROCKY BAY.', *West Australian*, 8 August 1895, http://nla.gov.au/nla.news-article4541634.

371 'LOCAL AND GENERAL.', *W.A. Record*, 28 December 1895, http://nla.gov.au/nla.news-article212345288.

TWENTY-ONE: MONSTER MEETINGS – 1895

372 'TRADES AND LABOUR COUNCIL OF WESTERN AUSTRALIA.', *West Australian*, 6 March 1895, http://nla.gov.au/nla.news-article4543070.

373 'THE ANTI-ASIATIC AGITATION.', *West Australian*, 13 March 1895, http://nla.gov.au/nla.news-article4540464.

374 Parliament of Victoria, 'An Act to amend the Factories and Shops Act 1890 and for other purposes.' fasa1896196.pdf (austlii.edu.au)

375 National Museum of Australia; 'National Museum of Australia - Harvester Judgement', https://www.nma.gov.au/defining-moments/resources/harvester-judgement.

376 'THE INFLUX OF CHINESE.', *Daily News*, 15 March 1895, http://nla.gov.au/nla.news-article78356661; 'THE ASIATIC QUESTION.', *West Australian*, 16 March 1895, http://nla.gov.au/nla.news-article4548696.

377 'THE LOCOMOTIVE WORKSHOPS', *West Australian*, 12 March 1895, http://nla.gov.au/nla.news-article4542590; 'THE RAILWAY WORKSHOPS.', *Daily News*, 16 March 1895, http://nla.gov.au/nla.news-article78361000; 'THE RAILWAY WORKSHOPS.', *Daily News*, 18 March 1895, http://nla.gov.au/nla.news-article78355832.

378 'WEDNESDAY'S DEPUTATION TO THE PREMIER.', *Daily News*, 18 March 1895, http://nla.gov.au/nla.news-article78355831.

379 'THE LOCOMOTIVE WORKSHOPS.', *West Australian*, 20 March 1895, http://nla.gov.au/nla.news-article4540302.

380 'THE LOCOMOTIVE WORKSHOPS.', *West Australian*, 21 March 1895, http://nla.gov.au/nla.news-article4542704; 'THE RAILWAY WORKSHOPS. DEPUTATION TO THE PREMIER. MR. MARMIONS SPEECH. SIR JOHNS REPLY. *Daily News*, 21 Mar 1895', http://nla.gov.au/nla.news-article78362122.

381 'THE LOCOMOTIVE WORKSHOPS.', *West Australian*, 21 March 1895, http://nla.gov.au/nla.news-article4542704

382 'REMOVAL OF WORKSHOPS.', *West Australian*, 30 March 1895, http://nla.gov.au/nla.news-article4546117.

383 'NEWS AND NOTES.', *West Australian*, 13 April 1895, http://nla.gov.au/nla.news-article4548458.

384 E. Jaggard, 'Vosper, Frederick Charles Burleigh (1869–1901)', in *ADB*, https://adb.anu.edu.au/biography/vosper-frederick-charles-burleigh-8933.

385 'COOLGARDIE NEWS.', *Inquirer and Commercial News*, 28 December 1894, http://nla.gov.au/nla.news-article66249260.

386 'THE ANTI-ASIATIC LEAGUE', *Daily News*, 27 April 1895, http://nla.gov.au/nla.news-article78357559.

387 'INDISPOSITION OF THE PREMIER.', *Daily News*, 27 April 1895, http://nla.gov.au/nla.news-article78357534.

388 'NEWS AND NOTES.', *West Australian*, 3 May 1895, http://nla.gov.au/nla.news-article4545933.

389 'Departure of Mr C. Y. O'Connor, District Engineer.', *Grey River Argus*, 25 March 1880, https://paperspast.natlib.govt.nz/newspapers/GRA18800325.2.6.5.

390 'Fremantle Stuff>buildings>Plympton House', https://freotopia.org/buildings/plympton house.html

391 'FASHIONABLE WEDDING AT FREMANTLE.', *West Australian*, 3 May 1895, http://nla.gov.au/nla.news-article4545931.

TWENTY-TWO: A QUESTION OF ACCOMMODATION - 1895

392 Mental Health Museum of WA, Aboriginal Patient Files, 'EJ', certification. Quoted in P. Martyr, '"Behaving Wildly": Diagnoses of Lunacy among Indigenous Persons in Western Australia, 1870-1914', *Social History of Medicine* 24, no. 2 (1 August 2011): 316–33, https://doi.org/10.1093/shm/hkq046.

393 P. Martyr, '"Behaving Wildly".

394 Chief Secretary's Department and Colonial Secretary's Office, 'Insane Half Cast Girl "Emily Jones" Belonging to the Swan N and H.C [Native and Half Cast] Mission Refused Enter to the Fremantle Lunatic Asylum' (Item, 29 May 1895), AU WA S675- cons527 1895/1175, SROWA.

395 Philippa Martyr, '"Behaving Wildly":

396 Martyr, 'Equal under the Law? Indigenous People and the Lunacy Acts in Western Australia to 1920', 498 Viewed at austlii.edu.au.

397 Martyr, 'Equal under the Law?', 335

398 'ROTTNEST NATIVE PRISON.', *Victorian Express*, 18 February 1888, http://nla.gov.au/nla.news-article212630377.

399 Western Australia Parliament, 'Report Upon the Lunatic Asylum at Fremantle for the Year 1895 by the Superintending Medical Officer. No. 6', 1896. RACPMHL

400 Philippa Martyr, 'Equal under the Law?', 317

401 'VIGILANS ET AUDAX', *West Australian*, 23 April 1895, http://nla.gov.au/nla.news-article4538433.

402 'FREMANTLE MUNICIPAL COUNCIL.', *Daily News*, 23 March 1895, http://nla.gov.au/nla.news-article78358203.

403 'THE BUDGET SPEECH', *Daily News*, 9 August 1895, http://nla.gov.au/nla.news-article81178534.

404 Hansard, Legislative Assembly, 8 Aug 1895, 556.

405 'THE GOLDEN FLEECE.', *Coolgardie Miner*, 21 November 1895, http://nla.gov.au/nla.news-article216664924.

406 'REPRESENTATION OR SEPARATION.', *Hannan's Herald*, 7 October 1895, http://nla.gov.au/nla.news-article227992381.

407 Additional Information - FPOL2107-3 - Fremantle Arts Centre Conservation Management Plan (2).pdf 28-29

408 '(Before Mr. Registrar Moseley.) Re D. ROGERS.', *Western Mail*, 28 June 1895, http://nla.gov.au/nla.news-article33116166.

409 'WATER CONSERVATION.', *Inquirer and Commercial News*, 8 November 1895, http://nla.gov.au/nla.news-article72375987; 'GENERAL NEWS.', *Daily News*, 1 November 1895, http://nla.gov.au/nla.news-article81385653.

410 'NEWS AND NOTES.', *West Australian*, 30 November 1895, http://nla.gov.au/nla.news-article4548579.

411 Western Australia Parliament, 'Report Upon the Lunatic Asylum at Fremantle for the Year 1895 by the Superintending Medical Officer. No. 6', 1896. RACPMHL

412 Hansard, Legislative Assembly, 1 Oct 1894, 834.

413 'Classified Advertising/Houses and Land', *West Australian*, 30 January 1895, http://nla.gov.au/nla.news-article4538126.

414 'Classified Advertising', *West Australian*, 20 November 1895, http://nla.gov.au/nla.news-article4540004.

415 'Classified Advertising/To Let', *West Australian*, 15 November 1895, http://nla.gov.au/nla.news-article4546200.

416 'Classified Advertising', *West Australian*, 23 January 1896, http://nla.gov.au/nla.news-article3078081.

417 'Classified Advertising/To Let', *West Australian*, 20 February 1896, http://nla.gov.au/nla.news-article3080786.

418 Supreme Court of Western Australia and Civil Court of Western Australia, 'Henry Calvert Barnett' (Item), AU WA S34- cons3403 1897/150.

TWENTY-THREE: RAILWAY BLUES – 1895 – 1896

419 Hansard, Legislative Assembly, 3 Sept 1895, 795ff.

420 'THE GOVERNMENT RAILWAYS.', *West Australian*, 16 September 1895, http://nla.gov.au/nla.news-article4544783.

421 'NEWS AND NOTES.', *West Australian*, 19 October 1895, http://nla.gov.au/nla.news-article4547821.

422 'NEWS AND NOTES.', *West Australian*, 19 November 1895, http://nla.gov.au/nla.news-article4540924; 'GENERAL NEWS.', *Daily News*, 19 November 1895, http://nla.gov.au/nla.news-article81383803.

423 'CAPE LEEUWIN LIGHTHOUSE.', *Southern Times*, 14 December 1895, http://nla.gov.au/nla.news-article157530774.

424 'PROBABLE WATER FAMINE AT WOOLGANGIE.', *Daily News*, 20 December 1895, http://nla.gov.au/nla.news-article81385271.

425 'THE GOVERNOR OF WESTERN AUSTRALIA.', *Australian Advertiser*, 23 December 1895, http://nla.gov.au/nla.news-article260528289.

426 'THE ENGINEER-IN-CHIEF AND THE AUDITOR-GENERAL.', *West Australian*, 16 February 1894, http://nla.gov.au/nla.news-article3058181.

427 'DEATH OF MR. F. W. MARTIN, M.I.C.E.', *West Australian*, 27 May 1895, http://nla.gov.au/nla.news-article4541126.

428 'THE GOVERNMENT RAILWAYS.', *Western Mail*, 20 September 1895, http://nla.gov.au/nla.news-article33118225.

429 'LOCAL AND GENERAL.', *Geraldton Advertiser*, 10 June 1895, http://nla.gov.au/nla.news-article252758610; 'THE LABOUR QUESTION IN AMERICA.', *Inquirer and Commercial News*, 14 June 1895, http://nla.gov.au/nla.news-article66259462.

430 Tauman, *The Chief*, 244.

431 'A GENERAL MANAGER FOR THE RAILWAYS', *Inquirer and Commercial News*, 13 March 1896, http://nla.gov.au/nla.news-article72370102; 'A NEW GENERAL MANAGER OF RAILWAYS.', *Kalgoorlie Miner*, 24 December 1896, http://nla.gov.au/nla.news-article87855812.

432 'MORE TRUCKS.', *Northam Advertiser*, 29 February 1896, http://nla.gov.au/nla.news-article211695715.

433 'FREMANTLE PIER GOODS TRAFFIC.', *West Australian*, 8 January 1896, http://nla.gov.au/nla.news-article3076428.

434 'THE BLOCK AT FREMANTLE', *West Australian*, 28 February 1896, http://nla.gov.au/nla.news-article3081663.

435 'THE WATER FAMINE AT WOOLGANGIE.', *West Australian*, 3 January 1896, http://nla.gov.au/nla.news-article3075913.

436 'THE PURCHASE OF RAILWAY ROLLING-STOCK.', *Inquirer and Commercial News*, 17 January 1896, http://nla.gov.au/nla.news-article72373803.

437 'THE GOVERNMENT RAILWAYS.', *West Australian*, 12 September 1895, http://nla.gov.au/nla.news-article4545843.

438 'Report of the Civil Service Commission (Appointed 13th April 1894) 1896.' (Parliament of Western Australia, 1896), page x (parliament.wa.gov.au)

439 Report of the Civil Service Commission, page 372

440 . Prior to going to New Zealand, O'Connor trained under Chaloner Smith in Ireland. There is no record of him ever working in England, so it is unclear why he said this. Possibly it was a mistake made by the person taking notes.

441 'THE NEW COAL CONTRACT.', *Daily News*, 23 January 1896, http://nla.gov.au/nla.news-article84727509; 'EXPANSION OF THE SHIPPING TRADE.', *West Australian*, 27 January 1896, http://nla.gov.au/nla.news-article3078450.

442 'THE BLOCK AT THE FREMANTLE JETTY.', *West Australian*, 25 January 1896, http://nla.gov.au/nla.news-article3078347.

443 'DEPARTMENTAL DIFFICULTIES.', *West Australian*, 26 February 1896, http://nla.gov.au/nla.news-article3081386.

444 'RUINOUS DEPARTMENTS.', *Inquirer and Commercial News*, 6 March 1896, http://nla.gov.au/nla.news-article72372654.

445 'THE COMMISSIONER OF RAILWAYS AND THE GOVERNMENT.', *West Australian*, 29 February 1896, http://nla.gov.au/nla.news-article3081836.

446 'THE SHORTAGE OF RAILWAY TRUCKS.', *West Australian*, 2 March 1896, http://nla.gov.au/nla.news-article3081934.

447 'THE DEPARTMENTAL DIFFICULTIES.', *West Australian*, 6 March 1896, http://nla.gov.au/nla.news-article3082418.

448 'GENERAL NEWS', *Daily News*, 9 March 1896, http://nla.gov.au/nla.news-article84725148.

449 'THE PREMIER AND THE RAILWAYS.', *West Australian*, 11 March 1896, http://nla.gov.au/nla.news-article3082865; 'THE PREMIER AND MR. VENN.', *West Australian*, 13 March 1896, http://nla.gov.au/nla.news-article3083101.

450 'REPORT BY THE ENGINEER IN CHIEF.', *Southern Cross Herald*, 13 March 1896, http://nla.gov.au/nla.news-article255688361.

451 'NEWS AND NOTES.', *West Australian*, 14 March 1896, http://nla.gov.au/nla.news-article3083189.

452 'THE VACANT PORTFOLIO.', *Inquirer and Commercial News*, 3 April 1896, http://nla.gov.au/nla.news-article72377930. Forrest became Colonial Secretary in December 1894 after the resignation of Stephen Parker. See F. K. Crowley, 'Forrest, Sir John (1847–1918)', in *ADB*, https://adb.anu.edu.au/biography/forrest-sir-john-6211.

453 'FREMANTLE HARBOUR WORKS.', *West Australian*, 14 March 1896, http://nla.gov.au/nla.news-article3083220.

TWENTY-FOUR: RUNNING AMOK – 1896

454 Western Australia Parliament, 'Report Upon the Lunatic Asylum at Fremantle for the Year 1895 by the Superintending Medical Officer. No. 6', 1896.

455 'Fremantle Stuff > cemeteries', https://freotopia.org/cemeteries/skinner.html. The Skinner Street cemetery closed in 1899.

456 'PUBLIC WORKS DEPARTMENT.', *West Australian*, 9 October 1896, http://nla.gov.au/nla.news-article3100540.

457 'FREMANTLE LUNATIC ASYLUM.', *West Australian*, 18 November 1897, http://nla.gov.au/nla.news-article3188215; 'NEWS AND NOTES.', *West Australian*, 12 June 1896, http://nla.gov.au/nla.news-article3092654; Western Australia Parliament, 'Report Upon

the Lunatic Asylum at Fremantle for the Year 1896 by the Superintending Medical Officer. No. 25', 1897. RACPMHL

458 'NEWS AND NOTES.', *West Australian*, 28 February 1896, http://nla.gov.au/nla.news-article3081655.

459 'DEATH OF AN OLD CIVIL SERVANT.', *Daily News*, 31 March 1896, http://nla.gov.au/nla.news-article84723565; 'BRAVERY REWARDED.', *Inquirer and Commercial News*, 10 April 1896, http://nla.gov.au/nla.news-article72371344.

460 Chief Secretary's Department and Colonial Secretary's Office, 'Superintendent Lunatic Asylum - Attack on a Warder - Reporting.' (Item, 3 July 1896), AU WA S675- cons527 1896/2039, SROWA; 'NEWS AND NOTES.', *West Australian*, 2 July 1896, http://nla.gov.au/nla.news-article3094782.

461 'NOTES AND COMMENTS.', *Coolgardie Miner*, 4 July 1896, http://nla.gov.au/nla.news-article216673257.

462 'CORRESPONDENCE.', *West Australian*, 27 August 1896, http://nla.gov.au/nla.news-article3098391.

463 'A CASE AT THE LUNATIC ASYLUM.', *West Australian*, 29 August 1896, http://nla.gov.au/nla.news-article3098508.

464 'CORRESPONDENCE.', *West Australian*, 5 September 1896, http://nla.gov.au/nla.news-article3098888.

465 'Victor Scanlan (1884-1897) - Find a Grave...', https://www.findagrave.com/memorial/206948272/victor-scanlan.

466 DEATH OF MR. W.E. MARMION, M.L.A.', *West Australian*, 6 July 1896, http://nla.gov.au/nla.news-article3095169.

467 'THE LATE MR. W. E. MARMION.', *Inquirer and Commercial News*, 14 August 1896, http://nla.gov.au/nla.news-article66540932.

468 'FREMANTLE LITERARY INSTITUTE.', *West Australian*, 3 October 1896, http://nla.gov.au/nla.news-article3100232; 'NEWS AND NOTES.', *West Australian*, 7 October 1896, http://nla.gov.au/nla.news-article3100412.

469 'NORTH FREMANTLE MUNICIPALITY.', *West Australian*, 12 November 1896, http://nla.gov.au/nla.news-article3102266.

470 'WHAT SHALL WE DO WITH OUR LUNATICS?', *Inquirer and Commercial News*, 19 November 1897, http://nla.gov.au/nla.news-article66693176.

471 . Chief Secretary's Department and Colonial Secretary's Office, 'Surgeon Superintendent Lunatic Asylum - Additional Accommodation Urgently Required.' (Item, 12 January 1897), AU WA S675- cons527 1896/3977, SROWA.

472 'PUBLIC WORKS DEPARTMENT.', *West Australian*, 9 October 1896, http://nla.gov.au/nla.news-article3100540.

473 'LATE ASSISTANT ENGINEER-IN-CHIEF.', *West Australian*, 23 December 1896, http://nla.gov.au/nla.news-article3104463.

474 'MR. DRAPER'S LECTURE.', *Coolgardie Miner*, 4 December 1896, http://nla.gov.au/nla.news-article216682343.

475 'VALEDICTORY TO MR. FRANCIS HART.', *West Australian*, 1 April 1896, http://nla.gov.au/nla.news-article3085072. Lillian accused him of abandonment in her divorce papers.

476 'TRAGEDY AT FREMANTLE.', *West Australian*, 4 December 1896, http://nla.gov.au/nla.news-article3103481; 'THE FREMANTLE TRAGEDY.', *West Australian*, 7 December 1896, http://nla.gov.au/nla.news-article3103599.

477 'A FREMANTLE TRAGEDY.', *Inquirer and Commercial News*, 11 December 1896, http://nla.gov.au/nla.news-article66537887; 'LOCAL AND GENERAL.', *W.A. Record*, 5 December 1896, http://nla.gov.au/nla.news-article211622291; 'TRAGEDY AT FREMANTLE.', *West Australian*, 4 December 1896, http://nla.gov.au/nla.news-article3103481.

478 'ACCUSED IN COURT.', *Daily News*, 4 December 1896, http://nla.gov.au/nla.news-article81329708.

479 'THE FREMAMTLE TRAGEDY.', *West Australian*, 12 December 1896, http://nla.gov.au/nla.news-article3103888.

480 'THE FREMANTLE TRAGEDY', *West Australian*, 19 December 1896, http://nla.gov.au/nla.news-article3104271.

TWENTY-FIVE: STANDING IN TIGHTS ON MOUNT BURGESS – 1897

481 'SANITATION AT COOLGARDIE.', *Daily News*, 25 September 1895, http://nla.gov.au/nla.news-article81385882; 'Goldfields Sanitation.', *Western Mail*, 25 October 1895, http://nla.gov.au/nla.news-article33119020.

482 'THE AVON AND COOLGARDIE.', *West Australian*, 29 October 1894, http://nla.gov.au/nla.news-article3068213; 'THE FOUNDER OF THE COOLGARDIE WATER SCHEME.', *West Australian*, 25 December 1902, http://nla.gov.au/nla.news-article24851061.

483 'NEWS AND NOTES.', *Inquirer and Commercial News*, 21 September 1894, http://nla.gov.au/nla.news-article66251407.

484 'RETURN OF MR. ALEX FORREST.', *Inquirer and Commercial News*, 24 July 1896, http://nla.gov.au/nla.news-article66534346.

485 'OPENING OF THE COOLGARDIE RAILWAY.', *West Australian*, 24 March 1896, http://nla.gov.au/nla.news-article3084232.

486 'THE GOLDFIELDS WATER SUPPLY SCHEME.', *West Australian*, 23 July 1896, http://nla.gov.au/nla.news-article3096595; 'THE COOLGARDIE GOLDFIELDS WATER SUPPLY SCHEME.', *Coolgardie Miner*, 25 July 1896, http://nla.gov.au/nla.news-article216674306.

487 Hansard, Legislative Assembly, 5 August 1896, 271-273; 'PARLIAMENT.', Inquirer and Commercial News, 7 August 1896, http://nla.gov.au/nla.news-article66541644.

488 Don Pugh, 'Constructing Australia: Pipeline Dreams', 5

489 Evans, *C. Y. O'Connor*, 168

490 'THE GOLDFIELDS WATER SUPPLY SCHEME.', *West Australian*, 23 July 1896, http://nla.gov.au/nla.news-article3096595.

491 The commission consisted of John Carruthers, George F. Deacon and William Cawthorne Unwin. 'GOLDFIELDS WATER SUPPLY SCHEME.', *West Australian*, 22 September 1897, http://nla.gov.au/nla.news-article3184160.

492 'NEWS IN BRIEF.', *Daily News*, 8 September 1896, http://nla.gov.au/nla.news-article84467031.

493 NEWS AND NOTES.', *West Australian*, 20 January 1897, http://nla.gov.au/nla.news-article3105895.

494 'THE PUBLIC WORKS DEPARTMENT.', *Inquirer and Commercial News*, 24 January 1896, http://nla.gov.au/nla.news-article72376576.

495 'WESTRALIAN NEWS.', *Western Australian Goldfields Courier*, 2 January 1897, http://nla.gov.au/nla.news-article250946994.

496 'CABLEGRAMS', *Kalgoorlie Miner*, 22 March 1897, http://nla.gov.au/nla.news-article87862480.

497 'THE AGENT GENERAL.', *Geraldton Advertiser*, 22 January 1897, http://nla.gov.au/nla.news-article252770197.

498 *The Saturday Review of Politics, Literature, Science and Art 1897-01-30: Vol 83 Issue 2153* (Out-of-copyright, 1897), 108 http://archive.org/details/sim_saturday-review_1897-01-30_83_2153.

499 'Western Australia and Its Public Works Policy.', *Coolgardie Miner*, 3 May 1897, http://nla.gov.au/nla.news-article216694289.

TWENTY-SIX: THE SULTAN ARRIVES – 1897

500 'FREMANTLE HARBOUR WORKS.', *West Australian*, 27 February 1897, http://nla.gov.au/nla.news-article3108137.

501 'JUBILEE HONOURS.', *Western Mail*, 25 June 1897, http://nla.gov.au/nla.news-article33141056.

502 'FREMANTLE HARBOR WORKS.', *Inquirer and Commercial News*, 30 April 1897, http://nla.gov.au/nla.news-article66518926.

503 'THE FREMANTLE BOATING FATALITY.', *West Australian*, 14 May 1897, http://nla.gov.au/nla.news-article3112052.

504 'THE FREMANTLE HARBOUR.', *West Australian*, 5 May 1897, http://nla.gov.au/nla.news-article3111538.

505 'NEWS AND NOTES.', *West Australian*, 5 May 1897, http://nla.gov.au/nla.news-article3111533.

506 'THE S.S. SULTAN.', *Inquirer and Commercial News*, 29 June 1894, http://nla.gov.au/nla.news-article66246709.

507 'THE S.S. SULTAN AND THE FREMANTLE HABOUR WORKS.', *West Australian*, 11 May 1897, http://nla.gov.au/nla.news-article3111849.

508 'THE LUNCHEON.', *Western Mail*, 7 May 1897, http://nla.gov.au/nla.news-article33133391; 'THE FREMANTLE HARBOUR.', *West Australian*, 5 May 1897, http://nla.gov.au/nla.news-article3111538.

509 'MP Biographical Register', Frederick Charles Burleigh Vosper, MP Biographical Register (parliament.wa.gov.au) Vosper and Ellis set up the Sunday Times in December 1897

510 'BOATING FATALITY AT FREMANTLE.', *West Australian*, 3 May 1897, http://nla.gov.au/nla.news-article3111440; 'THE FREMANTLE BOATING ACCIDENT.', *West Australian*, 7 May 1897, http://nla.gov.au/nla.news-article3111666; 'SUMMARY OF NEWS.', *West Australian*, 8 May 1897, http://nla.gov.au/nla.news-article3111741.

TWENTY-SEVEN: A VALUED GOVERNMENT OFFICIAL – 1897

511 'FREMANTLE GOVERNMENT HOSPITAL.', *West Australian*, 23 January 1897, http://nla.gov.au/nla.news-article3106115.

512 'NEWS AND NOTES.', *West Australian*, 19 January 1897, http://nla.gov.au/nla.news-article3105804.

513 'VIGILANS ET AUDAX.', *West Australian*, 18 November 1897, http://nla.gov.au/nla.news-article3188260.

514 'NEWS AND NOTES.', *West Australian*, 15 June 1897, http://nla.gov.au/nla.news-article3113656.

515 'NEWS AND NOTES.', *West Australian*, 11 February 1897, http://nla.gov.au/nla.news-article3107166.

516 Chief Secretary's Department and Colonial Secretary's Office, 'Superintendent Lunatic Asylum - Fremantle - Absence of Leave Doctor H.C. Barnet - Asking for - from March 5th for Three Weeks - Doctor Wheeler as Acting Superintendent during His Absence.' (Item, 4 March 1897), AU WA S675- cons527 1897/0537, SROWA.

517 Dr Paget, who had been in the colony only a few months, seems to have had no more experience in treating mental illness than any other general practitioner in the colony. His special interest was infectious diseases.

518 'THE FREMANTLE TRAGEDY.', *West Australian*, 4 March 1897, http://nla.gov.au/nla.news-article3108419.

519 'LADY FORRESTS AT HOME.', *West Australian*, 6 May 1897, http://nla.gov.au/nla.news-article3111638.

520 On 21 July, Mrs O'Connor advertised a white cockatoo missing, and asked for it to be returned to Park Bungalow in Barnett Street. 'Classified Advertising/Lost and Found', *West Australian*, 21 July 1897, http://nla.gov.au/nla.news-article3179839.

521 'THE QUEEN'S REIGN.', *West Australian*, 24 June 1897, http://nla.gov.au/nla.news-article3177968; 'AQUATICS.', *West Australian*, 29 June 1897, http://nla.gov.au/nla.news-article3178313; 'FREMANTLE ROWING CLUB BALL', *West Australian*, 6 August 1897, http://nla.gov.au/nla.news-article3181019.

522 'SPORTING NEWS.', *West Australian*, 9 November 1897, http://nla.gov.au/nla.news-article3187571.

523 'POISONING BY SULPHONAL.', *Journal of the American Medical Association* XVII, no. 11 (12 September 1891): 421–22, https://doi.org/10.1001/jama.1891.02410890039014.

524 'NEWS AND NOTES.', *West Australian*, 4 October 1897, http://nla.gov.au/nla.news-article3185030.

525 Supreme Court of Western Australia and Civil Court of Western Australia, 'Henry Calvert Barnett' (Item), AU WA S34- cons3403 1897/150, SROWA

526 Chief Secretary's Department and Colonial Secretary's Office, 'L. Wheeler - Superintending Medical Officer Lunatic Asylum When Vacant - for Post Of.' (Item, 15 October 1897), AU WA S675- cons527 1897/3127, SROWA

527 Chief Secretary's Department and Colonial Secretary's Office, 'Appointment of Superintending Medical Officer - Fremantle Asylum.' (Item, 7 January 1908), AU WA S675-cons527 1897/3176, SROWA

528 'DEATH OF DR. BARNETT.', *Inquirer and Commercial News*, 5 November 1897, http://nla.gov.au/nla.news-article66692364.

529 'DEATH OF DR. BARNETT.', *Inquirer and Commercial News*, 5 November 1897, http://nla.gov.au/nla.news-article66692364; 'DEATH OF DR. BARNETT.', *Western Mail*, 5 November 1897, http://nla.gov.au/nla.news-article33146178; 'DEATH OF DR. BARNETT.', *West Australian*, 4 November 1897, http://nla.gov.au/nla.news-article3187222. The third doctor is named as Cunningham in one account and Birmingham in another.

530 DOJ WA, Death Certificate for Henry Calvert Barnett.

531 'INQUEST.', Victorian Express, 3 July 1891, http://nla.gov.au/nla.news-article212531829; 'AN OVERDOSE OF MORPHIA.', *Kalgoorlie Miner*, 5 May 1896, http://nla.gov.au/nla.news-article87864022; 'AN OVERDOSE OF LAUDANUM.', *Australian Advertiser*, 28 March 1896, http://nla.gov.au/nla.news-article260682191. Inquests were listed in the Police Gazette, available online at Police gazettes | State Library of Western Australia (slwa.wa.gov.au)

532 'PERTH HIGH SCHOOL.', *West Australian*, 8 November 1897, http://nla.gov.au/nla.news-article3187487.

533 'DEATH OF DR. BARNETT.', *Inquirer and Commercial News*, 5 November 1897, http://nla.gov.au/nla.news-article66692364.

534 'FREMANTLE LUNATIC ASYLUM.', *West Australian*, 18 November 1897, http://nla.gov.au/nla.news-article3188215.

535 Hansard, Legislative Assembly, 6 December 1897, 849.

536 Hansard, Legislative Assembly, 17 December 1897, 1154.

537 'THE LIFE OF A LUNATIC.', *West Australian Sunday Times*, 7 October 1900, http://nla.gov.au/nla.news-article32722663.

538 Hansard, Legislative Assembly, 17 October 1900, 1094.

539 'MANAGEMENT OF LUNATIC ASYLUM', *West Australian*, 22 November 1900, http://nla.gov.au/nla.news-article23848192.

540 'NEWS AND NOTES.', *West Australian*, 21 June 1901, http://nla.gov.au/nla.news-article24753257.

541 'INSANE ASYLUM REFORM.', *West Australian*, 15 February 1902, http://nla.gov.au/nla.news-article24738618.

TWENTY-EIGHT: THE FINAL CHAPTER

542 Tauman, *The Chief*, 245

543 'THE ENGINEER-IN-CHIEF.', *West Australian*, 17 September 1897, http://nla.gov.au/nla.news-article3183858.

544 'FREMANTLE HARBOUR WORKS.', *West Australian*, 25 September 1897, http://nla.gov.au/nla.news-article3184408.

545 Evans, *C. Y. O'Connor*, 199

546 G. C. Bolton, 'Forrest, Alexander (1849–1901)', in *ADB*, https://adb.anu.edu.au/biography/forrest-alexander-6208.

547 'PARLIAMENT.', *West Australian*, 4 February 1902, http://nla.gov.au/nla.news-article24737718.

548 This was not the same newspaper that now carries the title 'Sunday Times'.

549 Evans, *C. Y. O'Connor*, 212-216

550 'RASON'S RICKETY RUSE', *West Australian Sunday Times*, 26 January 1902, http://nla.gov.au/nla.news-article32722020.

551 'CORRUPTION BY CONTRACT', *West Australian Sunday Times*, 9 February 1902, http://nla.gov.au/nla.news-article32722146.

552 'THE LATE MR. C. Y. O'CONNOR, C.M.G.', *West Australian*, 14 March 1902, http://nla.gov.au/nla.news-article24740578; Crown Law Department and Judicial Department, 'Re: Death of C. Y. O'Connor' (Item, 14 March 1902), AU WA S2664- cons997 1902/0976, online at s2664_cons997_1902_0976.pdf. SROWA

553 'THE LATE MR. C. Y. O'CONNOR, C.M.G.', *West Australian*, 14 March 1902, http://nla.gov.au/nla.news-article24740578.

554 Evans, *C. Y. O'Connor*, 248

555 Crown Law Department and Judicial Department, 'Re: Death of C. Y. O'Connor' (Item, 14 March 1902), AU WA S2664- cons997 1902/0976, online at s2664_cons997_1902_0976.pdf SROWA.

556 'Death of Mr. C. Y. O'Connor', *West Australian*, 11 March 1902, http://nla.gov.au/nla.news-article24740321.

557 'THE LATE MR. C. Y. O'CONNOR, C.M.G.', *West Australian*, 14 March 1902, http://nla.gov.au/nla.news-article24740578; Crown Law Department and Judicial Department, 'Re: Death of C. Y. O'Connor' (Item, 14 March 1902), AU WA S2664- cons997 1902/0976, s2664_cons997_1902_0976.pdf SROWA.

558 'Symptoms & Causes of Cirrhosis | NIDDK', National Institute of Diabetes and Digestive and Kidney Diseases, https://www.niddk.nih.gov/health-information/liver-disease/cirrhosis/symptoms-causes.

559 'THE FUNERAL.', *Western Mail*, 15 March 1902, http://nla.gov.au/nla.news-article37798673.

560 'THE OPENING OF THE WATER SCHEME.', *Western Mail*, 31 January 1903, http://nla.gov.au/nla.news-article37538596.

561 'ARRIVAL AT COOLGARDIE.', *West Australian*, 26 January 1903, http://nla.gov.au/nla.news-article24853440.

EPILOGUE

562 Evans, *C. Y. O'Connor*, 233-234; Hansard, Legislative Assembly, 16 September 1902, 1127ff.

563 'WOMAN'S REALM.', *West Australian*, 14 November 1941, http://nla.gov.au/nla.news-article47169202.

564 'Emily Barnett', marriage, 1899, Western Australian Pioneer Index, 1841-1905, Online Index Search Tool (www.wa.gov.au); Ancestry.com. *UK, Mechanical Engineer Records, 1847-1938* [database on-line]. https://www.ancestry.co.uk/search/collections/3149/ ($)

565 Ancestry.com England & Wales, Civil Divorce Records, 1858-1918 England & Wales, Civil Divorce Records, 1858-1918 | Ancestry®

566 'STABAT MATER.', *Sunday Times*, 19 January 1930, http://nla.gov.au/nla.news-article58372399.

567 'Classified Advertising', *West Australian*, 28 June 1898, http://nla.gov.au/nla.news-article3213484; 'AQUATICS.', *Umpire*, 2 July 1898, http://nla.gov.au/nla.news-article257732602.

568 'NORTH FREMANTLE MUNICIPAL COUNCIL.', *West Australian*, 14 April 1899, http://nla.gov.au/nla.news-article3224363.

569 Westminster, London, England, Non-Conformist Baptisms, Marriages and Burials, 1841-1964. Accessed at Ancestry.com

570 Wellcome Trust; London, England; Collection: The Medical Directory, 1920; Reference: b21330724_i13766028. Accessed at Ancestry.com

AFTERWORD

571 'What Is a Tragic Hero? Definition, Examples & Common Traits', Reedsy, https://blog.reedsy.com/tragic-hero/.)

572 'Isambard Kingdom Brunel's Great Western Railway', https://britishheritage.com/history/isambard-kingdom-brunel-great-western-railway.

573 'Man Of La Mancha Script - Transcript from the Screenplay and/or Don Quixote Movie Based on the Musical Play', http://www.script-o-rama.com/movie_scripts/m/man-of-la-mancha-script-transcript.html.

Also by Stella Budrikis

To learn more about these books, visit my website at stellabudrikis.com

The Edward Street Baby Farm

Published by Fremantle Press 2022.

In 1907, Perth woman Alice Mitchell was arrested for the murder baby Ethel Booth. The police soon discovered that at least 37 infants had died in Mitchell's care in the previous six years. It became clear she had been running a 'baby farm', making a profit out of caring for the children of 'unfortunate women'. The Alice Mitchell murder trial gripped the city of Perth and the nation. On everyone's mind was the question, "How did it come to this?

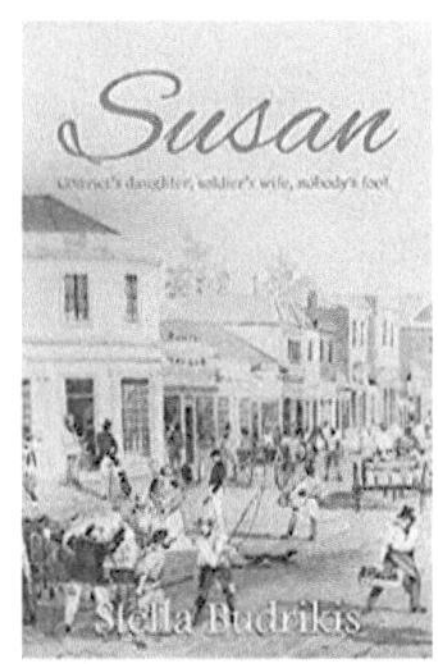

Susan: Convict's daughter, soldier's wife, nobody's fool

'Susan' is the true story of Susan Whybrew (nee Mason). Born in 1848 in Adelaide, South Australia, to Irish parents, she survived childhood destitution, the hardships of being an "off the strength" army wife and giving birth to fourteen children, all with a feisty spirit that refused to accept insults from anyone. In telling Susan's story, the author (her great great granddaughter) captures something of what life was like for those close to the bottom of the social ladder in the Victorian era, both in Australia and in Britain.

www.ingramcontent.com/pod-product-compliance
Ingram Content Group UK Ltd.
Pitfield, Milton Keynes, MK11 3LW, UK
UKHW041635190726
13854UKWH00006B/2499